THANKS FOR THE MEMORIES

Love, Sex, and World War II

JANE MERSKY LEDER

Westport, Connecticut
London

Library of Congress Cataloging-in-Publication Data

Leder, Jane Mersky.
Thanks for the memories : love, sex, and World War II / by Jane Mersky Leder.
    p. cm.
  Includes bibliographical references and index.
  ISBN 0–275–98879–1
  1. World War, 1939–1945—United States.   2. World War, 1939–1945—
Women—United States.   3. World War, 1939–1945—Social aspects—United
States.   4. Women—United States—History—20th century.   5. United
States—History—1933–1945.   6. United States—Social conditions—1933–
1945.   I. Title.
  D744.7.U6L43   2006
  940.53'1—dc22   2006015707

British Library Cataloguing in Publication Data is available.

Library of Congress Catalog Card Number: 2006015707
ISBN: 0–275–98879–1

First published in 2006

Praeger Publishers, 88 Post Road West, Westport, CT 06881
An imprint of Greenwood Publishing Group, Inc.
www.praeger.com

Printed in the United States of America

The paper used in this book complies with the
Permanent Paper Standard issued by the National
Information Standards Organization (Z39.48–1984).

10 9 8 7 6 5 4 3 2 1

Copyright Acknowledgments

The author and publisher gratefully acknowledge permission to reprint the following:

Letters from Damon Frantz Rarey, editor, *Laughter and Tears: A Combat Pilot's
Sketchbooks of World War II Squadron Life* (Santa Rosa, CA: Vision Books International, 1996) p. 4.

Extracts from Lorraine Bodnar, "Lorraine Remembers" (unpublished), pp. 50–52.

Extracts from Jack Havener, *Marauders in the Midst* (unpublished), p. 53.

Extracts from Donald Hyde, *Notes for His Children* (unpublished), 1988.

For Morris and Shirley. Your World War II stories ignited a passion and a vision. Your unwavering support and encouragement sustained me through the ups and downs of the journey.

CONTENTS

          Photo essays appear following pages 74 and 154

INTRODUCTION

The collective consciousness of World War II revolved around the virtues of bravery, sacrifice, and commitment. Whether it was joining the armed services, planting a victory garden, or going to work to keep the wartime machine rolling, Americans toed the political and social line in hopes of winning the war. Their privacy was invaded, their patriotism opened to question, their lives inundated by propaganda. Yet the members of "the greatest generation" fell into lockstep, asking very few questions and breaking few social and sexual mores.

Or did they?

Thanks for the Memories: Love, Sex, and World War II is the true story of how the World War II generation responded to the passions of war and how their lives and the relationships between the sexes were forever changed.

Not long after the country breathed a collective sigh of relief at the end of the Great Depression, it was plunged into a world war most Americans had hoped to watch from afar. The Japanese attacked Pearl Harbor on December 7, 1941, decimating the Navy fleet there, and, in an instant, young American men and women knew instinctively that their lives would never be the same. The "normal" sequence of events—education or work, marriage, children—had been blown to bits, and as they would soon discover, so had long-held attitudes toward love and sex. Millions of men and, eventually, thousands of women left home to join the military, and millions more young Americans pulled up stakes to find better jobs. The issue of sexuality, which had been submerged during the Depression, reemerged among young people, whose separation from their home communities and economic autonomy offered unprecedented opportunities for experimentation. But the mixed messages about venereal disease, birth control, and women's sexuality muddied the battle for morality and public opinion. The government's propaganda machine rolled overtime, and the military's hypocritical stance on love and sex ultimately failed to set and control the moral barometer of the troops. Soldiers were counseled to remember their girlfriends or wives back home and to remain "pure"; however, if they strayed (and stray they did!) the instructions were to use a condom or get to the nearest prophylactic station. Service wives who opted to follow their husbands during their stateside training were advised to go home and wait for their husbands there. And despite Uncle Sam's campaign to woo women out of their homes and into the workplace in a Herculean effort to keep the war industry booming, many—like lathe operator Bella Gillaspie, a minister's daughter and the only woman in a factory with 400 men—experienced the kind of sexual harassment that would lead straight to the courts today.

"The men came around and tapped me on the rear or put their arms around me. . . . I couldn't stand it," Bella, now 90, said. "I decided not to pay any attention, but that didn't help a bit. Even when the foreman eventually moved me and my lathe to a remote corner of the factory, the harassment didn't stop. It just got worse."[1]

As Bella and many other women workers saw it, they could try to keep a smile on their face or quit because the behavior they found so offensive was implicitly sanctioned as "normal." Neither the government nor business leaders across the country had any intention of altering traditional gender roles beyond what was absolutely necessary for the war effort. Once the war was over, women would return home and become housewives and mothers, as they'd "promised" to do, and the unprecedented way in which the war had shifted the balance between the sexes in work and in love would be all but forgotten.

Many of the books about life during World War II focus on the wholesome, American pie version of lonely but dutiful soldiers who desperately missed the girls back home but rarely gave in to the temptations of strangers. In "Big Night with the Broads," a section from Time-Life Books' *This Fabulous Century: 1940–1950,* the editors wrote: "All through boot camp and subsequent tours of duty, every serviceman lived for the days when he would go on leave or liberty. Burning in his mind were wild tales, told by veterans, of booze and broads and orgies. But when the eager GI or swab-jockey finally set off, . . . he was usually in for a sharp letdown." To illustrate the point, a photo of young soldiers asleep on chairs and couches in a hotel lobby is accompanied by a caption that reads: "Unable to dredge up any action—or even as much as a room—in Spokane, Washington, five defeated fighting men flake out in a hotel lobby." A "Sad Sack" cartoon by Sergeant Georgie Baker also drives home the point. A drunken soldier approaches a woman on the street, waving a wad on money in his hand. The well-dressed, voluptuous woman takes the money and the soldier's hand and leads him, not to her room as he had hoped, but to a church bazaar. The "poor" soldier has been duped, and his hopes of a wild night dashed.[2]

Despite such widespread attempts at characterizing young men in the military as striking out in sex, the truth was that long separations, the burgeoning independence of women who entered the workforce or traveled as service wives, and the reality of large numbers of postadolescent men thrown together and segregated from the rest of society created a pent-up sexual desire that was acted on much more often than not. As copilot Jack Havener put it, "War changes things. Guys who, at home, wouldn't be doing certain kinds of things, do them." And young girls and women who might not be doing "certain kinds of things" did them as well. At the onset of the war, the government and military campaigns focused on the professional prostitute, who was blamed for the increasing number of men with venereal disease (VD). Venereal disease had accounted for the loss of seven million man days in World War I, and the military was hell bent on not repeating such an abysmal record. The fear of those numbers increasing exponentially prompted the military, as well as social hygienists and local and federal lawmakers, to pull out all the stops in an attempt to combat this "special wartime threat." Former air/sea rescue pilot Bill Holbrook remembered the "horror" movies about VD that he and the rest of the troops were shown. "They tried to scare us by making it so explicit," he said. "But most of us just laughed." In one such film, "USS VD: Ship of Shame," produced by Paramount Pictures in 1942, a group of sailors on a night out enjoy a rollicking time with some local prostitutes. Not long after, many of them begin complaining about swollen penises and nasty discharges—not the ones that sent you home from the military. The men's ignorance about how to protect themselves from getting a sexually transmitted disease is laughable. The only doctor on the ship has the following discussion with one of sailors who is showing symptoms:

Doc: What did you use?
Sailor: I douched my canal with whiskey.
Doc: Well, whoever told you to do that?
Sailor: Well, that's the way we do it back home.

Doc: Well, that's a helluva use of good liquor.[3]

Equally ineffective at quelling men's sexual escapades was the closing of close to 700 red-light districts in towns and cities around the country and the variety of magazines and other publications that championed a campaign to eliminate VD through the suppression of so-called sexually deviant women. Publications like *The American Journal of Public Health* called for a "hard-hitting and planned attack" against prostitution and proclaimed, "Let's give neither aid nor comfort to the enemy."[4] But the "enemy" and their cohorts weren't going to let haranguing social hygienists or the law curtail their business relationships. When the brothels were closed in Norfolk, Virginia, the "working" women hired taxis that became known as "chippy wagons" and conducted their business in the backseats. In Seattle, the "forces of evil" never quit. Mayor William F. Devin summed up the frustration of city, state, and federal officials: "One day we get them down, but they just lie in wait ready to take advantage of any lull in the battle."[5]

In none of the government or military "battles" against prostitution was there an onus put on men and their role in the spread of prostitution, disease, and moral laxity. A double standard informed the public and military stance on sex. After all, boys would be boys. Male sexual restraint never became an issue; disease and deterioration of morals could only be transmitted in one direction. A promiscuous man was, by definition, an oxymoron.[6] In retrospect, the military's wartime attempt to control prostitution and the "promiscuous" woman problem seems both shortsighted and an exercise in hypocrisy. According to GIs, the first part of the "sex talk" when they arrived in camp was delivered by the base chaplain and went something like: "Remember your sisters and your mother and be good boys." Then came the second message from the company commander: "I know what the chaplain has told you. (*That's our way of covering our bases.*) But if you do go out (*and I suspect you will*), watch what you're doing (*protect yourself and use a condom*)." "If you can't say no, take a pro," became an oft-used military directive. Another reminder: "Put it on before you put it in!" Although the War Department's official position was that "continence and self-control not only develop character but are the only completely satisfactory methods of preventing venereal disease," orders from the top brass were to continue building prophylactic stations and to issue free condoms "*when* the foregoing educational efforts have failed."

When the "foregoing educational efforts" *did* fail, public attention was refocused on "promiscuous" girls, those of "loose morals" and commonly known as the "Khaki-Wackies," "Victory Girls," and "Good Time Charlottes." According to the authorities, "hordes" of these young women were replacing commercial prostitutes as sources of venereal disease. "War Time Girls Alarm Jurist" read a headline in the June 26, 1943, issue of the *Chicago Daily Tribune.* "Police War Urged on the Pick-Up Girl," read another in the July 27, 1944, *New York Times.* The federal and local governments waged a campaign on this "menace" to the servicemen. Police joined the attack by increasing their patrolling of trouble spots where these mostly teenage girls "preyed" upon the defenseless American soldier. One of Uncle Sam's most popular war posters features the picture of a fresh-faced girl next door with the caption: "She may look clean—But." At the bottom of the poster, it reads: "Pick-Ups, 'Good Time' Girls, Prostitutes Spread Syphilis and Gonorrhea. You can't beat the Axis if you get VD." There had always been teenage girls who "did it," of course; war made them more visible, more independent, more mobile. Yet one estimate had it that "Victory Girls" represented at most only 1 in 1,700 out of their age group. Still, a 1943 study made by the Third Naval District found that 80 percent of the cases of VD were *attributable* to girlfriends or pickups.[7]

The vast majority of young women were not pickups but many were courted to do their patriotic duty by entertaining the troops at United Service Organizations (USO) dances and other government-sponsored activities. As one USO volunteer put it: "It was hammered at us through the newspapers and magazines and on the radio. We were needed at the USO to dance with the soldiers. A young woman had a chance to meet hundreds of men in the course of one or two weeks, more than she would in her entire lifetime, because of the war. Life became a series of weekend dates." [8]

"Hail Hostess," a USO publication written for girls who volunteered to entertain the troops and "maintain morale," outlined "guide-posts" to becoming a successful Junior Hostess. Young women were instructed to, among other things, be sweet and clean, to consider their clothes carefully ("Men tell us that they like their girls to look like girls"), and to be cheerful. In the "Subtle X, Y, Zs," section, there was strong advice about romance:

> *Be realistic about romance!* Romance is wonderful in its place, but the USO is hardly ever the perfect place. For one thing, the boys have a lot of things on their minds, but you are probably not one of them. They love fun, but they're frightened to death of entangling alliances. And incidentally an amazing lot of them have dear little wives and sweethearts back home. (They may neglect to mention this, but take our word for it!)[9]

Despite such warnings, thousands of young women fell for soldiers at USO dances. Lois Bevens, then an 18-year-old from Sioux City, Iowa, met and danced the night away with a soldier named Eldon who was on his way from service in England to redeployment in the Pacific. The two saw each other for several months, during which time the war ended and Eldon awaited his formal discharge from the armed forces. Once discharged, he returned to his home town of Dallas, Oregon. The young couple carried on a long-distance relationship, and they were married almost three years later.

The most visible sign of the increase in sexuality during the war on the home front was the number of illegitimate births. Some 650,000 babies were born out of wedlock between 1942 and 1945, an average of 8.3 illegitimate births per 1,000. Soldiers discovered early on that appealing to a young woman's patriotism, as well as to her heart and libido, often got her into the sack. "I'm going overseas tomorrow, so stay with me tonight" became a quotable line. The passion of affairs in wartime was heightened by the need to make the most of every hour, and inevitably, chastity was an early casualty as lovers were forced to abandon the traditional drawn-out period of courtship. The number of illegitimate births in Great Britain was even more startling: Of the 5.3 million infants delivered between 1939 and 1945, more than a third were born out of wedlock. In 1945, the rate peaked at 16.1 per 1,000 births, up from a prewar average of 5.5 per 1,000 births. Moreover, neither British nor American statistics, which already indicate that wartime promiscuity reached its apex in the final stages of the war, take into account the number of pregnancies that were terminated illegally. Doctors who performed abortions appear to have been in great demand. And, surprisingly perhaps, the highest recorded rate of illegitimate births was not among teenage girls but among 20- to 30-year-old wives of servicemen, suggesting that their independence and loneliness often snapped the bonds of marital fidelity.[10] Total war subjected whole civilian populations to the extremes of violence and disruption. This stimulated the urge to love and be loved and led to the rapid increase in extramarital sexual activity. "Total war is the most catastrophic instigator of social change the world has ever seen, with the possible exception of violent revolution," wrote Francis E. Merrill, a professor at Dartmouth College, whose 1946 study explored how wartime duty had transformed America into a "people doing new things—grimly, protestingly, gladly, semi-hysterically—but all changing the pattern of their lives to some extent under the vast impersonality of war."[11] The birthrate for married couples in the United States skyrocketed as well; it rose to 22 per 1,000, the highest in two decades. Most of these babies were "good-bye babies," conceived just before the husbands shipped out, partly because of an absence of birth control, partly because the wife's allotment check would be increased with each child, and partly as a tangible reminder of a father who could not know when, or if, he would return.[12]

For lesbians, the wartime loosening of sexual mores led to something of a coming-out experience. Although they were strongly discouraged, same-sex relationships flourished in the women's branches of the armed forces and in the female dominated sectors of the war industries. There's a good story in Mary Ann Humphrey's *My Country, My Right to Serve,* when General Dwight Eisenhower called the head of his base's Women's Army Corps (WAC) into his office. He said that he'd heard that there were a lot of lesbians in the WAC brigade, and he wanted her to find them, and make a list of their names, to be discharged.

> She said, "All right, but, sir, you need to know that the first name on that list will be mine."
>
> Eisenhower's secretary then spoke up: "Excuse me, sir, but with all due respect, the major's name will be the second one on the list. Mine will be first."
>
> The major then pointed out that the lesbians were the best soldiers in the corps, they didn't go off base and carouse with men, there were no pregnancies.
>
> Eisenhower said, "Forget the order."[13]

There was no such recorded willingness to look the other way when a *man* was suspected of being gay. For those who could pass as straight, there was the constant fear of being dragged out of the closet because of a letter they'd written, fraternization with other homosexuals, or being "outed" by another gay man. If discovered, gay men were thrown into the brig; labeled a sex pervert, criminal, or even a psychopath; and eventually tossed out of the service with dishonorable discharges, stripped of all veterans' benefits. "I was put in a psychiatric ward for observation," said a homosexual who chose to remain anonymous. "I had no legal counsel and was eventually tried. After being convicted, I was dishonorably discharged. I was mortified, afraid to go home." Officially, more than 9,000 gay men suffered the same fate during World War II. Unofficially, the number was much higher.[14]

Thirty million American men and women were uprooted during the war, either as members of the military or as civilians in search of work and improved living conditions. Away from family and friends—living at a time of heightened fear and a heightened lust for life—young men and women tested limits and often broke the rules. For the first time, many gays and lesbians developed a camaraderie they had never known in their hometowns. Single women landed jobs once exclusively held by men, made more money than they ever could have imagined, and, in the process, discovered the freedoms of financial independence and work outside the home. "It was a very exciting time," said Mimi Saunders, who was 21 when she moved from Detroit to Washington, D.C., to take a job with the government. "I had a date almost every night of the week and, yes, there was a man who stole my heart and, well . . . my virginity."[15] For the young men who went overseas, 84-year-old Seymour Simon summed it up this way:

> World War II brought sharp focus on the immediate and dimmed the long term. The man-woman intimacy created by sharing private thoughts, emotions, as well as bodies became an urgent goal for most men in the military. Spending long periods of time with men only, as much as two years or more for many, living far from the comforts of home creates a passionate desire for female company. To see women, hear women talk, hold, touch, feel, kiss, smell women . . . eat with women . . . yes, even to argue with women. The ultimate thought in the foxholes was to share living with a woman, including clean sheets, a comfortable chair and a cold beer in the refrigerator.[16]

For all the past and current interest in World War II and the myriad of books and films, there are some stories that, after more than 65 years, have never been told. Perhaps those whose lives were so affected by the war just wanted to recreate some semblance of normalcy once the troops came home. Maybe a resurrected core of traditional values in the late 1940s and 1950s made tales of wartime sex and romance too risqué to share. Without question, soldiers who were unfaithful and wives who strayed wanted to keep their transgressions under lock and key. *Thanks for the Memories: Love, Sex, and World War II* opens the hearts and memories of a generation that is dying, by one estimate, at the rate of approximately 1,100 a day. It exposes the sexual and romantic escapades of the "greatest generation" and underscores the importance of how those four war years revolutionized relationships between the sexes, between gays and lesbians, and helped set the stage for the second wave of the women's liberation movement. Many who never thought their stories mattered now feel the pull of limited time and the importance of leaving an accurate account for their children and grandchildren of what it was like to be a young man or young woman during World War II.

This is their collective story.

NOTES

1. Isabella Gillaspie, factory worker. Interview by author. October 29, 2002.

2. Time-Life Books, *This Fabulous Century: 1940/1950* (New York: Time-Life Books, 1969), pp. 178–79.

3. "USS VD: Ship of Shame," Los Angeles: Paramount Pictures, 1942.

4. Harry P. Cain, "Blitzing the Brothels," *Journal of Social Hygiene* 29, No. 9 (December 1943): 594–95.

5. Agnes E. Meyer, *Journey through Chaos* (New York: Harcourt, Brace and Company, 1943–1944), p. 111.

6. Allan M. Brandt, *No Magic Bullet: A Social History of Venereal Disease in the United States since 1880* (New York: Oxford University Press, 1985), pp. 163–64.

7. Richard Lingeman, *Don't You Know There's a War On? The American Home Front 1941–1945* (New York: Thunder's Mouth Press/Nation Books, 2003), pp. 88–89.

8. Mark Jonathan Harris, Franklin Mitchell, and Steven Schechter, *The Homefront: America during World War II* (New York: G.P. Putnam's Sons, 1984), pp. 179–81.

9. Barbara Abel, "Hail Hostess!" *United Service Organizations Program Service Publication #522,* p. 9.

10. John Costello, *Love, Sex and War: Changing Values 1939–45* (London: Collins, 1985), pp. 276–77.

11. Lingeman, p. 92.

12. Costello, p. 279.

13. Mary Ann Humphrey, *My Country, My Right to Serve: Experiences of Gay Men and Women in the Military, World War II to the Present* (New York: Harper Perennial, 1990), pp. 39–40.

14. Arthur Dong, *Coming Out under Fire,* documentary film (Los Angeles: Deep Focus Productions, Inc., 1994, 2003).

15. Mimi Saunders, USO hostess. Interview by author. February 12, 2003.

16. Seymour Simon, World War II veteran. Interview by author. April 14, 2004.

PROLOGUE: TO MY PARENTS—MORRIS AND SHIRLEY MERSKY

The handwriting on the envelopes never changed, even when the world around them was falling apart. My parents, like millions of other young couples separated by World War II, depended upon letters to keep them connected to each other and to their families. Those neatly folded pieces of paper—now curled at the edges and tinged brown with age—preserve the dreams, fears, and passions of men and women whose lives were fast forwarded and turned upside down the day in 1941 when the Japanese attacked Pearl Harbor.

As the daughter of parents who both "served" in World War II, I had heard bits and pieces of their stories over the years. But like many members of what Tom Brokaw dubbed the "greatest generation," my parents rarely talked about the war and the fears, separations, sacrifices, losses, and life lessons associated with it. The wartime letters and scrapbooks that had somehow survived multiple moves and decades of annual spring cleanings were stuffed away in a corner of the basement, and it seemed their memories were, too. World War II had changed the psyche as well as the face of this country and of the world. Yet the survivors of that heady time who were closest to me were mum.

That all changed one Thanksgiving more than 10 years ago, when I listened in awe as my mother and her cousin by marriage, Lila Saulson, swapped stories of their time on the road as service wives and the challenges their husbands faced both stateside and overseas: crowded troop trains, shabby rooms with packrats and roaches, lusty landlords, near disasters while learning to fly, learning to play bridge in less than an hour to secure a place to stay, lonely days and nights, aircraft engine troubles behind enemy lines, and the births of their children into a chaotic, confusing world. It was suddenly clear that World War II had been the pivotal emotional experience of their lives; it had shaped their character and liberated them—at least, for a time—from traditional inhibitions and roles.

Shirley Saulson, a teacher, and Morris Mersky, a salesman in the grocery business, were married on December 22, 1940, after a one-year engagement. Theirs was a carefully considered marriage, not a "last fling" decision, as were an estimated half the marriages once war became increasingly imminent in 1941. By then, my parents had settled into married life in Highland Park, Michigan, where they enjoyed a large circle of friends and close family ties.

On December 7, 1941, my folks were visiting my mother's parents, watching my uncle and grandfather build a sailboat in the garage. When news of the Japanese attack on Pearl Harbor blared across the radio waves, my father jumped down the garage stairs. My grandfather turned white. And my mother just stood there, unsure of what it all meant. She learned quickly enough when my father announced he was going to enlist in the army air corps. But he was married, too old (24 years old), and too heavy to meet the army air corps' rigid requirements. Disappointed but intent on doing *something* for the war effort, he nabbed a job at the Continental Motor Corporation where small airplane engines were made. My father stayed at Continental Motor until he discovered that he could sign up for civilian pilot training and possibly use that experience as a flight path to the army air corps. At age 26, my father enlisted, training first as a civilian pilot in Wyandotte, Michigan, and then spending time at Washington University in St. Louis before heading to preflight training in San Antonio, Texas. His first letter to my mother from St. Louis dated May 17, 1943, described "quite a place" and closed with an uncharacteristic expression of love and sentimentality:

> I miss you like the devil already. I don't know what I'll do as time goes by. I certainly was proud of your saying good-bye. I think I cried more than you. You're a swell gal, and I love you with all my heart.

Two days later, he wrote:

> I think I will enjoy my stay here . . . There is only one serious thing wrong with the set up . . . you're not here. I do mean it. I'm terribly lonesome and it's only two days without you.
>
> Do you love me?

Mail call was one of, if not *the,* most important events of the day for a soldier away from home. For most servicemen, letters and magazines were their only contact with loved ones and old friends. There was no email or video phone, and phone calls were few and far between. You could always find soldiers carrying around letters, rubbed, worn, and crumpled after having been read over and over again. So many letters were sent during World War II that, to save shipping space to be used instead for war supplies, the War Department devised a miniaturized letter form known as the V-mail, or Victory mail.

The 37 bags required to carry 150,000 one-page letters could be re-placed by a single mail sack that weighed a mere 45 pounds versus 2,575 pounds. The specially designed V-mail letter-sheets were a combination of letter and envelope that were constructed and gummed so as to fold into a uniform and distinctly marked envelope. Once delivered, the V-mail was reduced to thumb-nail size on microfilm, and the rolls of film were sent to prescribed destinations for developing. Facsimiles were reproduced about one-quarter of the original size and then delivered to the addressee.

> I just returned from mail call and STILL NO LETTER FROM YOU. Have you forgotten me already? You have no idea how anxiously I wait for mail call and some word from you.

Finally, four days after my parents parted, a letter from my mother arrived.

In a letter my father wrote two weeks later, he talked about his first off base pass and his visit to St. Louis. His expressions of love took a back seat to his disgust for young soldiers' sexual appetites and the women who were appar-ently willing to do their "patriotic" duty and satisfy them:

> I ended up eating a steak dinner and then commenting on some of these "young fellows" who are under the impression that wearing a uniform entitles them to do a lot of things they wouldn't ever do as civilians . . . under the impression that the uniform makes them men. Out getting pickled and look-ing for women. And there are plenty of young gals in St. Louis. I guess it's all part of a country at war.

A country at war was a troubling, confusing place, with virtue and love under fire. As my father observed, young "fellows" in uniform were shedding socially acceptable behavior from back home, as were young gals. Sex and sexuality had become a significant part of the war experience—a hedonistic impulse that redefined relationships between the sexes. Who can say what part the fear of "young gals" played in my mother's eventual decision to join my father on the road? After more than seven months apart, my mother "made up her mind" to take a leave of absence from her teaching job to be with him during the remainder of his stateside training. "Nothing I would rather have," my father wrote. "But whether it's the sensible thing to do is another story." When it comes to love and war, *sensible* is not an operative word. And early on a frigid Detroit morning, my mother wedged a set of Mexican bookends into the trunk of her 1939 Chevy, slammed the trunk shut and slid into the driver's seat. With her mother, father, and two younger brothers assembled on the front porch, all waving furiously like the American flags flapping in the wind, she shifted into first gear and made her way slowly down Broadstreet Boulevard. My mother was driving to Corsicana, Texas, on the first leg of what would become more than a yearlong journey as a World War II service wife. She had no idea at the time that she was joining what the August 30, 1943, issue of *Time* magazine described as a "vast, unorganized army of women" estimated, by some, to include more than 1.25 million wives who were all following their husbands from one end of the country to the other.

The thousands of miles of travel, as captured in my mother's letters home to her family, often read like a movie script. Cadets at Corsicana's Perrin Field spent most of their time learning to fly PT 19As, trainers for the B24. Their time off was limited to Tuesday and Thursday base visits from 7:30 P.M. to 8:30 P.M., Saturday nights from 7 P.M. to 1 A.M., and Sundays from 8 A.M. to 10 P.M., if they didn't have to fly. But a few stolen hours here and there didn't add up to much. In a scheme to have more time with their wives, my father and a buddy of his volunteered for the staff of the *Flying Lines*, a weekly, 12-page newspaper with news items about the base and its personnel, cartoons, and weekly sections like "Locker Lovelies" (photos and bios of cadets' girlfriends and fiancées), a "Heroes' Corner," and "Girl of the Week." The last might feature a "classy lassie" like Mrs. Hazel Brenner, the wife of Corporal W.C. Brenner, or an 18-year-old like Miss Geraldine Bishop who, with her neatly-arched eyebrows, shoulder-length dark hair and seductive smile could win the hearts of many a young cadet.

My father had some limited experience doing advertising layout, and his buddy knew how to take a decent photograph. The *Flying Lines* staff was delighted to sign them on. Little did they know that the cadets' interest in journalistic pursuits had little to do with their willingness to serve. Armed with drafts of stories and page layouts, my father and his friend would leave the base to "go to the printer in town." Instead, they made a beeline to their respective wives' rented rooms to steal a few extra hours together each week. Of course, the boys couldn't return to the base without something to show for their time. So, my mother started writing articles and helped out with the typing. One of her poems, "'Twas Visitors' Night (with all due apologies to St. Nick)," appeared in the February 28, 1944, issue of *Flying Lines* and playfully described the one-hour base visits from the point of view of a cadet wife:

. . . In one sustained movement while the
moment was tense
They looked for their cadet: grabbed
their pass through the fence
Rushed through the gate; formed
into many a couple,
And raced for the reception room
on the double.
Holding hands, telling each other
the news
Both talking at once, 'cause there's
no time to lose…
At eight twenty-five just like Noah's
Ark,
They line up by twos for that kiss
in the dark.
It doesn't take long for wives to
learn
They no sooner arrive when it's
time to return.
Yet back on the bus they all cry
with delight
"Just 47 more hours 'til next
Thursday night!"

THE STRENGTH OF FRIENDSHIPS

While my father's military training accelerated, the friendships between service wives—all in the same boat—deepened. These wives of noncommissioned officers could not live with their husbands, and the amount of time they could spend with their spouse was limited. My mother's letters were filled with tidbits about dinners with other wives, roommates, and the trials and tribulations of looking for places to stay. Still, these young women, many barely out of their teens, persevered. An excerpt from one of my mother's letter follows:

Tonight I am having eight wives for a buffet supper in my room. Am going to have it really simple, but it should be fun. Baked a fudge cake using a recipe on the Hershey's Cocoa box.

> Spent last weekend packing, getting gas, loading the car. Planned to leave
> for Sherman, Texas, at 6 a.m. to beat all the other wives to rooms. Mary Jane
> and another girl from Detroit came with me . . . We looked and looked all day
> long. By late afternoon, we were getting desperate and finally decided that
> we'd have to find separate places. I landed a room with kitchen privileges but
> a shared bathroom with the family for $7.00 a week. The other wives are both
> within two blocks.
>
> I think Mary Jane will move in with me. We were planning on cooking to-
> gether, anyway. If she does move in, I won't be alone at night, and we'll each
> pay just $3.50 a week. On Saturday and Sunday nights when the boys come
> in, Mary Jane will take a room at a hotel.

While service wives like my mother were crisscrossing the country, World
War II, like all previous American wars, attracted another set of "unofficial"
service supporters: prostitutes. "Wherever these men are gathered, those who
seek to exploit them for gain will follow," wrote leading social hygienist Walter
Clarke. "And chief among the exploiters will be the procurer and the prostitute, spreading disease and disorder among those upon whom our protection
depends." My mother remembers hearing the story about a small Tennessee
town where there were no rooms for service wives to rent. And the only small
hotel was occupied by prostitutes. The service wives were determined to get
them out, so a group held sway in the hotel lobby. When the soldiers came to
"visit," the wives sang in unison, "We know where you're going!" The humili-
ated soldiers and ladies left in a hurry; the service wives got the rooms. This
"clash" between the prostitutes and the service wives represented for many the
larger battle for the health of the troops and the morality of the country.

The place of the service wife in this battle was up for debate. The wives
and their husbands saw their travels together as true love under pressure. The
wives provided comfort and a sense of normalcy in unsettling times. They
boosted their husbands' morale and, what was good for individual soldiers
was good for the country. In a letter from Sherman, Texas, where my father
was stationed at Perrin Field, my mother talked about my father not wanting
her to go home:

> Just sent in for my extension of leave of absence from teaching. Mor doesn't
> want me to go back while he's anywhere around . . . As long as I can be with
> him, I'm going to stay.

But magazines like *Modern Romances* criticized the wife who wanted to follow
her husband, both for her "jealous and mistrustful" nature and her failure
to understand her "mission" to "keep the home fires burning." One article

suggests: "Ask your soldier what *he* thinks of them," implying that they were unpatriotic and overly sexual. Neither my mother nor any of the service wives she knew read *Modern Romances*. Even if they had, such attacks on their character and motives wouldn't have meant a damn. They were on the road for the "duration."

BEGINNERS' LUCK

My father received his army air corps wings in August 1944. As an officer, he and my mother were finally allowed to live together—that is, if they could find a place to stay. One of my father's assignments took him to Davis-Monthon Air Force Base in Tucson, Arizona. That meant some 980 miles of nonstop driving with my parents taking turns at the wheel. Although the drive was uneventful, the stay in Tucson was anything but. There was absolutely no place to stay—no rooms or apartments or hotel accommodations. So, my parents spent their first night in the car. The next day, my father reported to the base, only to find that his name was not on the roster. More concerned about a place to stay, he decided to find a room first, then to settle his assignment. A colonel overheard him inquiring about a room.

"If you and your wife play bridge," the colonel said, "we have a space to rent in our home."

"We play a great game of bridge," my dad said, trying not to look the liar.

He'd never played a game of bridge in his life!

Never mind. My mother would teach him.

The colonel's home, nestled in the foothills of the Sierra Mountains looked like the Taj Mahal, at least after a night in the car. The "spare" room came with its own enclosed garden and European hand-carved furniture. My parents thought they'd reached Paradise. But the excitement over the room was quickly overshadowed by the reality that my father had to learn how to play bridge in a matter of hours.

"I am telling Mor as much as I can as quickly as I can," Shirley said. "How points are counted . . . how many points each card is worth . . . and he's writing it all down on the inside of his cuff."

Then there was a knock on the door. "Excuse me," the Colonel's wife said as she walked into the room. "There's been a change of plans. Some friends are visiting this evening, so we won't be playing bridge. We'll be playing poker."

The color returned to my father's face. He'd gotten a reprieve.

But now it was my mother's turn to panic. *She'd* never played a hand of poker in her life! So, with the tables turned, my father became the teacher, trying to quickly fill my mother in on the rules of the game.

Beginner's luck has a way of showing up just in the nick of time.

My mother played like a pro, winning $400. (Sixty-two years later, there is some disagreement as to the exact windfall. "It was more like $4," my father said.)

Whatever the amount, my mother had begun to like poker and hoped friends would be visiting the colonel and his wife regularly. She was counting her money when there was another knock on the door.

It was the colonel's wife. "Now that we have you to share expenses," she said excitedly, "we've decided to hire a house boy."

She left the room, and my parents knew they'd be looking for yet another place to stay. There was no way they could afford to help pay for a house boy.

The next day, my father went to the base, only to be told that there had been a mistake in his orders. He was supposed to be in Pueblo, Colorado, not Tucson, Arizona, and he was to make it there on the double.

The ride from Tuscon to Pueblo was a rough one, and the nausea my mother attributed to driving the highest highway in the world through the Rocky Mountains turned out to be the first signs of morning sickness. She was pregnant.

In a letter dated December 2, 1944, my mother made the big announcement:

> And now for the big news!!!!! You are going to be grandparents. We are so thrilled and excited it isn't funny. You'd think no one else had ever had a baby before . . . We're saving silver dollars like mad and already arguing about names and the poor child's future education. The baby's due at the end of July or the first part of August. With a miraculous break, there's a chance Mor might complete his mission and be home by that time. We know it won't be easy under the circumstances, but it will certainly be worth it.

In another letter written a month later, my mother talked about decisions that needed to be made before my father left for the European theatre. Her resolve to think ahead and face the possibility of having to raise her child alone is a poignant reminder of the realities of war. By the end of 1944, the Battle of the Bulge, the largest land battle in which American forces participated, was well under way. At its conclusion, 81,000 Americans would be killed, captured, or wounded.

> Where did you get the idea that I was going to resign from teaching? That would be a foolish thing to do now. I'm going on a maternity leave for two years. I hope I'll never have to go back to teaching, but until this war is over and Mor comes

home safe and sound, I wouldn't dream of resigning . . . He and I have gone over this thing backward and forward, and that's one of the reasons we want to register the baby at Merrill-Palmer (a nursery school in Detroit). If anything should happen and I'd have to go back to work, there would no better place to leave the baby. Naturally, we hope this will be unnecessary, but we're trying to face all the possibilities, solve them, then dismiss them and have faith.

With the war continuing to drag on and the number of American casualties continuing to mount, faith was not always easy to come by. "The war news from Europe is certainly not what we would like to hear," my mother wrote. "I wonder how long this damn war is going to last. Both Mor and I are sick to death of it, and it can't be over too soon to suit us."

In her last letter from the road, my mother tried to reassure her parents that there was no problem in her driving all the way from Pueblo, Colorado, to Detroit in her "condition."

Dr. Lang says driving home is perfectly fine as I will already be in my fourth month when I leave here. I'm beginning to feel a little better and will be just fine . . . Time is flying so fast that it scares me. I dread Mor's going overseas but the sooner he goes, the faster he'll get back.

* * *

After seven months stationed in Cerignola, Italy, my father did get back and not a moment too soon. There are no letters that record my birth on July 25, 1945—only the remembered event as filtered through the years.

Three strangers dressed in military uniforms came to my grandparents' home where my mother had been living since she had returned to Detroit. The somber soldiers handed my mother one of the dreaded missing-in-action telegrams that succinctly told of the loss of my father's plane behind enemy lines. The shock sent my mother into early labor, and she was whisked off to the hospital to give birth.

My father's plane had, indeed, gone down but just *outside* enemy lines. Despite the disabling of two engines, the crew managed to land the plane safely. However, due to a three-day communications blackout during which General Mark Clark and the 5th Army moved toward Rome, the whereabouts and status of my father and his crew were unknown. The telegram had been sent before the disabled plane limped back to camp. Upon hearing that a crew scheduled to fly several generals back to the States needed a copilot, my father added his name to the many other volunteers. He knew my mother's due date was fast approaching and would have done just about anything to be at the hospital. Miraculously, his name was chosen from all the other names in a hat.

Ten hours after the three strangers had appeared at my grandparents' home, my grandmother opened the front door again—this time, to see my father standing on the front porch. In between gasps, she was able to tell him that my mother had gone into labor early and was in the hospital. My father jumped back in to his rented car and sped off, only to return several minutes later looking rather ruffled. "Which hospital?" he asked.

In 1945, the nuns at Providence Hospital still wore long, flowing habits with starched white bibs and a collar securing the bib to a black veil. And in 1945, men were not allowed to be with their wives once they went into labor. My father would have none of it and demanded to see his wife. The attending nun was not sympathetic and instructed him to kindly take a seat in the waiting room until his baby was born. "But it's your patriotic duty," my father said, trying to appeal to the nun's sense of country.

She didn't buy it.

Frustrated, he took a seat—but not for long. Once the nuns had retreated to their various stations, my father spotted a portly nun, just beginning to climb the stairs to the second floor. Quietly, without drawing attention to himself, he placed himself directly behind the overweight nun in the flowing habit. Each time she took a labored step, he took a step. Slowly but surely, the two of them made it up the stairs, with my father virtually hidden behind her habit. Once at the top of the stairs, he darted past her and down the corridor.

When the overweight nun finally caught up with him, she acquiesced and volunteered to go in to the labor room and tell my mother to hurry up and have that baby because her husband was waiting in the hallway.

My mother didn't believe it for a minute. Her husband was missing in action. He might already be dead. And she was going to have to raise her child alone. The nun kept insisting that none of that was true and, finally, in a moment of calm, my mother asked to see a note from my father, if she could not see *him*.

She recognized his handwriting right away and, against the nuns' protestations, rolled over on her side, gingerly put her feet on the floor, and lumbered out into the hall. While she had recognized my father's handwriting, she didn't recognize *him!* He'd lost thirty pounds, his brown hair was bleached blonde, and his face was deeply tanned from the hot Italian sun. For an awkward few seconds, my parents stood frozen in time. Coming to their senses, they embraced—relieved, grateful, and very much in love. I was born at 4:40 A.M. Eastern War Time after one hell of a ride.

Through my parents' stories I had discovered a doorway to the larger story of love and romance, war and sex during World War II. Just like my mother 61 years ago, there was nothing that could stop me from getting up and walking through that doorway. What I found were women and men—single, married, military, and civilian—who had experienced firsthand the social and sexual upheaval of World War II and whose futures were, in a multitude of ways, molded by a war that changed the dynamics between the sexes for an entire nation and for subsequent generations like my own.

Although the paths of most of these men and women never crossed, their stories do.

One

DERAILED DREAMS

Ed Gannon carefully took coins from his back pocket and counted out the exact amount of money his oldest daughter would need for trolley fare to and from school. It was December 1933, and Olga, a high school senior, stood in the kitchen next to her father's chair, anxious to get the money and leave for school. Ed Gannon didn't look at his daughter as he handed her the change. His shoulders hung limp; his voice wavered as if he'd had the wind knocked out of him. "Whatever it takes, we'll have enough for the trolley fare," he said.

Like millions of other Americans, Ed Gannon was broke. He'd lost money in the stock market crash of 1929, lost the remainder of his savings when his bank and almost 3,000 others collapsed by the end of 1932, and now he'd lost the government job that then Senator Robert Wagner of New York had finagled to get for him. The father of six, who prided himself on being a capable and successful breadwinner for his wife and children, was overnight rendered penniless, unable to put food on the table. Embarrassed and dejected, he never fully recovered from the insults of the Great Depression and died in an automobile accident during a major storm at age 67.

No one suspected that the country was going to fall into a depression so severe that it would take 10 years to recover. On May 1, 1930, President Herbert Hoover said, "I am convinced we have passed the worst and with continued effort we shall rapidly recover." But by the end of 1930, there were more than 25,000 business failures and, as later studies would estimate, 4 million Americans unemployed. Still, Americans could think that the economic plunge was just a routine business-cycle downswing. Then, 600 banks collapsed in the last two months of 1930. "Mobs of shouting depositors shouldered up to the tellers' windows to withdraw their savings. The banks, in turn, scrambled to preserve their liquidity by calling in loans and selling assets. . . . They further drove down the value of assets in otherwise sound institutions, putting the entire banking system in peril."[1] By the end of 1932, 2,294 American banks had failed, nearly twice as many as in 1930. Well over 10 million Americans were out of work, almost 20 percent of the workforce. In big cities like Chicago and Detroit, the unemployment rate ran to almost 50 percent. That number, as large as it is, underestimates the impact of the Depression because the typical household had only one wage earner. When the wage earner lost his job, there was no other means of support. The Great Depression, which spanned over a decade from 1930 to 1940, with aftershocks up until America's entry into World War II at the end of 1941, ruined lives, derailed dreams, and changed the course of personal relationships.

Olga Gannon had dreamed of a career in architecture and, later, marriage. But as soon as she graduated from high school, she went to work to help feed her family. Only through a family connection did she land a job as an office girl at a beach club that lasted just a few months because no one had money to join swimming pools. Gannon wandered from one temporary job to another, working next for the telephone company, then as a convention registrar. "I walked home from those conventions at three in the morning, wearing an evening gown I sewed myself and my one pair of high heels," she said. "Trolleys didn't run that late at night. And taxi fare was out of the question. I spent a lot of time at the shoemakers, trying to save those brown pumps."[2] Her mother, who before the Depression had enjoyed cooking fancy French meals, now had to settle for spaghetti, soup, and other inexpensive dishes. Still, the Gannon family had food on the table and never stood in the long soup lines that wound their way up and down thousands of American streets. People scavenged garbage cans for food. Evicted families moved in with relatives or lived in cars or makeshift cardboard shacks.

With unemployment rates never dropping below 14 percent, reaching a national high of 25 percent in 1933 and, as late as 1941, eight million workers earning less than the legal minimum wage, men were reluctant to marry if they couldn't provide for a family. The marriage rate plunged from nearly 90 percent per 1,000 women in 1929 to just 60 percent per 1,000 only 10 years later. The Depression's gloom seeped into the country's bedrooms, too, as married couples had fewer children—15 percent fewer in 1933 than in 1929.[3] The Depression didn't play favorites; it hit almost every sector of the economy. One-third of American farmers lost their land from 1929 to 1932. Housing starts plunged by almost 90 percent between 1929 and 1933. The Dow Jones Industrial Average fell by almost 90 percent. Total wages dropped 60 percent.[4] Even the divorce rate declined by 25 percent, with the shrinking economy sealing the exits from unhappy marriages. As David M. Kennedy writes in *Freedom from Fear,* "Unemployment could also powerfully rearrange the psychological geometry of families. Out-of-work men experienced both the loss of a paycheck and the loss of respect from wives and children who couldn't understand why their 'man' could no longer support them."[5]

For single women like Gannon who were lucky enough to find work, the idea of fooling around on the job was absolutely out of the question. You did your work or you were fired. There were plenty of others waiting in line to fill your shoes. That didn't seem to faze Marshall Warfield. A runner, or errand boy, at the bank where Olga eventually settled as a file clerk, Warfield took one look at the full-lipped, brown-eyed clerk and was absolutely smitten. Gannon was oblivious. She didn't notice that the curly-haired young man with narrow brown eyes delivered packages, memos, and other office goods to her work station several times each day. Even when Warfield invited her to see *Gone with the Wind* at the Palace Theater, she brushed off his attention. Gannon was for quite some time the sole financial supporter in her family, with five children still living at home. Life was serious and challenging. There was no room for romance. Still, Warfield persevered. He took her to office parties and to the country on weekend jaunts to ride horses and visit relatives. He told her how much he loved her. Gannon called it "puppy love" and assured him that he'd quickly outgrow his feelings. Then, in 1939, he and his brother joined the National Guard to help protect their country and went off to train at Fort Mead in Maryland. The couple saw each other on the weekends and, on one of those visits, Warfield popped the question. "I'm like a six-year-old," Gannon told him. "I haven't had any independence and I'm not thinking of marrying anyone. Furthermore, I don't want to live as the wife of an enlisted man."

Warfield took care of that. He went off and became a First Lieutenant in the army's Ninetieth Infantry Division. Then he and Gannon did some serious talking. She honored a promise to pay for the flowers at her younger sister's wedding and then accepted Warfield's marriage proposal. An older bride at age 27, Gannon looked at a map and picked Asheville, North Carolina, as a convenient place to be married, halfway between Washington, D.C., where she still worked as a secretary and Fort Benning, where Warfield was then stationed. The bride wore a smoky blue dress, a spring coat that matched, and a hat with a wide brim. Following the ceremony officiated by a Jesuit priest in a Catholic church, the newlyweds stayed in a hotel wedding suite and shared a bathroom with her mother in the room on the other side. "There wasn't any birth control in those days," Warfield said. "Well, I knew about this jelly stuff but I didn't want to deal with that! I'd never heard of condoms. And I never thought *once* about the possibility of getting pregnant."[6]

THE COMSTOCK ACT AND THE ATTEMPTS TO END IT

Warfield may not have worried about getting pregnant, but birth control advocates did. By 1930, there were 55 birth control clinics in 23 cities in 12 states. However, the 1873 federal ban on disseminating birth control or birth control information through the mail or across state lines remained in force. The Comstock Act, as it was called, was named after its sponsor, Anthony Comstock, a dry goods clerk and then self-appointed crusader against obscenity. Comstock founded the New York Society for the Suppression of Vice and boasted about the number of "libertines" he had driven to suicide. He carried a sack of "lowbrow" material to Washington, including literature on contraceptives and abortion. It wasn't hard to find support for his position and, in 1873, Congress passed the Comstock Act that, among other measures, defined contraceptive information and materials as obscene and made their dissemination illegal. Scientific books were censored, pharmacists were arrested for discussing contraception, and hundreds were imprisoned. Comstock later bragged that he had convicted enough people to fill a train with 61 passenger cars—roughly 4,000 citizens.[7]

If he had been alive in 1916 (he died a year earlier), Comstock would have delighted in the arrests of Margaret Sanger, the leader of the birth control movement in the United States; her sister, Ethel Byrne; and another woman, Fania Mindell, for opening the first birth control clinic in America in the Brownsville community of Brooklyn, New York. Born into an Irish working-class family, Sanger witnessed her mother's slow death, worn out after 18 pregnancies and 11 live births. While working as a practical nurse and midwife in the poorest neighborhoods of New York City in the years before World War I, Sanger saw women deprived of their health, sexuality, and ability to care for children already born. Contraceptive information was so suppressed by clergy-influenced, physician-accepted laws that it was a criminal offense to send it through the mail.[8] Sanger and the other two women were tried and found guilty under New York State's Comstock Act. Sanger refused to pay a fine and served 30 days in the Queens County Penitentiary. Byrne was sentenced to Blackwell's Island, where she went on a hunger strike and became the first woman to be force-fed in an American prison. Fania Mindell was fined $50 for distributing copies of a pamphlet written by Sanger, titled "What Every Girl Should Know." Once released from jail, Sanger's passionate devotion to the birth control movement led to its growth both in America and around the world. She founded the American Birth Control League in 1921 and opened the Birth Control Clinical Research Bureau (BCCRB) in New York two years later. Despite the apparent progress in birth control education and distribution, the Comstock Act was used again in 1929 when police raided the BCCRB, arrested physicians and nurses, and seized supplies and confidential patient records. Photos of the arrested staff being loaded into a police paddy wagon were splashed on the front pages of newspapers across the country. A judge later dismissed the charges, citing insufficient evidence. But the publicity generated by the raid helped secure support from the medical profession and community leaders. By 1930, nearly 100 national, regional, and local groups had passed resolutions in favor of birth control.[9]

With the election of Franklin D. Roosevelt as President in 1932 and then again in 1936, those working in the birth control movement began convincing social workers of the importance of birth control. Caseworkers were desperate for information about contraception and the authorization to dispense it to clients. Despite their efforts, birth control was mainly available for middle- and upper-class women who had access to regular health care. For them, the vaginal diaphragm, the most effective form of contraception at the time, was the method of choice. But as Linda Gordon points out in *Woman's Body, Woman's Right,* a diaphragm needed to be individually fit, and its use required privacy, running water, and a full explanation—luxuries not available to most American women. Less complicated methods of birth control like the vaginal sponge moistened with some spermicidal substance or condoms were used more regularly.[10] Even though the harsh realities of the Depression had led to the disappearance of the fun-loving, sexually free flappers, those women still believed in sexual liberation. Their expectations continued to clash with society's view of contraception as a way to prevent the birth of children that families could not afford.

In 1933, Margaret Sanger decided the time was right to test the constitutionality of the Comstock Act. She had an order of pessaries (solid, bullet-shaped preparations designed for easy insertion into the vagina to be used as contraceptives) sent from Japan to a physician in New York and then leaked information about the order to the postal authorities. In a major victory for Sanger and the proponents of birth control, Judge Augustus Hand, writing for the U.S. Circuit Court of Appeals in the case of *U.S. v. One Package of Japanese Pessaries,* ordered a sweeping liberalization of federal Comstock laws as applied to the importing of contraceptives. Although the judge's decision stopped short of finding the laws unconstitutional, he found that birth control could no longer be classified as obscene, based on the recent data on the damages of unplanned pregnancy and the benefits of contraception. Though it would be nearly 30 more years before the U.S. Supreme Court effectively repealed the Comstock laws across the country, Sanger's ideas that had once been so controversial gradually became "entrenched" in American public life. Still, those women who did not have regular access to private doctors were deprived of birth control information—that despite a 1937 poll showing 79 percent of women believed in birth control. Interestingly, this overwhelming majority was not rebelling against a traditional family role for women. They wanted control over pregnancies in order to make their traditional housework easier, not to escape it.[11]

Warfield did not get pregnant, even though she and her husband never used birth control. (She discovered later that a girlhood accident in which a small tree branch had gone up her "middle" made conception impossible. Only after an operation was she told she would be able to conceive.) Following her wedding in March 1943, the new Mrs. Warfield packed her bags and followed her husband to three different military bases. Because he was an officer, Lieutenant Warfield and his bride were allowed to live together off base. "I remember the guest house on a beautiful estate in Columbus, Georgia," Warfield said. "We paid only $35 a month, and everyone was jealous. The house was furnished; all we brought were two pillows." Warfield knew that Marshall could be sent overseas "any minute," but the newlyweds made the most of their time together. Almost a year later, Lieutenant Warfield shipped out, first to Scotland, then on to France, and Olga, like so many other young wives, returned home to live with her parents in Washington, D.C. Warfield's division eventually made its way to France and, on August 8, 1944, Lieutenant Warfield was awarded the Silver Star for gallantry. The citation published in the *Baltimore Sun* in September 1944, read as follows:

> Lieutenant Warfield was leading a reconnaissance platoon riding in a quarter-ton truck advancing the rear of a light tank platoon which was leading a task force.
>
> Upon reaching a turn in the road an enemy anti-tank weapon fired on and hit the leading tank, which the crew immediately abandoned. Unable to bring fire

from other sources, Lieutenant Warfield worked himself forward to the disabled tank, found its gun unimpaired and used it to knock out the enemy gun and ammunition truck.

This gallant action permitted the column of the task force to advance rapidly and facilitated the mission of the whole force and was in keeping with the best traditions of the military spirit.

But Lieutenant Warfield's gallantry wasn't enough when, just six weeks later, he and two other men riding with him on yet another early morning reconnaissance mission were hit by enemy sniper fire. All three men were killed.

Olga Warfield never remarried. She had plenty of boyfriends over the years and almost married a second time, but the man was a divorcé, and Warfield's family would never have approved. She worked in a variety of jobs until she became "voluntarily unemployed" at age 65 and has spent the intervening 25 years doing all the things she was unable to do while holding down a full-time job. Until she was almost killed in an automobile accident five years ago when a driver ran a red light and hit her broadside, she was a strong and healthy woman. Since the accident in which her head was smashed open, her leg cut to the bone, and both shoulders injured, she has suffered a stroke and breast cancer. "I'm too old to do anything about it," she said. "I really don't give a damn." At age 91, she describes herself as a "hermit" who is glad to be alone. "I never had enough time," she said. "I am enjoying my solitude. And as I look back, there is no doubt that the Depression followed by World War II took the most important parts of my life."[12]

COURTING DURING THE DEPRESSION

With the family as a refuge from the difficulties of the Depression, public opinion polls confirmed that the overwhelming majority of Americans showed little interest in altering traditional gender roles or conventional sexual norms. Psychologists, family "experts," media, and advertisers perpetuated the view of woman as wife and mother and man as breadwinner. When it came to sex, women (and many men) were on their own. There was no such thing as sex education, and the topic was not one readily discussed, if at all, between parents and their children. The opportunity to leave home for coeducational colleges—many of them established in the 1920s—and to experience newfound academic and social/sexual freedom was denied many young Americans during the Depression. Ninety-nine-year-old David Kaufman was the valedictorian of his high school class in Collegeville, Pennsylvania. "I was scheduled to attend engineering school," Kaufman said. "But my parents lost everything in the Depression, and I was forced to leave high school in the middle of eleventh grade and go to work in a parking lot." Edith Bennett, now 85, suffered a similar blow. As a high school senior in 1939, she earned a scholarship to a college about 60 miles from her home in Everett, Washington. "It was the Depression," Bennett said, "and my parents literally did not have enough money for me to take a bus trip to see the college. That was a lost dream." After graduating from high school, Bennett went to work as a clerk at a Montgomery Wards store in her home town for $2.16 a day. "I didn't particularly like the work," Bennett said, "but it was a paycheck that helped my family. Just one of the facts of life at that time."[13]

At age 93, Mort Hahn of Chicago looked at a photo of two young women riding bicycles on a warm summer afternoon. He pointed to one of the two women and said to a tenant who rented the second floor of his two-flat, "She was the love of my life." "Oh," said the tenant. "Is that a photo of your deceased wife?" "No," Hahn said. "That is someone else." Hahn first met Florence at the Jewish temple he and his family attended. "She was a very warm person," Hahn said. "And she had a great sense of humor." One afternoon, the young couple sat in Hahn's car overlooking Lake Michigan. "Will you marry me?" *she* said. Very much in love, Hahn would have liked nothing more. But it was the Depression, and he didn't have any money. He had been forced to leave Crane College at the end of his junior year and go to work, and the job he found in the printing business paid very little. The couple continued to date until 1941, when Hahn received his draft notice in the second Illinois draft of World War II. He was 30 years old but very fit, and the army signed him up as a foot soldier in the infantry. Following 15 weeks of basic training, Hahn and his division sailed to England on an old, converted cruise ship, sleeping in hammocks five high. He wrote to Florence like "mad," maybe 1,000 letters total. Hahn fought in what was sometimes referred to as "hedge row country" in France. The hedges that separated properties could be 15 feet tall. Hahn would lean against one of the hedges and write part of a letter, while a couple of GIs dug a big hole. When enemy fire erupted, Hahn would jump in the hole for protection and return fire. When the firing stopped, he got up, crawled out of the hole, leaned up against one of the hedges and continued writing. It was in France that he got hit with shrapnel in his lower leg. He was first taken to a hospital in France, then flown to a second hospital in England to recover. Hahn was gone from Chicago for 52 months and, sometime during the last months, the tone of Florence's letters changed. Perhaps the years apart had diminished her feelings. Hahn decided to play it by ear. Shortly after his return home, he saw Florence, who introduced him to her new husband. Hahn was devastated. First, the Depression, then the war had prevented him from marrying the woman of his dreams.[14]

For those women and men who did get married during the Depression, many didn't have a clue about what to expect in the bedroom. Harriet Bloom, born in the Bronx, New York, in 1921, laughed when she talked about her sex life as a newlywed. Her soon-to-be husband bought her a book about sex which she read from cover to cover. "I wasn't sure I wanted to get married!" she said. "You know . . . in those days, my husband was considered 'ideal' because he'd never gone to a prostitute. But that made two virgins. But we finally got the idea." The Blooms decided not to start a family until after the Depression and, then, not until after Sidney's stint in the army during World War II. As a male high school teacher, Sidney's job was secure, even during the dark days of the Depression.[15] While the percentage of married women teachers doubled, the majority of school boards refused to hire them. And if a married female teacher got pregnant, she was summarily fired as soon as word of her "condition" reached the administration.

Jack Havener and his girlfriend, Mary Alice, lived in the small, rural town of Sterling, Illinois, population 12,000. They met in confirmation class at the local Lutheran church when they were 13 and 14, but didn't start dating until they were seniors in high school. Havener got his information about sex from the "dirty talk on the streets" and, somewhat surprisingly, from both his mother and father, who advised him to save sex for marriage and to "always be a gentleman." When they married on Christmas Eve, both Jack and Mary Alice were virgins. But they got the hang of things very quickly and tried to get pregnant right away. They were sorely disappointed when month after month passed and Mary Alice had not conceived. Several years later, after the war, it was discovered that she had an "infantile uterus" and could never bear children. Still intent on having a family, the Haveners adopted a 45-minute-old, nine-and-a-half-pound infant boy, delivered by an unwed mother in their hometown.[16]

SEX AND HOLLYWOOD FILMS

During the Depression, when couples like the Haveners and Blooms adjusted to married life and the economic pressures of the Depression, 60 million to 80 million Americans went to the movies each week. Movies had become a "universal form of entertainment" that "influenced the life of a nation" and, as such, producers were asked to acknowledge that impact and to adhere to a list of guidelines. When it came to sex, the Motion Picture Production Code, commonly known as the Hays Code, was crystal clear: The sanctity of the institution of marriage and the home shall be upheld. Movies were not to infer that "low forms of sex relationships" were the "accepted" or "common" thing, and producers were to adhere to a set of guidelines:

1. Adultery, sometimes necessary plot material, must not be explicitly treated, justified, or presented attractively.
2. Scenes of Passion

   a. They should not be introduced when not essential to the plot.
   b. Excessive and lustful kissing, lustful embraces, suggestive postures and gestures, are not to be shown.
   c. In general passion should so be treated that these scenes do not stimulate the lower and baser element.

3. Seduction or Rape

   a. They should never be more than suggested, and only when essential for the plot, and even then never shown by explicit method.
   b. They are never the proper subject for comedy.

4. Sex perversion or any inference to it is forbidden.
5. White slavery shall not be treated.
6. Miscegenation (sex relationships between the white and black races) is forbidden.
7. Sex hygiene and venereal diseases are not subjects for motion pictures.
8. Scenes of actual child birth, in fact or in silhouette, are never to be presented.
9. Children's sex organs are never to be exposed.

Along with forbidding nudity and profanity, this code included a long list of rules that now seem laughable. A few examples follow:

- Screen kisses had to be close-mouthed and were limited to six seconds.
- Whenever two characters embraced, at least one of them had to keep one foot on the floor.
- No plot would present evil "alluringly."
- Seduction could not be the subject of comedy.
- Such words as "broad," "pregnant," and "hold your hat" were prohibited.

In fact, anything Hays deemed "unnecessary" could be forbidden.[17]

Despite all of these moral dos and don'ts, Hollywood films were rife with sex, dirty talk, gender role, and identity reversals. In the 1933 film *Female,* Ruth Chatterton plays the head of a large car manufacturing company. She runs the company like a "drill sergeant" but spends her nights sexually testing several of her male employees. As her male assistant says, "Miss Dee is a superwoman. She's never found a man worthy of her, and she never will!" The men who mistake sex for love repulse her, and one of the film's running jokes is her daily instruction to transfer an unworthy man to Montreal.[18] M-

G-M's *Red-Headed Woman* (1932), starring Jean Harlow, ruffled many feathers when she, as a lower-class woman, seduced her wealthy, so-called happily married boss. Harlow used sex as a ticket to social and gender-role chaos, and audiences were "enthralled to see her breaking down class and sex barriers in one stroke by barging in on an exclusive country club to a make-out scene in a phone booth with her rich, respectable, married boyfriend." In *Red-Dust* (1932), Mary Astor, who plays a middle-class woman stuck in the jungles of "Indo-China," meets the sweating, sensual Clark Gable and jumps headlong into a hot romance. In John Ford's *Flesh* (1932), the female star, Karen Morley, is pregnant and broke, ditched in Germany by her criminal boyfriend. She marries a sweet wrestler and pretends that the baby is his. Morley then struggles, as does the audience, with doing the "right" thing and staying true to her husband and "yielding to the lure of fleshly pleasures with her sexy but no-good boyfriend."[19] As Gary Morris points out in his article about the M-G-M bad girls for *Bright Lights Film Journal,* the "bad girl" is bad because she rejects the sanctioned roles as wife and mother, breaks established class barriers, and uses her sexuality to get what she wants.

The male comedy duo of Bert Wheeler and Robert Woolsey starred in 18 films, all but one for RKO, and took "queerness" out of the closet and onto the big screen. The two didn't invent drag, but they cross-dressed often, with Wheeler often playing the femme to Woolsey's butch. For almost a third of *Peach O'Reno,* Wheeler poses as a completely convincing professional divorcé correspondent. When Wheeler's wig catches fire from a lit match, one of the characters remarks, "I smell punk," with knowing audiences aware of *punk's* meaning among homosexuals as a passive gay man. And when a female character says that Wheeler's character looks like a "loose woman," Woolsey assures her: "Don't worry, she'll be tight before the night is over." The cross-dressing and outrageous take on being "loved" or "kissed to death" in *So This Is Africa* so angered the National Board of Review that it condemned the film: "Nothing as salacious has ever come before the National Board in eight years of reviewing . . . it outrages every common standard of decency."[20] Despite such criticism, Depression audiences loved Wheeler and Woolsey and their attitude that just about anything goes. But the duo's films, in addition to numerous other sexually suggestive movies, not to mention gangster pictures, provoked outrage from Catholic and Protestant religious groups. A newly appointed delegate to the United States Catholic Church, the Most Reverend Amleto Giovanni Cicognani, called on Catholics to launch a "united and vigorous campaign for the purification of the cinema, which has become a deadly menace to morals." Fearing a significant loss of patrons and revenue, the Hollywood producers responded by getting serious about adhering to the Hays Code. In 1934, Hollywood established a bureau, later known as the "Breen Office" (named after its administrator, Joseph I. Breen) that reviewed every film before it was released. The Breen Office was given the power to grant or withhold a seal of approval, and without a seal, a movie could not be shown in the major theater chains. The Office dramatically changed the nature of films in the later 1930s. That change had at least one positive effect: It led Hollywood to cast more women in roles as independent career women, albeit only single women, instead of as mere sex objects. It also contributed to what Maury Klein called a "stylization of technique" as directors and screenwriters searched for "subtle, creative, and often witty ways to treat sexuality . . . while avoiding censorship."[21]

To boost movie attendance at a time of economic depression, theaters lowered admission prices by as much as 25 cents, gave away free dishes, offered double bills, and created Bank Night, in which a customer with the lucky number won a cash prize. Movies starring comedy teams like Wheeler and Woolsey and sexy starlets who broke the restricted vision of women as wives and mothers shook things up—at least, for a time. But once the religious moralists pressured Hollywood to straighten up its act, controversial issues like sex, homosexuality, and gender roles were, for the most part, shoved back into the closet. In their place were westerns, detective films, and screwball comedies like *It Happened One Night* or *My Man Godfrey*. The fantasy worlds created in these films helped, if just for a couple of hours each week, counteract the very real problems during the Depression and keep alive a belief in the possibility of individual success and a government capable of protecting its citizens. The films produced after strict enforcement of "The Code" did not, however, continue to explore more sexual equality in the bedroom or in the boardroom.

WAR

Time Magazine began a series of news broadcasts called "The March of Time" that was aired on CBS radio and shown as theatrical newsreels in movie houses across the country. The endeavor was one of the first big cross-promotion ideas and was a smashing success from 1931 through 1945. Beginning in 1942, soon after the United States entered World War II, other media giants like 20th Century Fox released newsreels called "Fox Movietonews," which covered important news of the day. Although conflicts and then all-out war had broken out in Europe and Asia in 1936, the United States had managed to stay out of combat. The country began to move ever so slowly out of the Depression, and the promise of renewed economic stability encouraged a spurt in marriage and in the birthrate. The so-called American Dream seemed possible once again, and life for many Americans improved. Then on December 7, 1941, the first wave of Japanese planes descended upon Pearl Harbor, dropping clusters of torpedo bombs on the unsuspecting naval fleet there. Within minutes, all eight of the American battleships had been hit, along with three destroyers and three light cruisers. Before the third wave of Japanese planes completed its final run, 3,500 sailors, soldiers, and civilians had lost their lives. It was the worst naval disaster in American history.[22] The surprise was complete, and the lives of American women and men would never be the same. The United States was now at war, a war that would forever change the landscape of American society and the balance of power between the sexes.

NOTES

1. David M. Kennedy, *Freedom from Fear: The American People in Depression and War, 1929–1945* (New York: Oxford University Press, 1999), p. 66.

2. Olga Gannon Warfield, secretary, World War II service wife. Interview by author. December 4, 2002, and March 4, 2005.

3. Kennedy, p. 165.

4. David M. Kennedy, "The First Measured Century." www.pbs.org/fmc/interviews/kennedy.htm.

5. Kennedy, *Freedom from Fear*, p. 165.

6. Warfield.

7. Mary Alden Hopkins, "Birth Control and Public Morals: An Interview with Anthony Comstock," *Harper's Weekly*, May 22, 1915, http://www.assumption.edu/acad/ii/Academic/history/Hi113net/his213/ComstockInterview1915.htm.

8. Gloria Steinem, "Margaret Sanger: Her Crusade to Legalize Birth Control Spurred the Movement for Women's Liberation." *Time*, April 13, 1998, pp. 93–94.

9. Planned Parenthood Federation of America, Inc., "1920s," "1930s," "1940s," http://www.plannedparenthood.org/pp2/portal/files/portal/medicalinfo/birthcontrol/bio-margaret-sanger.xml, http://www.plannedparenthood.org/pp2/portal/files/portal/medicalinfo/birthcontrol/fact-020709-contraception-history.xml.

10. Linda Gordon, *Woman's Body, Woman's Right: Birth Control in America* (New York: Penguin Books, 1990), p. 323.

11. Ibid, pp. 317–23.

12. Warfield.

13. Edith Bennett, Depression-era student, World War II service wife. Interview by author. October 3, 2002.

14. Mort Hahn, World War II soldier. Interview by author. June 7, 2005.

15. Harriet Bloom, young bride. Interview by author. March 13, 2003.

16. Jack Havener, World War II veteran. Interview by author. August 14, 2002.

17. "The Motion Picture Production Code of 1930 (Hays Code)," http://www.artsreformation.com/a001/hays-code.html.

18. Gary Morris, "Public Enemy: Warner Bros. in the Pre-Code Era," *Bright Lights Film Journal 17* (September 1996), http://www.brightlightsfilm.com/17/04b_warner.html.

19. Gary Morris, "The Bad Girls of M-G-M, 1932," *Bright Lights Film Journal 17* (September 1996), http://www.brightlightsfilm.com/17/04a_badgirls.html.

20. David Boxwell, "Wheeler and Woolsey Queered," *Bright Lights Film Journal 42* (November 2003), http://www.brightlightsfilm.com/42/wheeler.html.

21. "Hollywood and the Great Depression," Digital History, http://www.digital-history.uh.edu/historyonline/hollywood_great_depression.cfm.

22. Doris Kearns Goodwin, *No Ordinary Times: Franklin and Eleanor Roosevelt: The Home Front in World War II* (New York: Touchstone Books, 1994), p. 23.

Two

"PRAISE THE LORD AND PASS THE AMMUNITION"

It was an unusually warm and sunny December day in Bremerton, Washington, a fine enough day to wash a car. Edith and Frank Bennett had attended Sunday morning church services and were pulling up in front of the "cottage," the little home Frank had pretty much built himself. The Bennetts had the car windows rolled down and could hear their neighbor's radio blaring much too loudly. Frank had barely turned the ignition off when the McDonalds started waving their arms wildly in the air. Something was wrong. Frank and Edith hurried out of the car, and as they ran toward all the commotion, the McDonalds yelled in unison, "Pearl Harbor has been attacked!" Like millions of other Americans hearing the news simultaneously across the country, neither the Bennetts nor the McDonalds knew exactly where Pearl Harbor was. The four listened intently as the radio broadcaster filled in the blanks.[1] Just before 6:00 A.M. on December 7, 1941, Vice-Admiral Chuichi Nagumo's armada of destroyers, submarines, battleships, and cruisers headed due east toward Honolulu, Hawaii's Pearl Harbor, and the American ships and aircraft that lay serenely unsuspecting and virtually unprotected. Within minutes, 183 Japanese planes had lifted from the decks of the six Japanese carriers and were shaping their triangular formations for the first attack wave. By the time the second attack wave had been launched about an hour later, 350 aircraft were humming through the sky en route to their designated target. At that moment, most Americans were either asleep or relaxing on an early Sunday morning. And then all hell broke loose. For more than an

hour, bombs and bullets pounded the American arsenal, sinking or heavily damaging 18 U.S. naval ships, destroying 180 aircraft, crippling another
120, and killing 1,103 men. Another 1,178 men were wounded. The devastating attack had caught Americans and their government completely off
guard and rudely threw the United States into World War II. The picture
was grim, and in an address to a joint session of Congress the following day,
President Franklin D. Roosevelt issued a national call to arms. He expressed
outrage at Japan and confidence in the "inevitable triumph" of the United
States. On December 8, 1941, the United States declared war against Japan.
Three days later, Germany and Italy declared war against the United States.
The impact on Americans was immediate.

The navy town of Bremerton, Washington, where the Bennetts lived, went
in to an immediate lockdown. Rumors of Japanese submarines lurking in the
waters off Puget Sound ran wild. Restrictions at the navy yard were tightened,
with more guards posted around the clock. Total blackouts brought Bremerton and all cities along the West and East Coasts of the country to a standstill once the sun went down. Street lights and neon signs were turned off;
windows and doors had to be covered completely so as not to allow light to
escape; citizens were instructed not to drive a car (though many did with only
their parking lights on); and cigars, cigarettes, or pipes were not to be lit in
the open or near any windows. Wardens patrolled the streets like police officers looking for criminals. If any light was observed, they were quick to re-
spond with heavy footsteps and loud knocking on the offender's front door.
"It was wartime," Edith Bennett said. "It was expected of you. You were doing
your duty, and you learned to live with it." Overnight, the longtime Japanese
American residents of Bremerton and other west coast cities became suspect.
Friendships, many of them forged in elementary school between Japanese
Americans and whites, suffered under the pressure. When, in the summer of
1942, Japanese Americans were rounded up and put in camps, even sympathetic citizens like Bennett did and said nothing. "We weren't politically aware,"
she said. "They were shipped out, and we just went along with the program."[2]

Immediately following the Pearl Harbor attack, there was no clamor for
reprisals against the Japanese Americans. The editorial in the December 8,
1941, *Los Angeles Times* said that most of the Japanese on the West Coast
were "good Americans, born and educated as such" and predicted that there
would be "no riots, no mob law." The chief of the army's Western Defense
Command, General John L. DeWitt, initially shrugged off any discussion of
mass evacuations as "damned nonsense." "An American citizen, after all, is an
American citizen," he said. But all the sweet talk changed following the re-
lease of a government investigation at the end of January 1942. The report al-

leged without documentation that Hawaii-based espionage agents, including Japanese American citizens, had abetted Nagumo's strike force. As historian David M. Kennedy describes in *Freedom from Fear*, rumors from DeWitt and others about Japanese submarines and then an organized conspiracy in the Japanese community spread like hot lava flowing down an erupting volcano. Ultimately, the fact that all of DeWitt's "evidence" of secret communications between "the enemy at sea and enemy agents on land" was deemed false no longer mattered. Fear and prejudice toward Japanese Americans had reached a fever pitch; the damage had been done. In February 1942, DeWitt officially requested authority to remove all Japanese from the West Coast. Despite the fervent protestations of several members of the government, President Roosevelt was ultimately advised that DeWitt should move forward. One hundred ten thousand innocent Americans were interned in 10 relocation camps, one in Arkansas and the others scattered through the western interior.[3] The Office of Censorship made certain that photographs that revealed the ironies of the actions were kept out of view. One of these photos, taken by Dorothea Lange in 1942 during her brief time with the War Relocation Authority (WRA), showed a Japanese American, apparently a retired veteran, dressed in his military uniform as he reported to the Santa Anita Park assembly center.

> The uniform markings and ribbons showed that he had served in the United States Navy for at least twenty years, stretching back to World War I. WRA's internal shelf list of negatives says this photograph was one of several "impounded by Major Beasley," and as far as I know was not released during the war years. As the camps were being set up, the Office of Censorship and the BPR coordinated their efforts to review all photographs taken inside them. They released those that served the dual purpose of proving the inmates were confined securely enough to make certain they posed no threat to the country's safety yet showing they were not being mistreated.[4]

Eventually, 3,000 Japanese Americans were recruited from the camps into the 442nd Regimental Combat Team, an all-Japanese, segregated unit that fought bravely in Italy. Slowly, other "certifiably loyal" internees began to be released. Not until December 1944, however, following Roosevelt's reelection did the government declare that the period of "military necessity" was ended. "To this day," said Edith Bennett, "I regret this page of American history." She is not alone.

DOWN THE AISLE AND OFF TO WAR

The Selective Training and Service Bill that the U.S. Congress passed on September 16, 1940, launched the first peacetime registration of the country's men between the ages of 21 and 35 years. Despite the hectic promotional hectoring of men like Secretary of War Henry Stimson, the truth was that the armed services were not prepared for a large conscript army, and apparently, neither was the country. As reported in a *Life* magazine article at the end of 1940, only 18,700 men had registered for the draft. Young men did not flock to their local recruitment office, but they did make a beeline down the aisle. The provision in the Selective Service Act to exempt fathers from the draft, in combination with the infusion of billions of defense dollars into the economy and subsequent full employment after the Depression, created a marriage boom. The marriage rate jumped from a low of 56 per 1,000 unmarried females over the age of 14 years in 1932 to 69.9 in 1938, to 82.8 in 1940, to 88.5 in 1941, and to a high of 93.0 in 1942. "With both men and women in war industries," wrote the social scientists Andrew G. Truxall and Francis E. Merrill, "earning unusually high wages, plus an absolute minimum of unemployment, economic conditions were ripe for a rush to the altar."[5] The upturn in the business cycle, in combination with men and women's wartime-heightened needs for romance and intimacy, pushed the marriage envelope. In 1943, *Keystone,* a jewelers' trade magazine, announced that the supply of wedding rings was dangerously low, due to the number of weddings and the increasing popularity of double-ring ceremonies. Most of the couples who had deferred marriage in the 1930s finally acted on their dreams. And whether it was intended or not, wartime marriages did serve to exempt many newly married men from military service, once the wartime draft was enacted. Men who were married prior to or during World War II were "much less likely" to serve than those who stayed single. In fact, Selective Service officials were so upset by this fact that, in late 1941 and early 1942, the officials charged that many recent grooms were "trying to escape provisions of the Selective Service Act through dependency deferments." Bennett was one who congratulated herself on being married before the war, confident that Frank would not have to serve. But as news about the war got worse, Frank came home one night from his job at the navy yard job and announced that he was going to join the navy air force. Early the next morning, he took the ferry across Puget Sound to a navy air force recruitment office in Seattle. The six-foot, three-inch man who had worked construction for years looked like the model of good health. But he was married, and the navy air force was not accepting married men. Edith was elated; Frank was not. He persevered and went next to the army air corps recruitment office, where he took and passed all of the prerequisite physical and psychological exams. There was only one problem: He didn't have enough "opposing molars" in his mouth. His application was turned down. But Frank wasn't going to quit. He went to a local dentist and said, "Stick anything you've got in there to look like real molars." The dentist acquiesced, and $220 later (a sum equal to almost nine house payments for the Bennetts), Frank had "molars" that lasted for the next 63 years. He also had a place in the army air corps. In June, 1942, Bennett was sworn in but had to wait until that November before being called up. "I had no idea when I'd see him again," Edith said. "It was awful. But it was a time of unbelievable unity in the country. And there was so much support for the armed forces. I felt like just one of the crowd."[6]

OUT OF THE KITCHEN AND INTO THE WORKPLACE

Bennett joined what would eventually swell to an armed services of 15 million men and several hundred thousand women, three-quarters of whom eventually ended up overseas. Another 15 million Americans—one out of every eight civilians—changed their county of residence in the three and half years after Pearl Harbor in search of better jobs and living conditions. Before the war, about 30 percent of working age women, or nearly 12 million, were in the labor force. The vast majority were single women who held down so-called pink-collar sector jobs in nursing, clerical work, and sales. But World War II, with its enormous drain of man power, forced employers and the general public to not only accept women in the workplace but to woo them. In his 1942 Columbus Day Fireside Chat, President Roosevelt urged employers to open their minds and their doors: "In some communities," the President said, "employers dislike to employ women. In others they are reluctant to hire Negroes. . . . We can no longer afford to indulge such prejudices and practices." In 1943 and 1944, the height of war production, 50 percent of all adult women were employed, a larger percentage than ever before in the country. Seemingly overnight, 7 million women swarmed in to the workplace for the first time, taking the place of men in the factories, in the offices, and on the streets.

Twenty-year-old Phyllis Gould was one of the first female welders to be hired in the Richmond, California, shipyards. Like many married women with a child, she had "absolutely no plans of getting a job." Yet after the start of the war, Gould, who had thought for some time that welding would be a fun thing to do, made up her mind and went to welding school at the local high school. Her husband was not happy. After completing her welding training, Gould landed the job at the Kaiser Shipyards. The men at Kaiser didn't know exactly what to do with her, so the union waited until it hired five more women *and* a chaperone. "She was supposed to herd us around and make sure the men didn't approach us too closely or do or say anything out of line," Gould said. "They had no idea how the men would react." There was no obvious harassment, and the chaperone didn't last long. In retrospect, she probably should have stuck around. Gould started working the graveyard shift, and there was a foreman, she said, who thought he was "God's gift to women." He and everyone else on the shift knew that Gould hated it when one of the workers would shine a flashlight from his chrome hard hat into the back of her welding hood. The light would hit the glass of the hood and reflect back into her eyes, making it impossible for her to see. One night just before the end of her shift, a light hit her hood. Gould turned around and, in one quick move, swung the heavy stinger at the end of her welding rod, hitting the foreman in the head, knocking his hard hat off and onto the floor. Furious, he grabbed Gould's welding hat and jammed it down around her ears. "I'm going to write this up!" the foreman screamed, threatening Gould and her job. Even though he couldn't fire her because *he'd* instigated the little fracas, he made sure that Gould got only the "nothing" jobs. About a week later, he came sashaying up to her and said, "Well, are you tired of it?" "I'll do this for the rest of the war rather than make up to the likes of you!" she said. The foreman backed off, and Gould eventually resumed more challenging welding assignments.[7]

By 1942, with so many men gone, only employment of women could meet industry demands. The government's all-out publicity campaign to encourage women to work was wildly successful. Women were called to "arms" in a variety of ways, and their role was glorified and glamorized in posters and film images without ever sacrificing their femininity. One war poster pictures a young married woman wearing ruby red lipstick and painted nails to match. She grasps a handful of letters from her husband—her wedding ring is clearly visible—and stares longingly off into the distance. The poster admonishes her that:

> Longing won't bring him back sooner . . .
>   GET A WAR JOB!

Another poster features a cheerful young blonde, sitting or standing behind a typewriter. Placed in front of a red, white, and blue background, the perky single gal salutes the viewer, obviously delighted with the important role she is playing in the war effort. The poster reads:

> Victory Waits on *Your* Fingers—
>   Keep 'Em Flying Miss U.S.A.

Yet another poster shows a young married woman dressed in a red factory uniform with a red hat or hair net of sorts. She concentrates on what appears to be a long plastic or metal tube. The caption is straightforward:

The more WOMEN at work
  the sooner we WIN!

Women's war work was likened to housework, with images of knitting, icing a cake, or cutting bread. Operating a drill press was just like operating a can opener; wielding a welding torch was just like operating a mix master; handling a drill press was like ironing clothes. In Seattle an advertisement sponsored by I. Magnin & Company attempted to reassure women that they were capable of factory work, observing that "an American homemaker with the strength and ability to run a house and raise a family . . . has the strength and ability to take her place in a vital War industry." Not only that, according to an ad for Martin Aircraft, war work was "a lot more exciting than polishing the family furniture."[8] A group of 114 electric companies extolled the "modern magic" of electricity: "She's 5 feet 1 from her 4A slippers to her spun-gold hair. She loves flowers, hats, veils, smooth orchestras—and being kissed by a boy who's now in North Africa. *But, man, oh, man, how she can handle her huge and heavy press.*"[9]

For some women like Bella Gillaspie, work was an economic necessity. Her husband, Carroll Robert (whom everyone called Robert) was a navy enlistee stationed in Buffalo, New York, to help guard the Great Lakes against possible enemy attack. He made a measly $75 a month. Gillaspie, who left her job as a teacher in Mason City, Iowa, to be near him, couldn't make it on her husband's salary. She took an aptitude test at a company that made ball bearings for airplane wheels and scored higher in mechanics than anyone else who had ever taken the exam. She was trained as the first woman to do turret lathe work at the Buffalo-based company and was the only woman on the factory floor with 400 men. "The men were not happy," she said. "They'd come along and spit their chewing tobacco on the floor. It made me sick! I was a minister's daughter who had never been around anyone who had smoked." The job was very physical, and Gillaspie operated lathes with arms 5, sometimes 10 feet tall. But she got paid almost three times what she would have made as a secretary, leaping right up to "about $3 an hour." Her presence in the factory led to many changes, including the division of the men's bathroom to make a place for her, spittoons, and sawdust on the factory floor. Resentment among the male factory workers grew. They'd come around and tap her on the rear or put their dirty, sweaty arms around her.

But that harassment paled in comparison to the fear for her physical safety once the time engineer saw how many bearings she turned out each hour and the subsequent increase in the production quota for the entire factory. Gillaspie began to notice first one man from the factory, then another, then another riding her bus home after work. To make sure they didn't know where she lived, she got off at the wrong stop every day for over a week. Then she just up and quit. Her husband had been transferred to New York City, and Gillaspie followed him there. She lived in a small rental bedroom, worked as a secretary—resigned to the significantly lower salary—and saw her husband on weekends. After "following" him for two years around the United States, he was shipped to the Mediterranean Sea, where his ship was a watch dog for German submarines. Gillaspie went home to wait for her husband's return.[10]

When women managed to enter jobs that seemed still to be the prerogatives of men, they were sometimes mistreated or harassed, as was Gillaspie. "The point was that occupational segregation continues during the war, not at the same level that it had existed before the war, but still at a level which ensures that women will know their places when the war ends," said Alice Kessler-Harris, Professor of History, Columbia University. "The jobs that women took were separate and unequal. Now, I say that with a little hesitation, because they were certainly more equal than they had been before the war, and one doesn't want to dismiss the opportunities that were given to women," Kessler-Harris said. "But they still didn't get quite the same kinds of opportunities as they might have. Women were often paid less than men for the same work, and they rarely unionized. African American women suffered particularly. They were given the most dangerous jobs, the jobs which are the messiest and the dirtiest."[11]

AFRICAN AMERICAN WOMEN: NOWHERE TO GO BUT UP

For African American women, the majority of whom worked outside the home no matter what their marital status, the war was far less successful in breaking gender and color barriers. Discrimination against black women proved to be one of the most unyielding of prewar practices. Even employers who were willing to hire black men and white women balked at changing their practices to include black women. The reason most commonly given by employers was the fear that hiring black women would lead to resistance on the part of white workers. Karen Anderson writes of the acute situation in Detroit, where the hiring or promotion of black women led to five hate strikes in one two-week period. White women walked out, as did their male counterparts, objecting to sharing bathrooms and other facilities with black women. The racial stereotyping of African American women as carriers of disease, specifically venereal disease, underscored how much education and progress lay ahead. In order to skirt the government's fair employment practices, employers hired black women at the factory or office gate, only to fire them soon after, or told black women that there were no jobs available. Yet despite the persistence of discrimination throughout the war, the number of African American women working as domestics *did* fall from 72 percent to 48 percent, and the number of African American women farm workers dropped from 20 to 7 percent. Still, these women worked in a context of racism and oppression and in the lowest-paying jobs.[12]

THE SECRETARIES OF WASHINGTON, D.C.

The surge of women into heavy industry—never more than 10 percent of female workers in wartime—was overshadowed by larger numbers of new women in the workforce who took up clerical and service jobs.[13] Washington, D.C. became a mecca for young, single women who took advantage of the newfound freedom afforded them to live away from home, hold down a job, and have some fun. Arlington Farms, often called Girl Town, was a group of buildings that housed 8,000 young women, including 3,000 Waves, across the river from Washington.

> Most Girl Towners are slick chicks and bobby sockers in their teens and 20s. They left small towns or farms because they wanted to see the world, because the war had taken their boy friends, or through sheer patriotism. Many are amazingly naïve when they first check in . . . But they turn into young cosmopolitans after a few months of grown-up life and responsibility.[14]

Most of the girls, like Betty Henshaw, worked for the navy, the FBI, the Treasury, or in the Pentagon, "doing necessary little war jobs without benefit of uniform or glamour." Although single rooms rented for $24.50 a month and meals cost as little as 30 cents, young women had to watch every penny. Henshaw ate on a dollar a day—15 cents for breakfast, 35 cents for lunch, and 55 cents for dinner. The self-described "country girl" from Pennsylvania worked the day shift at the Pentagon doing clerical work with top-secret clearance and followed the movement of troops abroad. She and the other gals from Arlington Farms rode the bus to and from the Pentagon, but it didn't take long to figure out that many people stopped and offered them a ride. "We could tell by the sticker on the car windshield if it was a lieutenant, and you didn't want him to pick you up. He had to park too far away from the main entrance. But if it was a general . . . well, of course, you accepted the ride." Henshaw talked proudly about the time that General Dwight D. Eisenhower stopped. "All we said to him was 'good morning' and 'thank you,' but we drove right up to the main entrance."[15] After a day at the Pentagon, life continued to whirl at Arlington Farms with 800 young women in each dorm. The rooms were very small with a cot, a chest of drawers, a little cupboard, a desk, and a chair. But the cramped quarters didn't seem to matter. In an article titled "Twenty-Eight Acres of Girls" that first appeared in October 1, 1944, in the *St. Louis Post-Dispatch* and was later condensed in the November 1944, issue of *Reader's Digest,* Eleanor Lake describes what it was like in Girl Town around five in the afternoon when the day shift women came home from work:

> The first rush is to the mail desks, where squeals of joy greet letters with APO postmarks. Then, with an energy to make men quail, the girls plunge into activities—bowling, basketball, tennis, softball . . . Service men drop by to play the piano, shoot baskets with the girls in the gym, or bowl in the 12 bowling alleys . . . In a special, mirror-lined room, 20 girls at a time take the famous $50 beauty and personality course given by a New York beauty house—*free.* Here 5000 girls have learned such important arts as how to sit down and cross the knees gracefully while taking dictation, how to put on eyebrow make-up, how to find their most becoming color.[16]

Henshaw was raised a Methodist and still had "pretty good morals." She also had a boyfriend named Ed Hart, whom she met at Banana River Naval Air Station, now Patrick Air Force Base, outside of Cocoa, Florida. Henshaw wrote often but still dated other guys. That stopped the day she opened the mail to find an engagement ring stuck inside a cereal box. Later that year, Henshaw got a phone call from her fiancé. His ship, the *USS Barnett,* had been hit during the battle for the Pacific island of Okinawa and had limped back into Seattle's port for repair. Happy to be alive, her fiancé wanted her to meet him in Seattle and get married. She didn't skip a beat. Between the time in the morning when she announced to her bosses that she was leaving and the time she returned from lunch, the colonels had a big gift box waiting for her. Surprised, Henshaw opened the box and found a "gorgeous white nightie and negligee from a very expensive department store." One of the colonels said, "I don't know why the hell we got that for you. It's going to choke you all night!" Henshaw blushed and feigned appreciation for the boys' attempt at sexual humor.

Life was not so rosy for another young woman who lived down the hall from Henshaw. "She was a little promiscuous," Henshaw said. "Unfortunately,

I think she led a marine too far, and police reports stated that he strangled her to death with his belt."[17] "Single women may have been wooed into the workforce, but they were considered 'dangerous,'" said historian Elaine Tyler May. "Men were constantly being warned that these single women could take their money and give them diseases."[18] Who knows what led to the murder of the young secretary. But the stereotyping of young, single women during the war as "dangerous" set up a potential recipe for disaster, with men having the moral upper hand.

The train authorities opened the gates at Washington's Union Station, and a mass of humanity stampeded down the tracks. People squeezed through the train doors, pushing and shoving, all hoping to find a seat. The fastest in the crowd sat, only to ultimately share their coveted seat with one or two other passengers. Henshaw managed to sit on her suitcase in the aisle, swinging and swaying all the way to Chicago where she had to change trains. There, an official's voice blared over the loudspeakers, announcing that, due to the overflow of passengers, only the military and their dependents would be able to board. Flustered, Henshaw stood on the tracks when a sailor waltzed up to her and said, "Where you headed?" "Seattle," she said. "So am I. You're my wife!" The stranger grabbed her suitcase, nudged her toward a train door, and Henshaw and the sailor boarded the train together. The kind sailor never made an "unwanted advance," bought Henshaw a bag lunch at one of the whistle stop towns, and "escorted" her all the way to Seattle. After a grueling three-day train ride, Henshaw arrived in Seattle, with no fiancé in sight. He'd warned her that he might not be at the train station, if the ship was repaired early and he and the crew set sail back to the Pacific. But then there was the head of her six-foot, two-inch guy bobbing along, and she was never so happy to see anyone in her life. On May 14, 1945, a Monday, the two were married in a Seattle courthouse. That Friday, her husband shipped out, and the new Mrs. Hart got back on the train and returned to D.C. To this day, she regrets never having gotten the name of the sailor who took her as his "wife" and got her to Seattle on time.[19]

In her documentary film *Government Girls of World War II*, filmmaker Leslie Sewell interviews then-81-year-old Florence Orbach. Orbach, whose maiden name was Simon, remembered hunkering down in her bathtub in her one-room efficiency. She wasn't worried about German bombs. She had a roommate problem. "My roommate turned out to be a pathological liar and a nymphomaniac," said Orbach. Orbach, 21, worked as a secretary at the Pentagon during the war and lived at Arlington Farms and then in several apartments in Washington, D.C., by then needing a roommate to help share rent and other expenses. She'd been warned that she was "making a big mistake" to room with a woman named Dotsie, but she didn't listen. It didn't take long for her to understand why. One day after work, she came home to find Dotsie in bed with a sailor. Horrified, she ran into the bathroom and locked the door. On a double date some time later, the guys plied the gals with liquor and, the next thing she knew, Orbach found herself in a hotel room. Dotsie was already under the bed covers, servicing one of the men, and the other guy was making a play for Orbach. Again, she ran to the bathroom, locked the door, and waited until Dotsie had done her "patriotic" duty. "It was a miracle that I survived!" Orbach said. The landlady at the last apartment they shared loved Dotsie but disliked Orbach intensely. "I don't know if it was because I am Jewish or because she saw all my union mail. I was a member of the United Federal Workers Union that eventually became part of the CIO, and many saw us as subversives." Whatever the reason for her dislike, the landlady gave Orbach one hell of a talking to about morals and loose women after *Dotsie* had spent the entire afternoon shacked up in the room with some guy. Not long after, Dotsie went away for the weekend with her "general" or "captain" and never returned. Orbach never saw or heard from her again.

Orbach, a self-described shy gal from Hicksville, Long Island, New York, was struck not only by some women's loose morals but by the way African Americans were treated at places like People's drugstore in downtown Washington, D.C. "What they had was a long counter. White people could sit on the stools, and up to a point, then the stools disappeared and the black people had to stand and order the food or stand and eat there. I thought, That's horrible." A matter of months after the war, Orbach married, raised a family, and worked for the Montgomery County Department of Social Services as a secretary and later as a caseworker. Her disgust with racism prompted her to become active in the civil rights movement, picketing businesses and marching in protest. Today, 83-year-old Orbach hasn't slowed down a beat. She's busier than a "one-armed paper hanger," studying Italian through opera, teaching English to only Spanish-speaking persons (ESOL), volunteering three hours a week at an agency that helps Spanish-speaking people, exercising twice a week, and line-dancing. "Thankfully," Orbach said, "my husband does the grocery shopping and prepares the meals. Otherwise, to quote my husband, 'I'd be dead by now.'"[20]

By 1943, the need for more women in the workplace led to the recruitment of full-time homemakers. Another 2.8 million women were drawn into the workplace, preventing a decrease in wartime production quotas. At the height of wartime employment for women, 60 percent of those over 30 years of age held down jobs, 75 percent of whom were married.[21] Not everyone was pleased with this development. A writer in *Fortune* magazine lamented: "There are practically no unmarried women left to draw upon . . . This leaves, as the next potential source of industrial workers, the housewives . . . We are a kindly, somewhat sentimental people with strong, ingrained ideas about what women should or should not do. Many thoughtful citizens are seriously disturbed over the wisdom of bringing married women into the factories."[22] As disturbed as "thoughtful citizens" were, they were somewhat pacified by the "agreement" that women were in "men's" jobs only for the "duration"—only until the war ended and men could rightfully reclaim their work. There was never any intent to end gender discrimination in the workplace after the war. The dialogue in one of Uncle Sam's "Time Marches On" newsreels made the point:

Narrator: When your husband comes home, will you still be working?

Female worker: I should say not! When my husband comes home, I'm going to be busy at home.

Narrator: Good for you!

Female worker: When the war is over, this job belongs to some soldier and when he comes back, he can have it.

Narrator: Oh, that's swell! And you women will go back home and become housewives and mothers as you promised to do.[23]

Ads like the one for the Eureka Company that appeared in the *Saturday Evening Post* also reassured Americans that women would return to their traditional roles once the emergency was over. It read, in part, " . . . a day is coming when this war will be won. And on that day, like you, Mrs. America, Eureka will put aside its uniforms and return to the ways of the peace . . . building household appliances." "On the one hand, ads were very obvious," said University of Minnesota history professor and author Sara Evans. "Only for the duration. But for women who actually went to work, there were groups who really liked what they were doing. The income, independence, and camaraderie were all very satisfying. A certain percentage of the women who went to work for the first time would have stayed. But, for most, they were ultimately left with only two options: leave the workforce completely or downgrade jobs significantly."[24]

Temporarily, at least, World War II caused greater changes in women's economic status and outlook than a prior half century of reform had been able to accomplish. The attack on Pearl Harbor quietly erased opposition to hiring women—at least, for the duration of the war—and cleared the way for a massive expansion of the female labor force. Yet while the war widened women's opportunities, it also reflected the persistence of sexist values and discriminatory practices at work, within the family, and within society in general. As Marilyn E. Hegarty, senior lecturer at Ohio State University's Department of History, points out in "Patriot or Prostitute? Sexual Discourses, Print Media, and American Women during World War II," "When it came to sex, women were expected to help build the morale of the troops but not to compromise their own respectability and reputation. The virtuous wife/mother and virginal daughter, Hegarty writes, remained a symbolic measure of social stability. But as women's roles expanded and social anxieties about the sexualization of wartime women increased, the media dished out a confusing double message: Wartime women were urged to provide sexualized support for the military in public and private entertainment, yet the same media portrayed women accused of prostitution and promiscuity as sexually "deviant."[25] Hegarty sums it up:

> The double message positioned American women in a complex sexualized border zone with a shifting boundary line, which could lead to the designation of "patriot" in one instance and "prostitute" in another. Since the parameters between the categories were slippery, the dividing line was vulnerable to collapse. "Patriotute," a term government authorities coined, clearly indicates the instability of the boundary. "Promiscuity" was a word applied to a broad spectrum of behaviors occurring on an expanding and contracting continuum between patriot and prostitute.[26]

Soldiers' sexual dalliances, on the other hand, were considered a "normal" part of war. The real possibility of death or injury on the battlefield helped to break down social taboos, disrupt relationships, and propel young men to focus less on the long-term future and more on the moment. "It was a matter of getting my fun when I could get it," said World War II veteran Harry Willis, "because who knew if I was going to be alive the next day." Anyone who thought that millions of men were likely to take a vow of abstinence for the duration was sadly deluded. For soldiers, sex was here to stay; however, in contrast, sexualized women became the "enemy within."

NOTES

1. Edith Bennett, Depression-era student, World War II service wife. Interview by author. October 3, 2002.

2. Ibid.

3. David M. Kennedy, *Freedom from Fear: The American People in Depression and War, 1929–1945* (New York: Oxford University Press, 1999), pp. 748–60.

4. Geroge H. Roeder, Jr., "Censoring Disorder: American Visual Imagery of World War II," in *The War in American Culture: Society and Consciousness During*

World War II, eds. Lewis A. Erenberg and Susan E. Hirsch (Chicago and London: The Chicago University Press, 1996), p. 55.

5. William M. Tuttle, Jr., *Daddy's Gone to War: The Second World War in the Lives of America's Children* (New York: Oxford University Press, 1993), p. 19.

6. Bennett.

7. Phyllis Gould, welder. Interview by author. March 9, 2004.

8. Karen Anderson, *Wartime Women: Sex Roles, Family Relations, and the Status of Women during World War II* (Westport, CT: Greenwood Press, 1981), p. 28.

9. Sara M. Evans, *Born for Liberty: A History of Women in America* (New York: Free Press, 1997), p. 222.

10. Isabella Gillaspie, factory worker. Interview by author. October 29, 2002.

11. Alice Kessler-Harris, "The First Measured Century," www.pbs.org/fmc/interviews/kesslerharris.htm.

12. Anderson, pp. 36–41.

13. Kennedy, p. 778.

14. Eleanor Lake, "Twenty-Eight Acres of Girls," *Reader's Digest,* November 1944, p. 103. Condensed from *St. Louis Post-Dispatch,* October 1, 1944.

15. Betty Hart, secretary. Interview by author. May 12, 2004.

16. Lake, p. 104.

17. Hart.

18. Elaine Tyler May, author, historian. Interview by author. July 12, 2002.

19. Hart.

20. Florence Orbach, World War II secretary. Interview by author. March 18, 2005.

21. Doris Kearns Goodwin, *No Ordinary Times: Franklin and Eleanor Roosevelt: The Home Front in World War II* (New York: Touchstone Books, 1994), pp. 364–65.

22. *Fortune,* quoted in Evans, p. 221.

23. Connie Field, *Rosie the Riveter,* documentary film (Santa Monica, CA: Direct Cinema Limited, 1999).

24. Sarah Evans, historian, author, professor. Interview by author. November 20, 2002.

25. Marilyn E. Hegarty, "Patriot or Prostitute? Sexual Discourses, Print Media, and American Women during World War II," *Journal of Women's History* 10, No. 2 (Summer 1998): pp. 112–36.

26. Ibid.

Three

"EAT, DRINK, AND BE MERRY, FOR TOMORROW WE MAY DIE"

War is the greatest of all immoralities and leads always to sexual license.
—Unidentified Writer, *English Review,* 1916

President Franklin D. Roosevelt's concern with the morale among the troops and the negative impact the mobilization of thousands, then millions of young men was having on local communities propelled him to summon the leaders of the fledgling United Service Organizations (USO) to Washington, D.C., in January 1941, to meet with military chiefs and the director of the Federal Security Agency. The president's objective was clear: to solidify plans for a nationwide USO that would keep young soldiers in touch with the civilian life they had so abruptly left behind. When a stalemate developed over what areas would fall under civilian or military control, Roosevelt broke the deadlock with a pointed directive: "This is the way I want it done! I want these private organizations to handle the on-leave recreation of the men in the armed forces. The government should put up the buildings and some name common to the organization should appear on the outside." Roosevelt's photo appeared on some of the first USO posters, urging "every individual citizen" to support the organization. His direct involvement and the efforts of USO National Campaign chairman Thomas Dewey (who later ran as the Republican candidate for president and lost to Roosevelt in 1944) helped raise more than $16 million by the end of 1941. USO centers first operated in railroad sleeping cars, barns, museums, and churches.

On November 28, 1941, the first permanent government-built USO center opened in Fayetteville, North Carolina, for the soldiers at nearby Fort Bragg. Seemingly overnight, USO centers sprang up in cities and towns across the country and, eventually, overseas. By June 1942, *Time* magazine referred to the USO, with its 507 clubs and the 2 million men who visited every month, as the "biggest chain dance-hall operator in the world." Yet even with the large number of clubs, "stag lines" were almost always too long. "Dancing involves more than just space and music: USO usually has to provide the girls, too. This means searching homes, schools, clubs and businesses for dancing partners. When the girls have been found, they all must be carefully checked, then their interests, talents and characters inquired into. Then at the dance itself they must be carefully chaperoned."[1]

Eighteen-year-old Lois Miller and many of her girlfriends went to the USO dances in Sioux Falls, South Dakota. Small and blonde, Lois had more than her share of male attention. She often brought her "new" male friends home for a comforting meal whipped up by her mother, who was a wonderful cook. But Lois wasn't the least bit ready to find a man and settle down. She was just "having a good time," like thousands of other young women around the country who were being urged by Uncle Sam to provide support to the men in uniform and help them forget, if just for a few hours, the horrors of the war that lay ahead. USO volunteers and women as a group were counseled on everything from how to dress to how to act. USO instructions included seemingly unambiguous dictates on how to maintain a "ladylike" demeanor: smile and be friendly, listen as well as talk, accept all dances graciously, wear dresses rather than sweaters or slacks, wear stockings or leg makeup rather than bobby socks, wear makeup that is natural, and do not devote yourself exclusively to one man.[2] But, at the same time, ads like the one for Evening in Paris perfume featured a woman wearing a provocative dress, in a supine position, with this caption: "Spell It to the Marines." The same perfume was advertised as a product used by women who love "a soldier . . . a sailor . . . a marine." The line between being sexually alluring and being sexual was a thin one. Magazines like *True Story* ran articles that included "Be the Thrill of His Furlough" and "She Makes the Wounded Wiggle." *Negro Digest* published a piece titled "Plan to Land a Marine." And the June 1944 issue of *Woman's Home Companion* featured this article: "Just How Do You Land a Marine?" Typical magazine ads during the war promoted a variety of "beauty" products and general advice to help captivate a man, preferably one in the military. The caption in one ad read: "6 million soldiers and here I sit," and another with a puzzled woman, trying to sell kisses to servicemen at a bazaar and wondering: "Think 50 cents is too much?" Married women were also targeted by the media to stay the same, sexy women they were before their husbands went away. A married woman, it was suggested, might even enter a "cheesecake" contest or send a pinup picture of herself á la Betty Grable to her husband overseas. Single or married, women were to be sexy but "good," to pique a man's fancy but not to go "too far."[3]

Miller broke a cardinal USO rule the night she met Eldon Bevens, a B17 gunner on his way from the European theater back to the Pacific. The young gal from South Dakota didn't boost the morale of many men that evening, only that of the returning soldier. Bevens walked her home after the dance and, two days later, showed up at her house with a gift of marshmallows and almond candy. Miller's mother was immediately impressed. Her father, who came home from work and found a young soldier with "his feet under my table," was not so enthusiastic. Then he noticed the goodies the young solider had brought and later warned his daughter that this boy was "petting the cow to get to the cat!" Still, he grew fond of the soldier from Dallas, Oregon, and was sad to see him leave three months later. The then-18-year-old Miller had no intention of settling down and dated other guys, much to her mother's chagrin. Every time she went out on a date, her mother would worry about what Eldon would think. "I'm not married to him!" Miller said over and over again. But in August 1947, almost two years after they'd met, the couple got engaged, and they were married in a church wedding six months later. "It felt like I was marrying a stranger," Miller said. "But my parents were so set on the wedding that I figured I just had to go through with it." Fifty-eight years later and still happily married, she believes she made the right decision.[4]

BLITZING THE BROTHELS: A FAILED CAMPAIGN

As more and more women fulfilled their patriotic duty by catering to the needs of servicemen and by expressing their own fears and desires, the boundary between good girl and bad girl was drawn and redrawn. Within a short time, women, particularly single women, became suspect. They could spread nasty diseases, share secrets with the enemy, or cross the line from patriot to prostitute. Even before the war, plans for the campaign against "deviant" sexuality in women were set in to motion when, in January 1941, Representative Andrew J. May introduced legislation that made vice activities near military installations—primarily prostitution—a federal offense. Congress passed the May Act in July of the same year. Many would-be brothel racketeers were frightened off, with a survey at the end of the year revealing that prostitution, though not eliminated, had been dramatically reduced in 526 out of 680 local communities. The blitzing of the brothels might have been successful in checking a potential wartime explosion of "illicit" sex if not for the ingenuity of the professionals. Without brothels, many of the prostitutes took their trade elsewhere; they worked the streets, the alleys, even the backseats of taxi cabs. Prostitution had become an "expanding war industry" where in military towns like Fayetteville, North Carolina, the prostitute population had grown from 200 women before the war to around 4,000 to 5,000 at the height of the war. This mass movement of unsupervised prostitution encouraged some to suggest that regulated, inspected brothels be established for servicemen. Those who supported military houses of prostitution reasoned that if normal men didn't have an outlet for their uncontrollable sexual drive, they would seduce or rape "nice" girls. Supporters also felt such military-controlled houses of prostitution would help fight the battle against venereal disease (VD). But the guardians of morality would have none of it. They were against any premarital sex and felt that military brothels sanctioned promiscuity and undermined the moral fabric of a nation whose sexual behavior had already come under serious attack. This stance put them in direct conflict with those whose major concern was to curb the rate of VD any way possible.

No where else than in Honolulu, Hawaii, was the struggle between the "guardians of morality" and those concerned about the spread of VD more visible. Honolulu had a long history of laws and regulations against "illicit connections," including prostitution, dating back to 1820. But "disorderly houses" kept reappearing over the decades, and no law or police enforcement was strong enough to stop the illegal sex trade. By 1930, the "unofficial," hush-hush system had deteriorated to the point where regulated prostitution, sanctioned by both law enforcement *and* the military, was established. The Honolulu press knew about all this and apparently agreed with authorities that "silence was a policy in the best public interest." Harry A. Franck, a prolific travel writer at the time, commented on the 18 unlicensed and "officially nonexistent hotels and rooming houses" in Honolulu, each harboring from 6 to 10 "inmates" from the mainland. He detailed the "extreme liquor-forbidden orderliness" and the almost "puritanical decorum" of these "hotels." By 1932, General Briant H. Wells, commanding the Hawaiian Department of the United States Army, asked for a plan to officially regulate prostitution. According to the new regulations, all girls had to live in the houses where they worked, and no white girls were allowed on the other side of River Street. The new rules stipulated that the civil police with "full cooperation by the Army and Navy" would oversee the rules and regulations. Then sometime before World War II, a mainland prostitute by the name of Jean O'Hara arrived on the island paradise. O'Hara became the city's most infamous madam and, in her book *Honolulu Harlot*, described how the girls made it to Honolulu: Madams like herself sent mail orders to the mainland, usually San Francisco. Depending upon a woman's age, the going rate was anywhere from $500 to $1,000 per woman. A steamer carrying the women to Honolulu was met by a detective off port, who chaperoned the girls to a receiving station, often a hotel on Front Street. There, the vice squad made their pitch, stressing that any infraction of the rules would lead to banishment from the city. Once instructed, the new girls were taken to the police station for fingerprints and photos, then to a brothel to begin their shift.[5]

Ted Chemin, a junior radio engineer from San Francisco, came to Honolulu in December 1938. He had heard about the open red-light district from some of his fellow college buddies who worked summer jobs in the Hawaiian city. When Chernin asked about the brothels, he was quickly shown the "houses of ill repute," 11 of them crammed into the small area called Chinatown. According to Chernin, the girls were medically examined weekly. They were not allowed to peddle their trade outside of the brothel, and when they did go out, they were not allowed to be accompanied by men. Drugs and alcohol were strictly forbidden. "To this day," Chernin wrote in a 2000 article for *The Hawaiian Journal of History*, "I can still smell the disinfectant that was used to mop the floors and clean the walls and furniture every day. One could say that, except for their profession, the women lived almost like nuns."[6] When talking to the prostitutes, Chernin learned that many of their steady customers were married men from Honolulu who, after choosing a prostitute, would remain "more or less faithful." Chernin's "surrogate wife," a woman called "Bobbie," was the first prostitute he met, and it was love at first sight. But after the attack on Pearl Harbor and the influx of troops to Honolulu, the demand for prostitutes mushroomed. There were only 203 registered prostitutes—among whom was Chernin's "wife"—servicing "50,000-odd men." Prostitutes worked hard: Each one saw upward of 100 men a day for at least 20 days a month at the going rate of $3 for servicemen and $2 for locals.[7] Chemin, deeply tanned from many hours at the beach, was always taken for a local Hawaiian. When "Bobbie" saw him standing in line leading to the brothel door, she would pull him out so he would be her first customer of the day. "That was very thoughtful of her, yet when I left the Islands for a second time in 1944, I neglected to tell her goodbye, a thoughtless act that I have regretted," Chernin wrote. During his frequent visits to the brothel, Chernin witnessed an assembly line–like scheme to handle all of the men:

It consisted of enclosures with four small rooms that operated in this way. In the first room, the man was dressing, the girl having just left after finishing a cursory wash up of both. The girl was in the next room, having a "love affair." In a third room, a man was ready and waiting, and in the fourth room a man had just entered and was proceeding to undress. In this way, a girl could handle twelve or more men per hour, and when she tired, another girl took over. The rooms were called "bull pens" . . . It was customary to hand out rain checks when for some reason the man could not perform.[8]

Despite the "impersonal efficiency" of the factory-like system, it could break down. One story featured a regular customer who, at the end of his allotted three minutes, told his favorite girl, "Judy, you're the bummest fuck I ever had." As he recalled, she was so angry that she spent the rest of the night proving him a liar for free. However, that was not a regular experience in what was normally a carefully orchestrated system.[9] Efforts by a new member of the Honolulu police commission to shut down the brothels fell on deaf ears, both in the local government and in the military. Resolutions seemed to disappear behind committee doors. One member of the commission urged delay: "I don't think I know enough about prostitution. For ten years I've been studying it but there's certain information I lack."[10]

Immediately after the attack on Pearl Harbor, many of the prostitutes had rushed to the hospitals to help care for the wounded. Their brothels were closer to the waterfront than many other Hawaiian homes, and the madams opened up the prostitutes' living quarters to be used as temporary hospitals.[11] With some of their rooms occupied by the wounded and the prostitutes' "forced" entry in to more mainstream life, all restrictions on their comings and goings were lifted. The women could do anything they wanted as long as they did their "business" in the brothel. Less than a year later, emboldened by their elevated position, prostitutes went on a 22-day strike: They wanted the right to live away from the brothels when off duty. In the end, the police commission capitulated, but there was never a word about the strike and its conclusion in the press.[12] Citizens of Honolulu and the military brass worried throughout the war about the spread of VD. Yet during the period of regulated prostitution in Honolulu, rates were "phenomenally low." That fact allowed local authorities to more easily tolerate the 250 registered prostitutes who worked in the city in 1943 and 1944. However, regulation did not stop amateur houses from springing up in residential areas or "clandestine" prostitutes and pickup girls from applying their trade. And when the complaints of ordinary citizens grew too loud to ignore, police once again banned residential areas to prostitutes and ordered them to move back to the regulated brothels immediately. Madams were the beneficiaries. They raked in approximately $150,000 annually, while the yearly income of the brothels totaled between $10 million and $15 million. Many of the prostitutes earned $30,000–$40,000 a year at a time when a working woman was considered very fortunate to make $2,000 annually. Successful madam Jean O'Hara put it succinctly, "Honolulu has always proved a veritable gold mine for the prostitutes and the madams." But the axe was soon to fall.

On September 10, 1944, then Hawaii Governor Stainback ordered the closing of Honolulu's regulated houses of prostitution. Word of impending vice squad visits spread through the district. Captain Ed Hitchcock and his men started to make the rounds of the remaining 15 active houses:

> Flashes of the girls here and there: One wore a red apron, a short-short shirt and a pair of cowboy riding boots; one shouted "whoopee" when told she could leave the house; another one said, "I see here that this paper says we can't practice prostitution any more. Heck, I don't practice. I'm an expert." Several madams expressed concern for their girls, hoping they would have the chance to become barmaids, dancers, or taxi drivers. Yet another madam said the closing would spread prostitution throughout the city. What would all these hundreds of boys do? "Well, I guess there still are the amateurs and the back alleys," one person responded. A portly, motherly type . . . said, "Okay, boys, now I can go home and take care of Papa. We'll be closed right up. Thanks for everything." A madam on Smith Street said she would have a lot of furniture to sell, "and all of this swell bedroom stuff." One comment summed it all up: "Well, we really got no kick coming. We have been well treated in Honolulu."[13]

Ted Chernin left Honolulu in 1944 and, when he returned, the brothels had all been closed. Although he tried, he never found "Bobbie" again. His own postmortem on regulated prostitution was summarized in an unsigned, undated memorandum written by Police Commissioner Victor Houston: "The only definite conclusion that has been reached is that it [prostitution] is likely to exist as long as the passions of human beings remain what they are today." The memorandum went on to comment on the observations of a Dr. William F. Snow, who, in his position with the War Department, investigated the regulated prostitution in Honolulu and remarked that he had "never before seen such a common sense setup . . . and was astonished at the low venereal disease rate." The well-regulated, clean Honolulu brothel district was, wrote Chernin, "the best little red-light district in the U.S."[14]

VALUES UNDER FIRE

Regulated prostitution was the exception, not the rule. Politicians and moralists steered public opinion, and prostitution was officially banned in just about every other city in the United States. But the official ban was never enough to successfully squash the trade. Norfolk, Virginia, home to the world's largest naval station and the country's oldest shipyard, was a case in point.

Long before World War II, Norfolk was known as a city of bountiful pleasure. There, a sailor could satisfy any fantasy imaginable from shacking up with a girl in one of the 30 or so brothels located along a notorious stretch of East Main Street to enjoying the burlesque show at the Gaiety Theater, a "Tudor gothic" building first opened in 1850 as Mechanic's Hall, used for years as a recital hall by traveling musicians and also for political rallies. The theater ended its career as the Gaiety Theater, a burlesque house featuring Norfolk's dark-haired beauty, Rose La Rose. Yet once war was declared and the May Act passed, Police Chief John Woods determined to enforce the law. He didn't attempt to shut down the Gaiety Theater but was intent on ridding the city of the brothels on East Main Street. However, word about raids had leaked out, and by the time the police arrived at most brothels, the lights were out and the doors padlocked. However, there were some stubborn madams who refused to shut down and watched as their girls were carted off to jail, where they had to pay a fine and undergo a physical exam. Undeterred, many madams moved their places of business just outside the city limits to avoid city police, and taxis shuttled the sailors back and forth. It wasn't long before many of the taxi drivers got a piece of the action. With a prostitute in the front seat, the cabbies drove around the city looking for sailors who were, by now, well aware of the setup. The cab driver parked in a quiet place, went for a walk, and the girl serviced her customer or customers in the backseat. The charge for a trick in what became known as a "chippy wagon" rose as high as $8, half of which went to the taxi driver. "Chippy," an Americanism, first appeared in print around 1886 and, tellingly, that was in New Orleans. "This class of females," reported a local journal, "are known by the gang as 'chippies,' and most of them come from the slums." In his 1954 autobiography *Satchmo*, New Orleans–born trumpet player Louis Armstrong wrote: "I had been brought up around the honky-tonks on Liberty and Perdido where life was just about the same as it was in Storyville except that the chippies were cheaper."[15]

Not to be left out of the financial windfall, bar owners devised an ingenious scheme to take advantage of the sex-starved troops that flooded Norfolk during World War II. "Waitresses" at the bars along East Main Street boosted sales for the local establishments by promising sailors "shack-up" dates after closing. The catch? The sailor had to buy an expensive $7 bottle of champagne. When closing time arrived, half a dozen horny men would show up for their date.

In the brawl that predictably ensued once the sailors realized they were not alone, the "waitress" made a quick getaway. She kept her commission and control over her reputation, and the bar owner kept the money from the sales of the expensive champagne. Frustrated by the creativity of Norfolk's "entertainment" industry, federal law enforcement and Norfolk police finally organized a permanent shore patrol that managed to round up many a wayward sailor and prostitute. Still, this concerted effort failed to ever put a stop to men and women looking for and having a good time. As John Costello writes in *Love, Sex and War: Changing Values 1939–45*, "The sex drive is the most intractable of human instincts. Normally repressed by religious taboos and social convention, it bursts these restraints when social life is disrupted by war and the demands of armed combat."[16]

AH, THOSE "KHAKI-WACKIES"

Professional prostitutes were not the only women boosting the morale of the troops. The "Khaki-Wackies" (also known as "Victory Girls" and "Good Time Charlottes") were, for the most part, amateurs. Instead of cash, the price for their sexual favors was often a movie or a Coca-Cola at a local drugstore. One of the numerous articles about the "promiscuous" girl problem appeared in the June 26, 1943, issue of the *Chicago Daily Tribune*. In it, teenage girls "looking for wartime excitement and romance" were cited as a problem in the Chicago courts: "The girls wander recklessly in the parks and in the loop, inviting 'pickups' that often lead to tragedies." The article went on to quote a Judge Frank Bicek, who warned, "We must preserve the mothers of tomorrow. Indiscretions among teen aged girls are increasing and the resulting destruction of character of mind and body by disease will have its full effect on the coming generation." In view of the long association between war and sex—sexual exploitation and violence as par for the course—comments like those of Judge Bicek mirrored the misogynist platitudes ever pervasive in an American society that completely overlooked the role played by men in the "destruction of character of mind and body by disease." Men in the military had been thoroughly warned about the potential problems of unprotected sex, yet many failed to insist on using a condom when having sex with these young girls. It's no surprise then that the incidence of VD among amateurs was higher than the rate among the professionals.

In a talk given at the Buffalo Regional Conference of the Young Women's Christian Association (YWCA) on February 2, 1943, YMCA board member Norma M. Kimball cited the "teen-age girl" as the situation at the top of the day's problems. Kimball had just returned from a series of meetings that, she said, brought women into New York from all parts of the country. "I am freshly conscious of the seriousness of the situation women find themselves in as they face their new world," she said. "I am also freshly aware of the great opportunity that is theirs." She quoted the director of the USO, who said grimly, "No one of us yet knows what to do with a 16-year-old prostitute." She noted the report of another woman whose major job all summer in a big Southern center was "taking care of the soldiers' teen-age brides who keeled over almost one a day, with miscarriages." Kimball further supported her case by recapping a discussion with older "industrial girls" who, "in the growing disregard for any moral standards between the sexes, fear for their younger sisters and say, 'We older girls can handle our boy friends, but our little sisters don't seem to understand that it's up to the girl to set the standard. What we need is a course on the responsibility women have for keeping men straight.'" Following a litany of other teenage girl behavior like drinking and wanting to "play" when they were not working, Kimball ended her initial complaints with a woeful question: "Where is Mother while all this goes on?" She then rattled off a list of ways in which women's lives had changed since the war and how their time was no longer their own, what with the demands of work and family. But, she asked, "Does this mean that women have to be dropped out of the program to control social disease? It most emphatically does not." Women *and* men, Kimball suggested, will have to now work together to stamp out prostitution, end the teenage girl problem, and win a "victory at home that matches in importance the victory at the Front."[17]

In 1944, *Woman's Home Companion* printed a message from the U.S. Surgeon General. He spoke of the "haunting specter of venereal disease," and went on to accuse the enemy in the home front battle: "The noncommercial girl who is supplanting the prostitute as the main source of venereal infection." Such a girl was "doubly threatening" because she was "active not only around military centers where control methods are strict, but in war boom towns, trailer towns, cities and villages where control measures are less efficient. She is driving our national standards of morality down." New York City's local American Social Hygiene Association reported a sizeable increase in diseases among high school boys and girls, and recommended a midnight curfew for the *girls*. The onus for what some deemed a breakdown in morality was yet again placed on girls. Young and single, they were "defeating" the troops on the home front, spreading diseases, and undermining the strength of the nation. Magazines and professional journals offered all kinds of advice for eliminating the "problem." Suggestions included heightened surveillance, even containing girls in shelters "overnight or until individual situations can be explored."

In its own way, the military did try to take soldiers' minds off of sex by providing a host of movies, entertainment, and athletic activities. To bolster its effort, the Army developed a battery of pamphlets, films, and educational materials about VD with fear as the motivating force. Just out of high school, gunner Max Fellows definitely remembers the VD films. "One of the films showed a young fellow carrying his swollen testicles in a wheel barrow. That was the only thing that kept me out of trouble when I was overseas." But for every soldier like Fellows who stayed out of trouble, there were plenty more like Manuel Solis who found the military's anti-sex campaign truly laughable. "They gave us condoms! And there was a pro [prophylactic] station right there in the post." (Eventually, there were prophylactic stations on military bases both in the United States and abroad. Military orders required that all personnel returning from pass or leave report to the unit prophylactic station. The location of these stations was stamped on all military passes. There, preventive chemical treatment for VD was always available.) Ultimately defeated in its fight to keep young men's sexual urges under control, the Army launched measures to prevent the spread of VD that had so crippled U.S. soldiers in World War I. As Solis said, troops were issued prophylactic kits that contained a leaflet titled "Sex, Hygiene and Venereal Disease"; a soap impregnated cleansing tissue; a five-gram tube of ointment made from calomel, or mercury chloride; sulfathiazole; and a condom for a future sexual encounter. As many as 50 million condoms were sold or freely distributed each month during the war. And the wartime efforts to decrease the number of men who came down with VD were, in an overall view, successful. Lost service due to VD was 30 times less in World War II than in World War I, although 606 men were diagnosed with a VD every day during the second World War.[18]

"SOME PLAY TIME"

In August 1942, Seymour Simon went off to the navy and eventually served overseas in North Africa, Italy, and France. "The war was a total shock for guys like me," the 84-year-old retired president of an advertising agency said. "We had grown up in the Depression. War was not to be in our time. World War I was supposed to have been the war to end all wars. I kept thinking this wasn't happening to me." For Simon and many men like him, the war put all future plans on hold. The idea of finding a wife and setting down was "eight million miles off." Even before many men arrived overseas, where sexual liaisons became the norm, the opportunity to have "play time" on the home front was never far away. And Simon knew the unwritten "rules" well: There were, he said, two kinds of girls—the ones who were sure to be virgins when they got married and the "other" kind of girls you pursued when you wanted to have sex. "You wanted to be sure to spend some time with the 'good' girls to learn all about them because they were the kind you were going to marry some day." And Simon did just that. He met a girl in the spring of 1942 whom he eventually married after the war. Though he'd been sexually active since the age of 16, he went "very slowly and carefully" with his future bride and never attempted to compromise her virginity. However, during intensive naval training in Chicago, Simon was fixed up with a woman to "weekend" with. She was a "gorgeous gal" who loved to drink and party, If Simon didn't have duty, he could leave the naval base at noon on Saturday until 7 P.M. Sunday night. "The gal and I would meet at a great Italian restaurant, eat and drink, and then rent a room at the Sherman Hotel. My dad was a big deal in the National Jewelers' Association that always held its conventions there, so I could always get a room, usually a suite. I had good weekends."[19]

Dorothy Oberman (not her real name) never felt she was *that* kind of woman. A tomboy nicknamed "The Tiger Woman" as a kid, Oberman was a virgin when she left home at age 21 to work as a secretary in Washington, D.C., during the war. There, she fell for a skinny soldier who played the fiddle. One afternoon, she and her roommate went to Walter Reed Hospital to visit the wounded soldiers. "The shock of seeing all those young men missing arms and legs made me so upset," she said, "that when I had a date with the soldier that night, my thought was: 'What do I have to lose?'" She lost her virginity. Some time later when the man she ultimately married asked her out, word had spread that she'd "gone all the way." The young man, hoping to get her in bed and lose *his* virginity, fell in love instead. He proposed two weeks later. Oberman thought he was "nuts." That was in the spring of 1945. On November 11 of the same year, the two were at union headquarters and talked about their salaries and how they might combine them. This time, Oberman said yes. The couple was married the following February at a synagogue in Hicksville, Pennsylvania. "Those were crazy, crazy times," Oberman said. She and her husband will celebrate their sixtieth wedding anniversary this year.[20]

WOMEN, MILITARY SERVICE, AND MORALS

Labor shortages affected the military as well as industries on the home front and, from the beginning of the war, women's groups demanded that women be allowed to serve their country. The idea was met with resistance in public opinion and by Congress. Opposition was generally based on some mix of both disdain and protectiveness toward women. But in the spring of 1941, U.S. representative Edith Nourse Rogers of Massachusetts introduced a bill that would give women full military status. The War Department wasn't interested, and the bill died in committee. Not long after, Army Chief of Staff General George C. Marshall became convinced that a manpower shortage would develop in the army if America went to war. With his support, Rogers's bill was reintroduced on Christmas Eve, 1941. Congressional opposition to the bill centered on Southern congressmen. With women in the armed services, one representative asked, "Who will then do the cooking, the washing, the mending, the humble homey tasks to which every woman has devoted herself; who will nurture the children?" But after a long and hostile debate that filled 98 columns in the *Congressional Record,* the establishment of the Women's Auxiliary Army Corps (WAAC) was approved by the Senate and signed into law by President Roosevelt on May 14, 1942. Within a matter of months, four other women's military branches were established: the navy's WAVES (Women Appointed for Voluntary Emergency Service); SPAR (an acronym based on the Coast Guard's Latin motto "Semper Paratus"); the Marines ("They are Marines. They don't have a nickname and they don't need one"); and the WAFS (Women's Auxiliary Ferrying Squadron). The WAACs attracted the most attention and, according to WAAC Director, Major Oveta Culp Hobby, "The gaps our women will fill are in those noncombatant jobs where women's hands and women's hearts fit naturally. WAACs will do the same type of work which women do in civilian life. They will bear the same relations to men of the Army that they bear to the men of the civilian organizations in which they work." During the war, only 20 percent of WAACs were assigned to ground forces, and most of these women worked in secretarial jobs and motor pools. In September, 1943, the word *auxiliary* came out of the WAAC's name, and WAAC became the Women's Army Corps (WAC). Women who elected to stay in the Corps—and 75 percent of them did—could now enjoy full military status, insurance, and pension rights.[21]

Jackie Sarge described herself as "free, white, and 21." Her dream was to drive an ambulance in the WAAC. But the fact that she'd been a secretary for the civil aeronautics administration in Alaska showed up in all of her records, and she was sent to army administration school at Fort Des Moines in Iowa, then on to Conway State Teachers' College in Conway, Arkansas, to become a noncommissioned officer. Sarge performed her duties well and ultimately became the first female sergeant major of army air corps cadets. "I remember they ran a picture of me in the base newspaper with a cadet coming to my desk and saluting," Sarge said. "The photo caption read: 'First time a male cadet salutes a woman!' The men in those days were absolutely wonderful. I had no problems." Despite her success, Sarge refused suggestions that she go to officers' training school. The money wasn't that much better, she said, and officers had to pay for their uniforms, whereas she did not. But when asked if she wanted to volunteer for overseas duty, she agreed. There weren't many women going abroad at the time and, among the list of equipment initially issued was a prophylactic kit. "Most of us had never seen a condom!" she said. "It turned out that we had the same list as the men had—obviously a mistake. Suddenly, the condoms were removed and never issued to WAACs again."[22] Apparently, *New York Daily News* columnist John O'Donnell didn't do his homework—or chose not to. In a June 9, 1943, column for the *New York Daily News,* he wrote that contraceptives and prophylactic equipment would be furnished to members of the WAACs, according to a super secret agreement reached by the high-ranking officers of the War Department and the WAAC chieftain, Mrs. Hobby. The following day, WAAC Director Hobby declared that there is "no foundation of truth" for such a report. Following this public exchange, the press was abuzz with the story. In a column that ran in the June 14, 1943, issue of *Newsweek* in a section titled "WAAC Whispers," more details were disclosed:

> It all began when Rep. Beverly M. Vincent, Kentucky Democrat, took the House floor to oppose the assignment of Waacs abroad. He said there had been "trouble" about the women soldiers in North Africa, and he had read somewhere that they "had to be given protection, probably by the convents or by the Mothers Superior." Vincent observed: "When you send girls over there remember that with our soldiers you also have Arabs, you have Senegalese . . . There is (sic) bound to be complications."[23]

This "rumor" was recorded in the *Congressional Record,* and, according to the same *Newsweek* column, congresswomen led by Representative Margaret Chase Smith of Maine met with female reporters to discuss how to scotch the unfavorable rumor. Representative Nourse Rogers, author of the bill that created the WAACs, noted that rumors of WAAC immorality had "sprung up simultaneously all over the country" and the worst, she thought, was the story that one group of WAACs "had been guilty of misconduct down to the last member and that several had been sent home pregnant":

> Mrs. Rogers had investigated and found that of 500 Waacs shipped to North Africa only two had returned. One was indeed pregnant—but she was married and wanted to have her child born on American soil.[24]

(An article in the *New York Times* dated June 27, 1943, put the total of WAACs in North Africa at 202. One girl did come home to give birth on

U.S. soil. One came home to have a gall bladder operation, and another because of a "nervous disorder.")

A week after the *Newsweek* article appeared, the June 21, 1943, issue of *Time* ran a column titled "O'Donnell's Foul," in which journalist O'Donnell was taken to task:

> Many an honest U.S. newspaperman was outraged last week when flashy, pompous *New York Daily News* Columnist, John O'Donnell, whose hatred for Franklin Roosevelt* and all his works sometimes leads him to flout the standards of his own profession. O'Donnell wrote, as a plain statement of fact, that contraceptives and prophylactic equipment were to become Government Issue for the WAACs.
>
> For days Washington and the U.S. have hissed with rumors of WAAC immorality and misconduct, which have made many women reluctant to enlist. O'Donnell gave the rumors wings and beak, reporting the rumors and then refuting them in such a way as to leave doubt whether he was taking it back or not.
>
> His last report came, O'Donnell admitted later, from the usual "intelligent and trustworthy official." O'Donnell saw it as " . . . a victory for the New Deal ladies who [think that] girls who want to go into uniform and fight. . . have the same right here and abroad to indulge their passing fancies." He also quoted "a lady lawmaker": " . . . You men think that there is nothing wrong if a solider sleeps with a girl so long as he keeps his health. Well, the same argument goes both ways . . . "
>
> *On Dec. 18, 1942, the President was so displeased over an article O'Donnell wrote—sniping at U.S. censorship—that he informally awarded him a German Iron Cross.[25]

The final nail in O'Donnell's coffin and the rumors he spread came in the form of a June 27, 1943, *New York Times* article in which reporter Eleanor Damton Washington disputed the "sinister rumors " aimed at destroying the reputation of the WAACs. She quoted Rep. Edith Nourse Rogers as saying that "no other country in the world would allow a newspaper to attack the character of its women." Secretary of War Henry L. Stimson got into the act: "My attention has been attracted to sinister rumors aimed at destroying the reputation of the Waacs. I have made a thorough investigation of these rumors. They are absolutely and completely false." Mr. Stimson went on to say that since June, 1943, "approximately 65,000 fine, patriotic women had joined the corps, each of whom relieved a soldier for front-line duty, and that anything that would interfere with recruiting for the corps or destroy its reputation interfered with the combat strength of the Army, and so was of value to the enemy."[26] (The number of women joining the WAAC dropped drastically for a time due to the backlash of public opinion against the employment of women in the armed forces. Enlisted soldiers tended to question the moral values of any woman attracted to military service and expressed their sentiments in letters home. The O'Donnell scandal made matters even worse.) Even General Marshall joined the chorus in a speech before the Conference of Governors at Columbus, Ohio. He dismissed the rumors as "most atrocious," if not "subversive," and glowingly described the WAACs as "as fine an organization of women as I have ever seen assembled." O'Donnell had his comeuppance and then some.

However, despite comments to the contrary made by the army brass, some WAACs were sexually active, particularly if they served overseas. Jackie Sarge met a guy the first day she was in England and went with him for about a year. "I think we thought we were going to get married," she said, "but the love affair didn't last." When asked whether she had had sex before she married in 1946, she said, "Oh, sure! Didn't everybody?" When it came to using a condom, well . . . that was a different story: "The military films were all about VD, not about getting pregnant. We never thought about that possibility. Never! We were so dumb . . . so dumb!"[27]

LaVerne Gibrich Schaffer Fefferman, now 84, also joined the WAACs. As a Jew, she felt she had to do something in the effort to defeat Hitler. "I felt very patriotic," she said. "I felt I was doing something very special. People were amazed to see women in uniform. We were on display and felt we were representing our country. So we behaved. We didn't get drunk, didn't fraternize with the men for the first year. But the minute we became part of the army, there were more weddings than you can imagine." After basic training, Gibrich was assigned to Camp Polk, Louisiana, where she sat at a machine all day long and tracked aircraft on a map. Sitting at a desk for hours at a stretch got to be very boring for Gibrich, and she put in for the chance to serve overseas. In early June 1944, she sailed to England on the *Queen Elizabeth*, arriving right after D-Day. One Friday night she told the guys that she was going to attend Sabbath services at a local synagogue. One of the soldiers whom she assumed was anything but Jewish stepped forward and offered to escort her. Melvin Schaffer, a radioman in the army air corps, turned out to be a nice Jewish boy from Miami, Florida. The two hit it off from the start and waited anxiously for passes that allowed them to spend time together. In one of his letters dated August 15, 1944, Schaffer talked about love and marriage:

Listen, Funnyface. For the present, get marriage out of your head, before you get it into mine. You know damn well that it is the wrong time . . . Please, Hon, have patience. I'm going crazy enough now. The fellas call it absentmindedness, but I know it isn't. Lately, I keep thinking of you and I forget a lot of things.

I can't help it. I have you on my mind, and there isn't room for anything else.

"War turned up the romance," Gibrich Fefferman said, "and the sex." A virgin until she met Schaffer, the couple made the most of their limited time together. And Schaffer's resolve not to tie the knot evaporated over time. One morning after the lovers had managed to spend the night together, Schaffer awoke and announced, "We'd better get dressed and get married." The couple went to London, where they were married by a local rabbi at the West London Synagogue. The new Mrs. Schaffer, who wore her uniform and a green orchid pinned to her lapel, was the first WAC in the 1st Allied Airborne attached to the unit to be married overseas. After their marriage and during their courtship, the couple never used birth control. "We didn't even think about it," she said. "We didn't think like people think today."

This wartime love story does not have a happy ending and, to this day, Fefferman isn't sure how her mother-in-law was able to insinuate herself in between her and the love of her life. She remembers the letters that started arriving once the couple had returned to the United States, begging her son to return home, to divorce his new wife, and to finish his education. She recalls a very uncomfortable visit to her in-laws' home in Miami and how everyone treated her harshly. And she'll never forget the day when her husband dropped her on the doorsteps of the Chicago apartment managed by her parents and left her for good. Fefferman was three months pregnant. "Our marriage was a legal romance that should have been written up in a novel years ago," she said. "And the divorce . . . well, that was devastating!" Fefferman married two more times, and her third marriage was a charm. The couple enjoyed more than 40 years together before her husband, now 93, was put into a nursing home.[28]

In 1942, the first full year of U.S. involvement in World War II, 321,000 couples were divorced. By 1945, the total had jumped to 485,000, and in 1946, the first full year of peace, the number soared to 610,000.[29] One out of every three American servicemen was married by 1945 when, for every 100 couples getting married, 31 were legally separated.[30] By 1950, a million veterans had been divorced. So many factors conspired to send couples to the divorce courts: hasty marriages, long separations, battle fatigue, the newfound independence of women at work and in the home, children, and wartime passion mistaken as love. In an environment of confusing messages about relationships between men and women, a time in which women were often cast as the "predatory enemy," it is a wonder that even more marriages didn't end in divorce and that suspicion and mistrust did not completely undermine the possibility of true and lasting love.

NOTES

1. "USO: In Peace and War It Has Proven Its Worth," *Time,* June 29, 1942, pp. 72–78.

2. "Camouflage," *Time,* June 21, 1943, p.78.

3. Marilyn E. Hegarty, "Patriot or Prostitute? Sexual Discourses, Print Media, and American Women during World War II," *Journal of Women's History* 10, No. 2 (Summer 1998): pp. 112–36.

4. Lois and Eldon Bevens, World War II couple. Interview by author, July 27, 2003.

5. Richard Greer, "Dousing Honolulu's Red Lights," *The Hawaiian Journal of History* 34 (2000): pp. 185–87.

6. Ted Chernin, "My Experience in the Honolulu Chinatown Red-Light District," *The Hawaiian Journal of History* 34 (2000): p. 205.

7. Beth Bailey and David Farber, *The First Strange Place: Race and Sex in World War II Hawaii* (Baltimore: The Johns Hopkins Press, 1992), p. 100.

8. Chernin, p. 208.

9. Bailey and Farber, p. 105.

10. Greer, pp. 189–90.

11. Emily Yellin, *Our Mothers' War: American Women at Home and at the Front During World War II* (New York: Free Press, 2004), p. 313.

12. Greer, p. 192.

13. Ibid., p. 197.

14. Chernin, pp. 208–10.

15. Kelley Kawanot and Meilina Wilkinson, "The Mavens Word of the Day," *Words @ Random,* May 24, 2001, http://www.randomhouse.com/wotd/index.pperl?date = 20010524.

16. John Costello, *Love, Sex and War: Changing Values 1939–45* (London: Collins, 1985), p. 120.

17. Norma M. Kimball, "Women on the Home Front," *Journal of Social Hygiene* 29, No. 7 (October 1943): pp. 425–28.

18. "The WWII Medical Department," submitted by Alain Batens, July 12, 2003, http://home.att.net/-steinert/wwii_medical_department.htm.

19. Seymour Simon (alias), World War II veteran. Interview by author. April 14, 2004.

20. Dorothy Oberman (alias), Washington, D.C. secretary. Interview by author. March 12, 2005.

21. Yellin, pp. 111–17.

22. Jackie Sarge, World War II WAAC. Interview by author. April 21, 2004.

23. "Wac Whispers," *Newsweek,* June 14, 1943, pp. 34, 36.

24. Ibid.

25. "O'Donnell's Foul," *Time,* June 21, 1943, p. 90.

26. Eleanor Damton Washington, "Comment about Mrs. Roosevelt Denouncing Immorality Reports as Nazi Propaganda," *New York Times,* June 27, 1943, Section B, p. 1.

27. Sarge.

28. Laverne Fefferman, World War II WAAC. Interview by author. April 9, 2004.

29. William M. Tuttle, Jr., *Daddy's Gone to War: The Second World War in the Lives of America's Children* (New York: Oxford University Press, 1993), pp. 219–20.

30. Costello, p. 274.

Four

DISCRIMINATION IN THE RANKS

"ALL MEN LIKE TO FIGHT . . . EVEN GAY GUYS"

John McPherson, a staff sergeant in the army's Quartermaster Corps, patted a young sailor on the shoulder and told him he was good-looking. Mortified, the handsome sailor yelled "Rape!" and ran off to alert the military police. As Mary Ann Humphrey documents in *My Country, My Right to Serve,* McPherson was incredulous but never believed for a moment that his military career was in jeopardy. He'd been in the service for more than two years and had been cited by his company commander as one of the best men in the outfit. But the military police badgered him with questions about his sexuality; eventually, McPherson told them he was gay. Naively, he assumed his admission would not tarnish 28 months of exemplary behavior. He was wrong. McPherson was handcuffed, then driven from town to camp and forced to spend a night in solitary confinement. A "lousy" MP forced him to have sex that night. A different MP attempted to rape him on another occasion, but McPherson managed to fight him off. The disgraced soldier was then confined to a neuropsychiatric ward in the station hospital for three weeks and, on February 25, 1944, he was "unceremoniously dumped" outside the main gate of camp in civilian clothes with a blue discharge certificate in his pocket. (Enlisted men had nicknamed undesirable discharges "blue discharges" after the color of paper on which they were printed.) "I was left without pride, self-esteem, and in disgrace," McPherson said. "Army psychiatry stinks!"[1]

Gay soldiers died on the decks of the USS *Arizona* in Pearl Harbor and spilled their blood on the sands of innumerable South Pacific islands. They fought and died in Europe, Japan, and everywhere else American troops battled. Yet despite their many contributions and sacrifices during World War II, gays were discriminated against in the U.S. armed forces as they had been from the time in 1778 when General George Washington issued orders to remove defendants court-martialed for sodomy. In Washington's army, the accused were subjected to a gauntlet of fifers and drummers marking their ouster and disgrace as they were literally "drummed from the corps." These methods have changed only slightly with the passage of time. It was during World War I that the punishment of homosexual soldiers was first codified in American military law. The Articles of War of 1916 included assault with the intent to commit sodomy as a felony crime. Homosexuality was deemed a criminal act, a move that led to the imprisonment of huge numbers of gay soldiers and sailors. By World War II, homosexuality was transformed from a crime to a psychiatric illness, and regulations were adopted that banned all those with "homosexual tendencies" from the military. In 1942, the first regulations instructed military psychiatrists to differentiate between the homosexual and the "normal" person, with the former deemed "unsuitable for military service." In 1943, the final regulations were declared, banning homosexuals from all branches of the military.[2] Discrimination against gay men in the military was (and is) based on long-held prejudices: Gays undermine cohesion and morale; their "promiscuous" lifestyle encourages high rates of venereal disease (VD) and drug and alcohol abuse; and they are not "man enough" to fight. During World War II, the military was just as intent on preemptively screening for homosexuals at the enlistment phase as it was on curbing the spread of VD. Would-be soldiers and sailors were asked about their sexual preferences. For gays who wanted to serve their country, the only way in was to lie, and the only way to remain was to continue to lie.

Mental health tools during World War II included the "drawing a man test," where, over pen and ink drawings, prospective recruits and enlistees were asked to draw a man. Psychologists claimed that gay men often drew a man with noticeable feminine characteristics and that they could weed out homosexuals before they ever took one more step toward joining the military.[3] Of course, many homosexuals "passed" such harebrained tests and managed to enlist without being discovered. In fear, some never came out of the closet during their entire wartime experience. Others claimed to have a girlfriend or wife back home to prove their manliness. Still others tried to be as cautious as possible with varying degrees of success. The number of homosexuals in the military during the war is not known. (In his 1948 study of

American male sexuality, *Sexual Behavior in the Human Male,* Alfred Kinsey found 4 percent of white males he surveyed to be "exclusively" homosexual throughout their lives after adolescence and 10 percent to be "more or less exclusively homosexual" for at least three years between the ages of 16 and 55.)[4]

"ONE OF THE BOYS WITH A SECRET"

An interview done for the Library of Congress Veterans History Project documents the wartime experiences of former army master sergeant Paul Jordan. Jordan didn't get to graduate from Bangor High School in Bangor, Maine, with the rest of the class of 1933. His father had lost his job during the Depression and urged Paul to join the army where he'd be certain to get food, shelter, and clothing, essentials that his father could no longer provide. Reluctantly, Jordan paid a visit to the army recruiting sergeant, where he made his position clear: "I'm not wearing that monkey suit in the United States because I look in any bar window and see a sign that reads, 'No soldiers or dogs allowed.' If you don't have something for me in foreign service, then I prefer to go to the Civilian Conservation Corps (CCC) and do road work." The sergeant took one look at Jordan's records and his three years in the Reserve Officers' Training Corps (ROTC) and signed him up on the spot. Jordan was shipped off to the 33rd Infantry at Fort Clayton in Panama, where he advanced quickly up the chain of the command, becoming a corporal by the end of his first enlistment. Before he joined the army, Jordan had had several experiences of "rather pleasurable excitement in the presence of certain types of other men" that disturbed him deeply. He read what he could, searching for an explanation, and found one in a book about abnormal psychology in the local Bangor Library. Jordan was gay. The struggle to live with and accept his sexual orientation while concealing it during his 12 years in the army was not an easy task. He took great pains to emulate the "more masculine types" in the military and did a very good job of acting: Jordan was accepted as "one of the boys—one of the boys with a secret."[5]

"You can't go around in the military with a limped wrist," Jordan said in a 2003 interview in *Bay Windows Online.* "You learn in a hurry how to walk and how to talk as a heterosexual. Because I was able to be inconspicuous, I never had any difficulty . . . I mimicked whatever I saw that looked masculine."[6]

By the time of the attack on Pearl Harbor at the end of 1941, Jordan had already planned on making the military a career. And he'd successfully managed to hide his homosexuality, knowing full well the prejudice against gays and the penalties if discovered. After his stint in Panama, Jordan returned to the United States, moved up and down the East Coast, and was, by 1944, a division artillery sergeant major supervisor in charge of eight clerks in an office —a job about as far away from the action as a soldier could get. Like a fenced-in wild horse, Jordan would have done anything to get free and to join the thousands of American troops about to invade France from the sea. He went straight to his colonel and asked to surrender his rank and pay in exchange for a transfer to a division headed for Europe and the D-Day invasion. When told he needed to find a replacement in order to be transferred, Jordan lost no time in finding someone to take his place. Within a short time, now demoted Private First Class Jordan sailed to Southampton, England, where in the middle of the night, his battalion was ordered down to the water's edge and loaded onto a troop transporter en route to storm the beaches of Normandy, France. "It was every man for himself," Jordan said. "We were well-trained, but things started going wrong right away. There was yelling and screaming and small arms fire. You were lost in a crazy nightmare . . . And it never stopped for fifteen months . . . all the way across France, Belgium, and right into Germany. . . . When you take stock, you realize that something has happened to you, all along those weary miles, those dangerous, weary, sticky, stinkin' miles. And you realize it's pretty hard to distinguish between courage and foolhardiness."

Jordan was one of the lucky ones. Through good training, a keen military mind, and some luck, he came home in November 1945. The transition from the military to civilian life was not easy: It took him many months to get his "head unscrewed" and screwed back into place. He worked for the Northern Paper Company in Bangor until someone who sat down next to him in a bar told him about the GI Bill. The Act, signed into law by President Roosevelt on June 22, 1944, paid for part or all of a veteran's education, depending upon how long he had spent in the military and the amount of time he was in a combat zone. By 1947, veterans made up 49 percent of U.S. college enrollment. Nationally, 7.8 million veterans trained at colleges, trade schools, and in business and agriculture training programs across the country. Jordan joined the beneficiaries of the GI Bill and eventually earned a degree in medical technology from the Franklin School of Medical Arts and Sciences Radiology in Philadelphia. Upon graduation, he went to work for Dupont, where he spent the next 15 years. Long after his retirement from Dupont, Jordan was sitting alone in his home, thinking. He had known he was gay for more than six decades but had never felt comfortable letting all but just a few people know. Why, he wondered, had he kept hanging on to the young boy with a secret? Because it was a safe place to stand. But he no longer had to worry about being safe. He'd survived 12 years in the military as a "macho guy" and years more in the workplace where he dared not divulge his sexuality for fear of being fired. He had plenty of money, a secure home, and memories of a war that no one could take from him. At age 85, Jordan picked up the phone, called a local newspaper reporter, and told his story for the first time.[7]

A FEW "QUEERS" TO ENTERTAIN THE TROOPS

As Allan Bérubé points out in his book, *Coming Out under Fire,* and filmmaker Arthur Dong pursues in his highly praised documentary of the same name, under wartime pressure to use every available man and woman, "military officials sometimes let known homosexuals serve and even found ways to utilize behavior ordinarily perceived as 'queer.'" Tom Reddy, born in 1925, served in the military's celebrated Special Services and provided entertainment for the troops. Like all Marines, Reddy wore a backpack even though his had costumes in it. Military officials used the entertainment, and drag routines in particular, to boost troop morale. Bérubé and Dong point out that vaudeville and Hollywood had already developed a variety of characters in comic effeminate roles, played by such actors as Bert Lahr, Grady Sutton, Edward Everett Horton, and Franklin Pangborn. "In the barracks, and particularly during soldier variety shows," writes Bérubé, "men with the most extreme effeminate qualities—especially if they were witty and funny—could be similarly valued as company comedians, clowns, screwballs, and entertainers."[8] It took a "particular form of bravery" demonstrated by gay servicemen who performed in drag. They chose to "risk visibility when hiding would have been safer."[9] A tall, skinny man with a high tenor singing voice, Reddy was garbed in a red dress and sent on stage to sing and dance. As he discusses in Dong's film, "I mean it took nerve to put a dress on and run out there in front of 500 or 1,000 of your peers that were all pretending to be so macho. I felt I could punch anybody in the face—you want to call me 'faggot,' go ahead. But watch your teeth when you do it because 'faggots' got a lot of teeth in it when you say it." Reddy really loved performing in drag for the troops because he understood how far a little laughter could go. Who wanted to look at a whole bunch of Marines in Marine Corps uniforms out there singing songs? "They wanted to laugh," said Reddy. And they wanted to forget the horror of war that tested their sanity and their ability to survive. "I used to look out there at all those boys and wonder who would not be back to see another show." Reddy received an honorable discharge when he left the Marine Corps after the war and ultimately settled down in California with a longtime companion.[10] Carroll Davis, another World War II entertainer, performed in drag shows all over the United States. "We could do more for the boys," he said, referring to the fun and laughter such shows brought to the men in uniform. And for the first time, Davis and many other gay soldiers realized that they were not alone in their sexual orientation. "The effect of World War II was really profound," Davis said. "The country would never be the same again. Gay people began to realize that there were others like themselves across the country, even though most were totally closeted. At the end of the war, many gays settled in port cities where they could be anonymous but could enjoy the camaraderie and support of an underground gay community." [11]

Men like Davis and Reddy had quite a grand old time in the military during the war. But for the majority of homosexuals in different circumstances, the war was devastating. Humphrey writes about navy man Charles Schoen, who enlisted in the U.S. Navy in 1942. His decision, he said, was "95 percent patriotism." Pearl Harbor had been bombed, war had been declared, and Schoen, like most young men, felt a call to take up arms for his country. Schoen had been sexually active before he enlisted and could tell that some of the sailors on board his ship were interested in him. As a means of self-protection, he ignored them. But when the ship docked in San Francisco, Schoen was careful but "game." "I was cautious about talking with people and accepting a time out with just anybody. Not that I could detect any better than the next guy, but I tried to analyze a person and say, 'Okay, this is the guy to go with—he isn't one that will turn me in.'"

One of the most common ways for a gay man to have his cover blown was to be turned in, often by another homosexual under pressure to name names and protect himself. That's exactly what happened to Schoen. He was presented with names of people he knew and told that the affidavits were from men that had sex with him and had agreed to testify against him. It's easy to assume that someone like Schoen would be furious at these men who ratted on him. He was not. "Let me tell you," he said. "I know exactly how they made those agreements. Hell, they intimidated them to agree to those kinds of things in order to receive speedy discharges for themselves. They even tried to get me to give names. God, they were such lowlifes, such worms! They got those 'witnesses' when they showed my picture in Norfolk to different people: 'Do you know this person?' Someone who would identify me would then be pressured into making statements to save their own butts." Schoen panicked and decided to resign instead of being dishonorably discharged. "I still don't know how my personal life, my sexual preference, had any damn thing to do with the navy way and the completion of a mission. It's still a complete mystery to me!" Schoen loved navy life and would have stayed in for 30 years, even under the pressure of hiding his homosexuality. His resignation and the stigma attached to his discharge followed him like a bad dream for years. He couldn't go through a security check in order to get a job, and his feelings of worthlessness made his life difficult. But once his own drapery and upholstery business did well and he was able to live as an openly gay man, his life took on new meaning. Among his many missions was a change in military law with regard to homosexuals. He joined a group called Veterans Care with a national goal of the acceptance of gays and lesbians in the armed forces. He has yet to see that mission accomplished.[12]

"Clark," one of two gay GIs who produced possibly the earliest newsletter by and for gay people, relates his story in Dong's documentary, *Coming Out under Fire*. First called *The Myrtle Beach Bitch* (with subsequent titles of *The Myrtle Beach Belle* and *The Bitches Camouflage*), the publications were sent to gay service members and featured lighthearted stories about themselves and "finding" each other. "Clark," born in 1921, and one of his air corps buddies produced the mimeographed newsletters by typing up tidbits of the day and the comings and goings of gay soldiers stationed around the country, eventually around the world. For many gays, it was like receiving a letter from home. The newsletter encouraged a sense of belonging in an often hostile military environment and was just plain fun. Unfortunately, it was the gay newsletters that led to "Clark's" demise. He and his fellow newspaperman were court-martialed in South Carolina for "the sending of vile and obscene matter through the mail . . . calculated necessarily to injure public morality and to prejudice the morals of other soldiers who receive such publications." Both soldiers were brought to trial without legal counsel and sentenced to a year of confinement at the Army Disciplinary Barracks in Greenhaven Federal Prison in Stormville, New York, where they found a prison crowded with homosexuals who were segregated from the rest of the prison population. "Clark," like thousands of other World War II homosexuals, was handed one of the dreaded blue discharges that effectively labeled him an "undesirable unfit for military service" and prevented him from ever receiving veterans' benefits. After the war, he was one of the first gay men to protest the military's anti-homosexual policy by petitioning to change his undesirable discharge. That was in 1945 and, according to the documentary notes written by Dong at the time the film was completed, "Clark's" requests continued to be denied.[13] As Randy Shilts writes so eloquently in *Conduct Unbecoming*: "The military's policies have had a sinister effect on the whole nation: Such policies make it known to everyone serving in the military that gay men and lesbians are dangerous to the well-being of other Americans; that they are undeserving of even the most basic civil rights. Such policies also create an ambience in which discrimination, harassment, and even violence against gays and lesbians is tolerated and to some degree encouraged."[14]

"To be honest, I haven't the slightest idea how gay soldiers coped with it all," said Lara Ballard, who serves as American Veterans for Equal Rights' national coordinator for the Library of Congress Veterans History Project. "It continually astounds me what these average Americans were asked to do, and what they did, without batting any eye. Added to the stress of combat was the stress of concealing your sexual identity, and I don't know how anyone could have coped. But the fact is, they did, and they performed heroically."[15]

"LESBIANS? OH, NO . . . WE HAD NOTHING LIKE THAT"

> Lesbians? Oh, no, that never came up! I don't know who would say that! Oh, no
> . . . We had nothing like that. And I was right in the middle; I was with those
> girls all the time. What if the women had been discovered? They would have been
> kicked out of the service immediately!
>
> —*Jackie Sarge, former WAAC*[16]

Sarge may have had her head in the sand when it came to lesbians in the Women's Auxiliary Army Corps (WAAC), which later became the Women's Army Corps (WAC). Or she, like many others, may have been blindsided by the secrecy in which lesbians were forced to conduct their relationships. Even today, it's difficult to get lesbian veterans from World War II to speak out about their experiences. "This is principally because of the secrecy in which they had to live," said Zsa Zsa Gershick, author of *Gay Old Girls.* "Most women in that age group that I've talked to wanted to steer entirely clear of any talk about sexual orientation. Lesbians had to hide their sexuality because just the suspicion of such tendencies ensured all-out persecution in mainstream society."[17] Yet anecdotal evidence contradicts the impressions that there were no lesbians in the women's branches of the armed forces during the war. Humphrey writes that "Women in service at the time have told me that a large percentage of all women in the military . . . were gay."[18] In her essay "Rosie the Riveter Gets Married," professor of American Studies and History at the University of Minnesota Elaine Tyler May writes about the not "fully effective" campaigns against "homosexuals and other 'deviants' in military and civilian life." "Lesbians found . . . opportunities, especially in the military," May writes. She quotes Phyllis Abry, who quit her job as a lab technician to join the WACs because she "wanted to be with all those women." Psychologists hadn't devised any tests to weed lesbians out of the military as they supposedly had with gay men, and demonstrations of affections like kissing and hugging were considered socially acceptable among women. In truth, homosexual activity was not considered as disgraceful when practiced by women in uniform as by men. Although it posed the same inherent threat to military discipline, it did not attract the same penalties. WAC officers in 1943 were officially instructed that "homosexuality is of interest to you . . . only so far as its manifestations undermine the efficiency of the individuals concerned and the stability of the group." Officers were warned against "hunting and speculating" about enlisted women's close attachments. And army psychologists perpetuated the theory that the development of close camaraderie among women was an important element in the building of esprit de corps.[19] Still, the witch hunt for lesbians who might undermine "efficiency" and group "stability" continued. Prospective female enlistees were often asked if they had any homosexual feelings or attitudes, and women "spies" were sometimes tapped to report any lesbian activities. Abry knew how to beat the system. When she was asked how she handled the questioning about her sexuality at the enlistment phase, she said, "I just smiled and was sweet and feminine." She understood that looking and acting feminine could easily put recruiters' minds at ease because the military and government went to great lengths to promote the military woman as a dedicated patriot who would be a good housewife and mother once the war ended. "Every effort was made to dispel prevailing notions that military work would make women 'masculine' or ruin their moral character," writes May. "The military presented the image of the female recruit as very 'feminine' as well as domestically inclined. A guidebook for women in the armed services and war industries, for example, included a photograph of a young WAVE with a caption that described her as 'pretty as a picture . . . in the trim uniform that enlisted U.S. Navy Waves will wear in winter . . . smartly-styled, comfortable uniforms . . . with a soft rolled-brim hat.'"[20]

Born in 1920, Abry was the "model WAC" and even served as a recruiter. "I was chosen for a lot of publicity work, not because I was the prettiest by any means, but because I represented the kind of woman they wanted in the service. I was a good WAC."[21] Arbry was also good at being able to identify other lesbians in her unit. She dropped hints and then monitored her friends' responses. "You'd start talking about anything," she told author Allan Bérubé, "and then you'd start talking about women—where you went with other women or what you did with other women. And pretty soon it's becoming obvious that you're not mentioning any men. And so then you get a little bolder, and the next thing you know they're telling you about their love life. It certainly took many days to get to the point of feeling, 'OK, I can be open with this person'—that they're not going to run and turn me in."[22] Abry's "method" worked, and she met another woman who was her lover for the entire time she served in the military. When the two were stationed in Lubbock, Texas, Abry talked about how they would get a pass and go to a hotel and make love: "We stayed in the hotel most of the time, because that was something we couldn't do in the barracks.

Our primary interest was getting somewhere where we could have privacy."[23] Ironically, Abry's partner was ordered to report any activity she observed that might be of a "homosexual nature." "And it's amazing," said Abry in Dong's documentary, "but she never did see anything to report. So she was an honorable woman, a trustworthy woman. And gay as they come." After the war, Abry returned to civilian life with an honorable discharge but, without a support network of other gay women, she did what many other lesbians of her generation did: She met a man, got married, and raised four children. Abry died of cancer in 1993 at the age of 73.[24]

In June and July of 1944, during a trial in which four lesbian "couples" became the primary focus of an investigation into "lesbian acts" in the WACs, a WAC psychiatrist who was "treating" most of the women established two types of women who engaged in lesbian behavior. The first group, she determined, got into relationships with other women accidentally and were thought to be experimenting with lesbianism. The women in the second group were unrepentant and were described as "homosexual addicts," especially those called "oral perverts." The point was to determine those women who were "reclaimable" to go on to more treatment and those who would be discharged or court-martialed. When the lead investigator, Lieutenant Colonel Birge Holt, asked the psychiatrist whether having sex with other women was a disease, she responded:

> No, it is not a disease. . . . It is a trait of character. It is an abnormal bent. It is a personality trait, not necessarily depraved, because she could in any other respect be of the highest order. This particular girl has high moral ideas. . . . She would not steal. She would not kill. She would not take advantage of anybody. She is a generous person. She has never done anything evil. . . . It is a certain bent of character and is part of the personality, but not an illness. Very unfortunate.[25]

Joining the military was ultimately a very "unfortunate" experience for aviation machinist mate, Sarah Davis, who joined the Women Accepted for Voluntary Emergency Service (WAVES) for "the adventure, the excitement." Davis, another subject of both Dong's and Bérubés, was going "to save the world for democracy." Born in 1923 and raised in the small town of Independence, Iowa (ironic as that may now seem), Davis's mother did not want her to enlist. She expected her daughter to go to college and then get married. Unlike Abry, Davis did not join the military to meet other women. She didn't even know what the word *queer* meant. When the psychiatrist at the induction center asked her if she liked men, she could honestly answer yes. When pressed as to why she had not yet slept with a man, Davis said that she'd been brought up not to have sex until marriage. Davis passed muster and was sent to Norman, Oklahoma, to the Naval Air Technical Training Center, where she trained as a machinist. She loved her work and her position as drill sergeant for the entire company of WAVES in Norman. "It was something like ballet and very interesting," she said. Davis liked the military life—the discipline, the order, the marching, and the tunes—and she eventually liked another woman.[26] "I was sitting in the barracks . . . and this one woman that I admired greatly—she was a little older than I, a beautiful body, very articulate and a lot of fun. We were sitting next to each other on the couch with our feet propped up on the table and she started stroking my leg and I thought, 'Wow! What's all of this!' I was instantly enchanted with this woman and had a lot of sexual attraction toward her. Eventually, we got in bed together."[27] Davis never thought of herself as queer. As she recalled, she and her lover never talked about being gay, to others or to themselves. Silence—refusing to say they were gay, let alone putting a name on their sexual orientation—seemed a good first line of defense against getting caught or reported.[28] One day, without warning, Davis was told to report to the company commander. "Do you know why you are here?" the commander asked. "No," Davis answered honestly. "Have you ever slept with a woman?" Only then did Davis understand the seriousness of the situation and determine to lie through her teeth. "Well," she said with a straight face, "I used to sleep with my sister." Davis bobbed and weaved her way through the "interrogation" so successfully that she left the commander's office unscathed, her reputation intact. But the fear of being "outed" and the threat of a dishonorable discharge mitigated her love life and the very strong feelings she had for her lover. Davis stopped corresponding with the other woman, who by then had been reassigned to another base. But the lapse in communication did not diminish her feelings and, once Davis completed her tour of duty with the WAVES, she contacted her lover and arranged to meet her in New York City. The two enjoyed the day together, and Davis expected that her lover would stay the night. She did not, and the women never spoke or saw each other again. "I assumed it was just an episode in her life because I expected that we would spend the rest of our lives together," Davis said. "But that isn't what happened. That was very sad." Devastated, Davis became a very "guarded person for years and years." Her military experience took away what "power" she thought she had and made it difficult to recover. Not until 1990 as a 67-year-old did she come out publicly as a lesbian. Davis competed in the Gay Games and won seven gold swimming medals in the senior category.[29]

POSTWAR HYSTERIA

After the war, as the need for troops decreased, the number of lesbians discharged (and women soldiers, in general) increased. Those women who remained in the military were seen as social misfits who deviated from social norms. Instead of returning home, getting married, and starting a family as the propaganda promised they would do, women who had enjoyed their military experience and wanted to stay saw the welcome mat pulled out from under them, just as many women workers on the home front received their pink slips. The doors that had opened for women were, as touted, opened for the "duration" only. With the war at an end, millions of boys returning home to assume their "rightful" place in the workforce, and still hundreds of thousands others deciding to make the military a career, women were once again pushed back into civilian life as purveyors of the home and family. For most gays, the return to a society still completely unwilling to accept their sexual orientation meant resuming their secret lives behind closed doors. The sense of liberation and camaraderie many had experienced in the military—despite the fear of being discovered and punished—quickly waned when these men and women returned to their families and hometowns. Beginning in 1950, then Senator Joseph McCarthy from Wisconsin made a speech claiming to name a list of 57 members of the Communist Party in the State Department. So began two years of intense Senate investigations in an attempt to rout out Communists in the government, in Hollywood, and in other sectors. McCarthy often used accusations of homosexuality as a smear tactic in his anti-Communist crusade. By early 1953 under President Dwight Eisenhower, homosexuality became by executive order a necessary and sufficient reason in itself to fire any federal employee from his job. Most defense industries and others with government contracts followed suit, and the U.S. Postal Service aided these industries by putting tracers on suspected homosexuals' mail in order to gather enough evidence for dismissal and possible arrest. The war that gays had fought in the name of freedom and democracy abroad failed to ensure them the same rights and liberties at home. It took a police raid on the Stonewall Inn, a gay bar in New York's Greenwich Village, on June 27, 1969, and three days of riots that followed to spark an organized struggle for gay rights and acceptance. Homosexual veterans of World War II, some of them still not out publicly, supported the movement in ways small and large. Whether it was continuing the effort to have dishonorable discharges thrown out, fighting for veterans' rights, or joining the fight against AIDS, the gay and lesbian members of the "greatest generation" continued to wage their battle on the home front decades after the end of World War II.

"LET US, TOO, MAKE AMERICA GREAT FOR DEMOCRACY"

As Americans migrated in numerous different directions during the war in search of jobs, many struggled with the country's unresolved issue of race.

Three out of every four African Americans still lived in the South at the beginning of World War II. The so-called Jim Crow laws enforced segregation by imposing legal punishments on people for "consorting" with members of another race . . . on buses, in toilet facilities, in restaurants, and, without question, in personal relationships. Service wife Betty Lou Rarey remembered walking alone down a very quiet street in Selma, Alabama. As she approached a black man walking toward her, he stepped off the sidewalk and walked past her. "I couldn't figure it out," she said. "There was plenty of room for both of us. Then it dawned on me that he had 'given way' because I was a white woman." And service wife Geraldine Greene talked about her visit to her husband's family in Texas. The couple stopped in Dallas, and Greene saw her first "colored" and white drinking fountains. She walked right up to the "colored" fountain and, in front of her six-foot-something husband, took a drink. He sat and laughed. Later, on a train en route from the north to Florida, Greene noticed that everyone started changing cars. When she asked what was going on, her husband, a southerner, said, "We've just crossed the line." She knew immediately that he was talking about the Mason/Dixon Line, the border between Pennsylvania and Maryland that separated free states to the north and slave states to the south. Once the line was crossed to the south, "coloreds" were not allowed to sit with whites. Green found it all absolutely ridiculous and later became very active in the Civil Rights Movement.

At the beginning of the war, three-quarters of adult African Americans had not finished high school. One in ten had no schooling at all, and many were functionally illiterate. African American men earned, on average, 39 percent of what whites made. Most employed black men were stuck in unskilled occupations and barely eked out a living. Despite urging by Roosevelt and others, large companies like Standard Steel in Kansas City refused to hire Negroes: "It is against company policy," Kansas City's Steel Corporation announced: "We have not had a Negro worker in twenty-five years, and do not plan to start now." The armed forces of the United States followed suit and replicated the patterns in civilian society by confining blacks to segregated units and assigning the majority of them to noncombat service and construction duty. A 1925 Army War College study had stated that blacks were "physically unqualified for combat duty" because the black brain weighed 10 ounces less than the white brain. Blacks, moreover, "subservient" by nature and believing themselves "inferior" to whites, were "susceptible to the influence of crowd psychology" and unable to control themselves in the face of danger. Therefore, the War Department would not "intermingle colored and white enlisted personnel in the same regimental organization." Neither would it assign "colored Reserve Officers other than to the Medical Corps and Chaplains" to existing black combat units in the regular army.[30] What blacks called the "Negro is too dumb to fight" policy crushed the chances for the vast majority of black soldiers to move through the ranks—or, in many cases, to join the military at all. The peacetime U.S. military at the beginning of 1940 included only five black officers, three of them chaplains, in the regular army. The navy accepted blacks only as messmen, cooks, and stewards. The air corps and marines barred blacks completely. Under pressure from a drive led by the National Association for the Advancement of Colored People to end discrimination in the military and amendments introduced by two U.S. Senators, President Roosevelt, who was then facing a race relations crisis in the election of 1940 with 19 percent of black men still unemployed, capitulated and opened all branches of the military to blacks. The official new government policy also ordered that black strength in the army reflect the percentage of blacks in the population as a whole and that blacks have the opportunity to attend officer training schools. But all officers in present and future black units, except for three existing black regiments, would remain white. And although blacks and whites would enjoy equality of service, they would not be integrated because that would "produce situations destructive to morale and detrimental to the preparation for national defense."[31] In *American Patriots,* author Gail Buckley spotlights the separate, vastly inferior living quarters for blacks; separate and vastly inferior training; and vastly inferior weapons and equipment: "In some Army camps," Buckley writes, "black soldiers were forced to sit behind German or Italian POWs for all entertainment, including USO shows.[32] Discrimination in the military and discrimination on the home front led to a "rising mood of militancy" in the black community. The editors at the *Pittsburgh Courier* called for a "Double V" campaign—"victory over our enemies at home and victory over our enemies on the battlefields abroad." Picketers outside a Washington, D.C., restaurant in 1944 carried placards that read: "Are you for Hitler's Way or the American Way?" and "We Die Together, Let's Eat Together." Black Americans faced obstacles on their way to becoming soldiers that most whites never encountered. Still, more than 2.5 million blacks registered for the draft, with about 1 million being called to serve. Perhaps the sentiments of boxer Joe Louis best summed up the reasons black men volunteered: "There may be a whole lot wrong with America, but there's nothing that Hitler can fix."[33]

"ONLY SO MUCH BASEBALL AND BASKETBALL CAN BE PLAYED"

In 1942, the army activated two all-black infantry divisions, the 93rd "Blue Helmets" and the 92nd "Buffalo Soldiers." The training base for the two divisions was Fort Huachuca, Arizona, a base in the middle of nowhere and about as far away from any American city as one could get and still be within the borders of the continental United States. With Tucson some 70 miles away and smaller towns accessible only by car, the army attempted to fill the soldiers' free time by building enlisted and officers clubs (segregated according to race), booking entertainment programs, and organizing all kinds of sports activities. But as Maggi M. Morehouse details in *Fighting in the Jim Crow Army: Black Men and Women Remember World War II,* for single soldiers at the base, prostitutes provided perhaps the main recreational outlet. The cluster of Quonset huts where prostitutes plied their trade was nicknamed the "Hook" because "anybody who went there was going to get hooked by something—the clap, a knife blade, or if he was lucky, just a tough black fist."[34] A local businessman rented the makeshift huts to the one hundred or so prostitutes and pimps who took advantage of the easy market of 18,000 potential customers. More than $100,000 was paid out to the soldiers every payday, and a good chunk of change was spent at the Hook. By 1943, the rise in VD that plagued the military around the country also made its mark at Fort Huachuca, with 368 cases out of every 1,000 soldiers. Alarmed, the army increased its efforts to reduce the disease, and those soldiers in the medical battalion worked overtime. The prophylactic station on base became de rigueur for any solider who visited a prostitute. If a soldier didn't go through the pro station and came up with a disease, he risked a court-martial. The combination of fear and medical treatment worked; by November 1944, the rate of VD had dropped to 157 out of every 1,000 soldiers. Ultimately, the military brass at Fort Huachuca decided to make the Hook off limits and to discipline soldiers who disobeyed orders. But as one soldier put it, "When men are stuck out literally a hundred miles from nowhere, only so much baseball and basketball can be played."[35]

Morehouse observes that it took a brave woman to follow her husband to Fort Huachuca. For those who did, there was limited housing, no work, and little, if anything, to do. When a service wife did make the trek, she was first put up in the "guesthouse," where she could stay until permanent housing could be found. The guesthouse, such as it was, included a converted barracks lined with rows of single beds, one latrine, and an infestation of bugs. Any dreams of privacy and comfort were shattered the moment a service wife stepped inside. "Military wives today don't know about roughing it; they only know a life of luxury compared to the women in Fort Huachuca, Arizona, in the 1940s," said service wife Susie Moore.[36] With housing at a premium, quarters for black officers' families were not available. The original, old fort and "officers' row" on base were open to white generals, colonels, and majors only. Lower-rank black (and white) officers had to find accommodations for their families in the surrounding towns and neighborhoods. One of these "neighborhoods" was the four-sided Quonset structure that housed the prostitutes. The Hook had 50 rooms, 25 of which were ordered to be rented to "colored officers." So, 25 officers moved into the Hook, where the rooms had two cots, a hot plate, and a bathroom down the hall. Initially, the men's and women's restrooms were close together. But Joseph Hairston talked about how that arrangement didn't last for long:

> I was in the shower one day, and a woman was taking a shower. I didn't quite know how to get out of there. I wasn't a very sophisticated guy at the time.
>
> Later I told the other guys; I knocked on the door and sort of whispered the word around, and then all the men took a shower. Well, the wives wondered what was going on, and they went down and checked it out. So, then the wives made that off limits to us. They put a sign on the restroom at our end, which would rotate. It would say, "Men" or "Women." It's funny to think of us living in a whorehouse![37]

Hairston and his wife eventually moved to Benson, a tiny town not far from the base, where they shared half a house. The wives, he said, had nothing to do during the day. In the evenings, the men, who had driven to the base first thing in the morning, would often return to Benson, pick up their wives, and go back to Fort Huachuca to either walk around or take in a movie. "There was always a whole drove of soldiers following you and explaining how they can do a better job with your wife than you were doing and suggesting they would like the opportunity. That kind of put pressure on us," Hairston said.[38] Whatever the pressure, married soldiers and their wives were just happy to have *some* time together, understanding that orders for the men to depart for overseas could come at any moment.

"NOW IT'S TIME FOR YOU BLACK BOYS TO GO GET KILLED"

It wasn't until early 1944 that the tide holding black soldiers from going to war receded. The number of U.S. combat-qualified recruits was running low. And white mothers were angry that their sons were dying while black soldiers were not being sent overseas. In his book *Lasting Valor,* Vernon Baker, an officer reassigned to the 92nd Infantry Buffalo Division and the only living black World War II veteran to receive the Medal of Honor, describes the makeup and poor morale of the 92nd Infantry Division at Fort Huachuca. Baker bemoans the fact that African Americans who, like himself, had gone to Officer Candidate School and had once been a close group were then scattered around the country. The War Department decided to put white Southerners in charge of black troops, and those white officers, Baker charges, changed "as often as Mae West changed lovers."[39] They spent a month, six weeks at the most, before moving on, totally uninterested in commanding black troops. "White officers weren't dying to command black troops so the thirty-day wonders we saw at the 92nd often weren't Uncle Sam's brightest and best."[40] There was, writes Baker, very little communication between black and white officers: "The only real communication from the top officers centered on making sure we recognized our place. . . . When we were summoned we knew to expect some phony assignment or a dressing down for reasons that were never made clear. We speculated that the chewing out was some sort of practice drill for the white officers."[41] Many of the black draftees who trained in Arizona knew the army didn't want them and felt the sting of white officers who spent too much time demeaning their character and potential contribution to the war effort. Most came from the rural South, had little education, and clearly understood that they had been recruited for tokenism, not the fight for freedom. By this time, roughly 10 percent of the U.S. military was black, a percentage that reflected the percentage of blacks in the overall population. Baker details an event in the spring of 1944: All black officers were ordered to the commander's headquarters. The chief of staff confirmed that men from Fort Huachuca would join a regimental combat team comprised of the best officers and enlisted men from several infantry companies. "All these years, our white boys have been going over there and getting killed," the chief of staff said. "Well, now it's time for you black boys to get killed."[42] Although they didn't know it at the time, Baker and his men were about to be sent against Germany's Gothic Line, its line of defense in the Northern Apennines of Italy.

As he details in *Lasting Valor*, Baker's luck with women never matched his success in the military. He married for the first time on June 25, 1941, the day before he left for the army. Leola, his teenage bride, had initially refused his rather sudden marriage proposal, ostensibly because he did not have a job. That's when Baker got the bright idea to join the army, make some money, and win Leola's heart. Following a one-night honeymoon in a Cheyenne motel, the newlyweds clung to each other on the train platform, the train that would take Baker to Camp Wolters in Mineral Wells, Texas. It was in those moments that his new bride reminded Baker to make sure to put her on the wives' allotment. That was the last time Baker saw or heard from Leola. A letter from a buddy informed him that she had moved back in with an ex-boyfriend the day Baker left for the army. Instead of divorcing her the minute he read the letter, Baker clung to the hope that Leola would tire of the boyfriend and rediscover her love for him. As soon as he graduated from Officer Candidate School, he took leave for Cheyenne to find Leola. His officer's uniform was so "stunning" that Leola would have to be blind not to come to her senses. But Leola refused to see him. She was nowhere to be found. According to a mutual acquaintance, the only time Leola ever thought of Baker was when the monthly allotment check arrived. (A $50-a-month allotment check was paid to every GI's wife. A really ambitious woman might decide she needed four, five, even six husbands to support her in style. These women, dubbed "Allotment Annies," developed the wartime racket of bigamous marriage for allotment checks.)

Marrying his second wife, Helen, wasn't exactly an "impulse, not in the same spirit as marrying Leola." He met her at a USO club in Birmingham, Alabama, and was immediately smitten by her model-like face, slender fingers, and the single strand of pearls around her neck. On their second date, Helen suggested that the couple take a walk after dinner. She led Baker to a park bench, where she "instantly melted into tears." Helen, a school teacher, was pregnant. She'd only been with a man once, she sobbed, at a party where she'd accidentally had too much to drink. Helen pleaded for Baker's help and, being the kind (and naive) man that he was, he offered to marry her. She named her daughter Vernon and, when Baker was sent back to Arizona, then on to Italy, Helen moved to Chicago to be with her family. Baker never heard from her again. "Tell the Army to stop her allotment checks," a friend suggested. "Then you'll hear from her." They say "three is a charm," and, for Baker and wives, the third was a keeper. They met in Tucson after the Korean War, married in 1953, and shared a happy marriage until she died from a heart attack/stroke one-two punch in 1986. Three years later, Baker fell in love a final time. He likes to joke and say he married "the enemy": Heidy Baker was born and raised in Germany.[43]

THE TUSKEGEE AIRMEN

In July 1941, a select group of men reported to Tuskegee Institute in Tuskegee, Alabama. The first blacks to ever be admitted in to the U.S. army air corps, many like Charles McGee held a college degree, and all had a passion to fly. In 1940, President Roosevelt was running for a third term. His opponent, Wendel Wilke, had already proposed a program to advance the black cause. Roosevelt knew he had to do something as well and made several concessions to the black community, among them the promotion of Colonel Benjamin O. Davis to Brigadier General and the creation of the first black fighter squadron. Based on the campus of Tuskegee Institute in a segregated unit, these men fought two wars—one war against the enemy and another against racism at home. "It wasn't easy," said McGee. "But our loyalty ultimately rested with the United States. We wanted to be responsible as individuals, and there was no thought of anarchy against our country." The men who trained at Tuskegee were considered part of an "experiment," a test as to whether black men had the intelligence and physical abilities to fly in combat. The pressure on them to succeed was enormous. They were not merely individuals trying to make the grade as pilots but representatives of a race in an unwelcoming military and in a country racked by discrimination and racism.

By July 1942, there were enough Tuskegee Airmen to form the 99th Pursuit Squadron. Hopes of going overseas and joining the fight for freedom and democracy were high. But as current Tuskegee Airman National Historian, William Holton, explained, it would take more than successful training to get black pilots into battle. No American fighter unit wanted the 99th. Despite the grave need for pilots in intense fighting overseas, the Tuskegee Airmen were not called to duty. Not until April 1943, after intense politicking and vocal support from the President's wife, Eleanor, did the 99th land in North Africa for what would be the beginning of their time in combat.

Still, there were those in the U.S. military who did not want the 99th overseas. They circulated unfavorable reports about the squadron's shortcomings, and the company commander was called home to Washington, D.C., to defend his men. Though he was successful, there was now more than ever no margin for error. The 99th needed to prove itself in a big battle and put to rest the myths that black men could not fly and fight. They got their chance defending American troops landing on the beachheads of Anzio, Italy, fighting side-by-side with the white pilots of the 79th group. In three weeks of combat, the 99th destroyed 17 enemy aircraft. Still, the Tuskegee Airmen were segregated overseas. They had no problem with the Italian populace but had to establish their own officers' club because they were not allowed to attend those for whites only.

The 332nd Squadron from Tuskegee followed the 99th into battle. At the controls of P 51 Mustangs, the top fighter aircraft of World War II, this second batch of black pilots was dubbed the "Red-Tail Angels" after the red tail markings on their planes. These pilots flew in the Mediterranean theater of operations. They completed 15,500 missions, destroyed more than 260 enemy aircraft, sank one enemy destroyer, and demolished numerous enemy installations. In all, 450 Tuskegee Airmen served overseas. Sixty-five were killed in action, and 23 were shot down and taken German prisoners of war. But when the war ended and the members of the Tuskegee experiment returned home, they were immediately reminded that in their own country they remained second-class citizens. In the Perkins and Reifenberger documentary *Tuskegee Airmen,* Tuskegee Airman Percy Sutton vividly recalls the homecoming experience that, to this day, causes him great pain. Sutton and his wife were traveling by train to San Antonio, Texas, to visit Sutton's family. He was anxious to impress his bride and treat her to dinner in the train's dining car. Sutton wore his army air corps uniform, proud of his military rank and service. The couple sat down at a table, enjoying each other's company, planning the future that lay ahead. Sutton noticed a young, white major standing in the aisle. For a moment, he worried about potential trouble over eating in what some might consider a whites-only dining car. But the major's accent was definitely northern, and Sutton relaxed. He picked up the dinner menu and began reading it when, out of the corner of his eye, he saw the white major standing next to his table. His body language spoke volumes before he uttered a word. Terrified, Sutton's wife became hysterical, screaming "Please let me leave! Please let me leave!" Sutton's anger roiled in his stomach like a bomb about ready to explode. He wanted to kill the major in the worst way. Instead, he stood up, took his wife's arm and led her out of the dining car. "Of all the things segregation had done to me, nothing hurt so badly as being embarrassed in front of my wife," said Sutton. "Absolutely nothing!"[44]

When Tuskegee Airman Dean Mohr returned from service overseas, he found a country unwilling to welcome black executives into its system. A graduate of Tuskegee Institute in engineering, Mohr had worked as an intern for Detroit's Ford Motor Company before he left for Officer Candidate School in October 1940. He dreamed of a full-paying engineering position with Ford or another company after the war and of supporting his young wife, Mary Louise, whom he had met through one of her neighbors. The Mohrs were married on October 22, 1942, in a very small church wedding, followed by a reception at the bride's home. Like the other black men who had been accepted into the army air corps, Mohr headed back to his alma mater for training. Mary Louise joined him there as soon as she could. Tuskegee Institute—both the school and the military base—remained an oasis of freedom and learning in the middle of a racist southern town. The townspeople of Tuskegee, Alabama, fought the training of an all-black corps with petitions and demonstrations—but to no avail. And as long as the cadets and their wives stayed on campus, they were safe from verbal, even physical, abuse. Dean Mohr was stateside for less than a year. When his crew was staging for overseas duty in Oscota, Michigan, Mary Louise went, too. There, the couple said their heartbreaking good-byes and didn't see each other again for almost two years. Back in Detroit, living with her parents, Mary Louise went to work helping to build airplanes at the

Ford Motor Company. "Our country was extremely patriotic," she said. "So we did everything we could. We bought war bonds, we turned off our lights at night during blackouts, and women worked in factories to support our men." She has no recollection of how much money she earned but does remember getting along just fine with the older men and those who weren't drafted. One morning in 1945, Mary Louise, who by then had left Ford and was off visiting her sister-in-law in Chicago, woke up and said, "I ought to go home today." She'd had a premonition. Mohr packed her bag and took the train back to Detroit. She hadn't been home for long before a taxi drove up in front of her parent's home. The back door of the taxi swung open and out walked her husband. "That was the most thrilling day of my life," she said. The reunited couple didn't talk much about the war. Instead, they focused their attention on getting on with their lives, planning for the future. But the immediate future was not as bright as they had hoped. Doors for college-trained black men were still closed, and Dean could not find a job as an engineer. He was forced to rejoin the air force in order to do what he loved and ultimately became a communications officer who, with his wife and, later, two children, traveled from Alabama to Alaska and to states in between. After 32 years in the military, Mohr retired in 1973. He died suddenly of a stroke in 1986. "I miss him to this day," said Mary Louise, now 82. She's been courted by men since her husband's death but has never remarried. "It would be quite unfair to expect any man to be like him."[45]

Anecdotal evidence suggests that wartime marriages like the Mohrs' survived because of the strong foundation of love, trust, and respect on which they were built. Indeed, the divorce rate among black and white Americans was relatively the same in the 1940s, around 18 percent. "Allotment Annies" aside, the vast majority of black wartime couples whose marriages were well considered survived months, often years, of separation, and the couples managed to rebuild their relationships once the men returned home. (By comparison, the divorce rate among blacks was 40 percent higher than whites by the mid-1960s. Today, the racial difference in divorce is quite large, with African American couples more than twice as likely as European American couples to divorce. The divorce rate for Hispanics doubled between 1970, the first year for which data are available, and 1998, compared with a quadrupling of the African American divorce rate and a tripling of the white rate over the same period.)[46] There were couples like Elmer Jones and music student Frankie Manly, who met at Tuskegee Institute and got to know one another a lot better on a train ride back to Tuskegee from Washington, D.C.: "I asked her how she made music out of a coronet," Jones said. "She puckered up her lips to show me and, bang, I was right in there with a kiss." They were married a month later, lived together for 6 months at Frankie's home while Elmer finished his training, and survived 26 months apart. Frankie died from colon cancer in 2003 after 60 years of what Elmer described as a "lucky" marriage, and, at 88, Elmer now spends his time as an amateur radio operator and member of the East Coast chapter of the Tuskegee Airmen.[47] And there were others, like Lois and Vance Marchbanks, who weathered the disruption of war and an 18-month separation, their marriage kept alive through V-mail. By the time Vance returned home, the younger of his two daughters, who was born not long before he went overseas, didn't know the man she would call "Father." The segregated world Vance had left wasn't much different when he returned. The Marchbanks stayed in the service and moved first to Fort Knox in Kentucky, where the troops remained segregated, the housing for black families substandard, and the feeling of being ostracized just as dispiriting. Lois couldn't take it and returned to Tuskegee until her husband got his next assignment in Columbus, Ohio, as the commander of an all-black hospital. Until his retirement from the military in 1964, Vance and his family traveled from one coast to another, also spending time in Japan. A victim of Alzheimer's, Vance died in 1988. "There was not a man in this world who loved so dearly," said Lois who, at 90, is "doing well."[48]

The evidence from World War II onward shows that the military is slow to follow the path of social change. Whether it is gays in the military, women among the ranks, or integrated units with African Americans marching and fighting alongside whites, the military has dragged its feet. The debate has been driven by clichés, stereotypes, and misconceptions at times in the country's history when the rest of the nation, like the military itself, is undergoing wrenching and still uncompleted changes over how to define the roles of women and men in our society. The military, intent on staying ahead of the curve when it comes to the weapons of war, still clings to archaic thinking about the makeup of its troops, assignment of positions, and promotions within the ranks. Despite the military's unwillingness to integrate the troops and to welcome gays and lesbians into its ranks, the love for their country compelled millions of blacks and homosexuals to serve during World War II. Historians note that, although it is not a straight line from the war to the fight for civil rights, gay rights, or women's rights, World War II set the stage for these struggles between the sexes and between the races.

NOTES

1. Mary Ann Humphrey, *My Country, My Right to Serve: Experiences of Gay Men and Women in the Military, World War II to the Present* (New York: Harper Perennial, 1990), pp. 33–34.

2. Ibid., p. xxiii.

3. Bruce R. Brasell, "Bullets, Ballots and Bibles: Documenting the History of the Gay and Lesbian Struggle in America," *Ceneaste* 21, no. 4 (Fall 1995), http://www.lib.berkeley.edu/MRC/ComingOut.html

4. Allan Bérubé, *Coming Out under Fire: The History of Gay Men and Women in World War II* (New York: Plume 1991), p. 3.

5. Paul Jordan, World War II veteran. Interview by Ed Armstrong for Library of Congress Veterans History Project.

6. Scott A. Giordano, "Vets: Serving in Silence," February 13, 2003, http://www.baywindows.com/media/paper328/news/2003/02/13/LocalNews/Vets-Serving.In.Silence-369501.shtml.

7. Ibid.

8. Allan Bérubé, *Coming Out under Fire: The History of Gay Men and Women in World War II* (New York: Plume 1991), p. 54.

9. Ibid.

10. Arthur Dong, *Coming Out under Fire,* documentary film (Los Angeles: Deep Focus Productions, Inc., 1994, 2003).

11. First Run Features, *Before Stonewall,* VHS (New York: First Run Features, 1985).

12. Humphrey, pp. 43–47.

13. Dong.

14. Randy Shilts, *Conduct Unbecoming: Gays and Lesbians in the U.S. Military* (New York: Fawcett Columbine, 1994) p. 4.

15. Lara Ballard, American Veterans for Equal Rights' national coordinator for the Library of Congress Veterans History Project. Email to author. May 15, 2005.

16. Jackie Sarge, World War II WAAC. Interview by author. April 21, 2004.

17. Zsa Zsa Gershick, author of *Gay Old Girls.* Email to author. May 18, 2005.

18. Humphrey, p. vii.

19. Elaine Tyler May, "Rosie the Riveter Gets Married," *The War in American Culture: Society and Consciousness during World War II,* ed. Lewis A. Erenberg and Susan E. Hirsch (Chicago: University of Chicago Press, 1996), pp. 134–35.

20. Ibid., p. 135.

21. Dong.

22. Bérubé, p. 100.

23. Ibid., p. 105.

24. "Coming Out under Fire: Veterans' Biographies," www.itvs.org/external/Coming_Out_UF/vets.html.

25. Emily Yellin, *Our Mothers' War: American Women at Home and at the Front During World War II* (New York: The Free Press, 2004), pp. 323–24.

26. "Coming Out under Fire: Veterans' Biographies."

27. Bérubé, pp. 42–43.

28. Ibid., pp. 104–29.

29. "Coming Out under Fire: Veterans' Biographies."

30. Gail Buckley, *American Patriots: The Story of Blacks in the Military from the Revolution to Desert Storm* (New York: Random House, 2001), pp. 258–59.

31. Ibid., p. 264.

32. Ibid., p. 261.

33. Maggi M. Morehouse, *Fighting in the Jim Crow Army: Black Men and Women Remember World War II* (Oxford: Rowman & Littlefield Publishers, Inc., 2000), p. 8.

34. Ibid., p. 79.

35. Ibid., p. 81.

36. Ibid., p. 54.

37. Ibid., pp. 54–55.

38. Ibid., p. 55.

39. Vernon J. Baker, *Lasting Valor* (New York: Bantam, 1997), p. 74.

40. Ibid., p. 74.

41. Ibid., p. 75.

42. Ibid., p. 76.

43. Ibid., pp. 146–53, 268–73.

44. W. Drew Perkins and Bill Reifenberger, *The Tuskegee Airmen: They Fought Two Wars,* documentary film (Los Angeles: Rubicon Productions, 2003).

45. Mary Louise Mohr, wife of Tuskegee Airman. Interview by Author. June 30, 2004.

46. Douglas J. Besharov and Andrew West, "African American Marriage Patterns," Hoover Press, www-hoover.stanford.edu/publications/books/fulltext/colorline/95.pdf.

47. Elmer Jones, Tuskegee Airman. Interview by author. April 20, 2005.

48. Lois Marchbanks, wife of Tuskegee Airman. Interview by author. April 14, 2005.

A World War II poster designed to warn men about the potential dangers of getting a venereal disease from a woman who looks as clean and innocent as the girl next door. Courtesy National Library of Medicine.

Formal photo of Lieutenant Morris Mersky and his wife, Shirley, taken on the day Mersky earned his wings in the army air corps.

Army air force cadet Mersky and wife, Shirley, together in Sherman, Texas, during Mersky's stateside military training.

Morris and Shirley Mersky with the author, Jane, shortly after her birth in July 1945.

Olga J. Gannon's wedding announcement photo that was eventually published in the *Baltimore Sun*.

Edith and Frank Bennett stand in front of the one-bedroom cottage they rented in Balboa Beach, California, in 1943.

A World War II poster that sings the praises of women for their contributions to the war effort. Courtesy of the Library of Congress.

Some of the women welders, including the women's welding champion, of Ingalls Shipbuilding Corp., Pascagoula, Mississippi, take a break. Courtesy National Archives.

Longing won't bring him back sooner...
GET A WAR JOB!
SEE YOUR U. S. EMPLOYMENT SERVICE
WAR MANPOWER COMMISSION

Married women were urged to get a war job, instead of wasting time longing for their husbands overseas. Courtesy National Archives.

Bella and Carroll Robert Gillaspie take advantage of precious hours together.

Washington, D.C., wartime secretary Betty Henshaw enjoys some time with her fiancé, Edward L. Hart, on October 16, 1943.

Florence Simon Orbach (center) hams it up with a first cousin and older sister's sister-in-law. The whiskey is a prop.

Florence Simon married Leo Orbach on February 24, 1946.

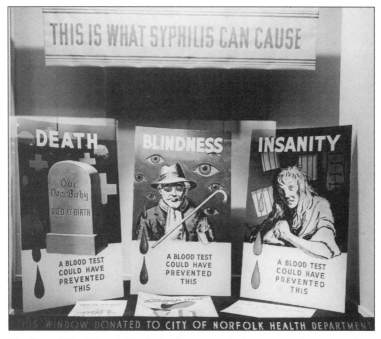

The City of Norfolk put this display in a store window to warn its citizens about syphilis and its potential consequences. Courtesy of the Sargeant Memorial Room, Kirn Library, Norfolk, Virginia.

Rose La Rose, the burlesque queen of the Gaiety Theater in Norfolk, Virginia, entertained servicemen throughout the war. Courtesy of the Sargeant Memorial Room, Kirn Library, Norfolk, Virginia.

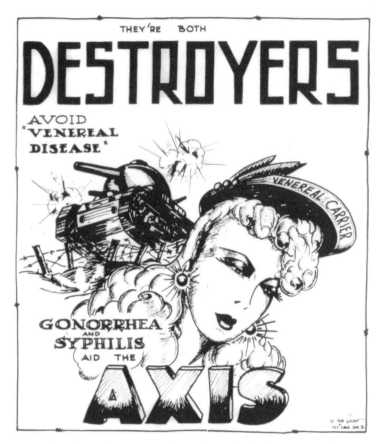

Posters throughout the war warned GIs about the double dangers of venereal disease and the Axis Powers. Courtesy National Library of Medicine.

Once the armed forces were opened to women, posters like this one wooed young women to join the WAACs. Courtesy Library of Congress.

After the war, LaVerne and Melvin Schaffer returned to the United States and posed for this photo on January 13, 1946.

Military officials sometimes let known homosexuals serve and perform in drag like this soldier impersonating Carmen Miranda in the U.S. Army show "Contact Caravan." From the film *Coming Out under Fire*. Courtesy of Deep Focus Productions, Inc.

WAC radio technician Phillis Abry (left) is shown with her lover, Mildred, on base during World War II. From the film *Coming Out under Fire*. Courtesy of Deep Focus Productions, Inc.

U.S. Army psychological assistant Stuart Loomis (right) pictured with a friend. From the film *Coming Out under Fire*. Courtesy Deep Focus Productions, Inc.

Five

AN ARMY OF SERVICE WIVES

The "army" of married women that followed their husbands during their stateside military training—estimated by some to number well over a million and a quarter women—came from large urban areas and from small country towns. From secure middle-class families and from broken families still struggling from the devastation of the Depression. Some had college degrees. Others went to work straight out of high school. They were Christian and Jewish but almost exclusively white. It was just about impossible for black wives to find housing anywhere south of the Mason/Dixon Line (with the exception of the small Arizona towns near Fort Huachuca and the oasis of Tuskegee Institute). Many of the service wives were young—girls, really. They cut their college education short. Or quit their jobs. Many wed their sweethearts in hastily arranged ceremonies, dressed in two-piece suits instead of the traditional long, white gown. Their country was at war. Uncle Sam was taking their men. And these women—most of whom had never seen the military in their future—joined the unofficial rank of service wife, determined to stay with their husbands for as long as possible.

Betty Lou Hodge met her future husband, George Rarey (fondly called Rarey) on a blind date in the slightly bizarre setting of a Thanksgiving breakfast in Washington, D.C. He was a 21-year-old transplanted Oklahoman working in the art department of the *Washington Star*; Hodge, the 19-year-old daughter of an itinerant newspaperman, was finishing business school and working part-time as a secretary. Although it wasn't love at first sight, Hodge said, things started to "percolate" a few weeks later, and the couple began talking marriage "darn soon." The rub: Neither of them had any money. So in the fall of 1940 Rarey moved to New York City to seek work as a cartoonist. Letters flew in both directions, and after just one semester, Hodge dropped out of school, packed her bags, and followed Rarey to Manhattan. She landed a job at the New School for Social Research working on a program for refugee scholars, a program funded by the Rockefeller Foundation and dedicated to getting Jewish and anti-Nazi scholars out of Europe. On December 7, 1941, the war in Europe became America's war, too, and in less than a month Rarey was drafted into the army.[1] He reported to a Greenwich Village induction center at 6 A.M. on a bleak day in mid-January 1942, carrying his toothbrush and shaving gear in a shabby brown pouch, a sketchbook under his arm, his pockets bulging with pipes, tobacco, pencils, and brushes. Hodge tried to settle down and wait for news. Quite amazingly, she received a postcard that same afternoon, a quick and telling cartoon of a bewildered, disheveled little civilian saying adieu to the world as he had known and loved it.[2] On his second day of military service, after a battery of dizzying psychological and I.Q. tests, Rarey, who had never learned to drive a car, was asked if he'd like to try to qualify for fighter pilot training. Twenty-four hours of buck private status convinced him that anything would be an improvement, and he said yes. A few days later he was sent south to Maxwell Field west of Montgomery, Alabama, for preflight training. The envelopes of Rarey's letters to Hodge were always a delight to both her and the mailman. In the upper right-hand corner (where all servicemen were instructed to write "free") Rarey drew a little cadet saying "Thanks." "And there were always airplanes zooming over the flap, parachutes in wild descent, and befuddled birds trying to find an empty piece of sky. . . . One bird, ultimately dubbed the Rarey Bird, became a permanent trademark on Rarey's letters and the letters of many other cadets."[3] Aviation cadets were not allowed to marry until June 1942. At the end of May that year, Hodge received the following "marriage proposal" in the mail:

> I think the 6th of June would be ideal for your arrival in Ocala. It can't come too soon. . . . We can get the license and be married the same day. . . . You must write me and tell me what you think. I'm no damn good at arranging such things. As to the finances, I think we're all set. We will be paid tomorrow or Tuesday and I should draw in the neighborhood of 85 bucks. I think that'll see us through. I wish it were a thousand. Oh, how I love you, gal![4]

With every penny she had saved stuffed in her purse, Hodge boarded a train in New York City bound for Ocala, Florida. Early on a warm Saturday morning, she stepped off the train and into the waiting arms of her Rarey who, "beneath the crisp summer khakis, a half-inch haircut, and a sunburned nose was absolutely and wonderfully the same." Rarey had made reservations for his bride-to-be at the Candle-Glo Inn, a haven for three just-married cadet wives who were not allowed to live with their noncommissioned husbands. With a lot of time on their hands, the "Candle-Glo Gang" took on Betty Lou's wedding as a welcome project. As detailed in *Laughter and Tears: A Combat Pilot's Sketchbooks of World War II Squadron Life,* it didn't take long for plans to fall in to place:

1. Everyone would donate precious sugar ration stamps, and the Candle-Glo cook would make a splendid cake. (It would be cut with the sword of Class 42J's one West Pointer.)
2. Gardenias from the inn's back yard would decorate the church and reception.
3. Someone was going to magically produce champagne.
4. Music would be provided by one standard-issue record player.
5. The bride-to-be would please take a book to the veranda and stay out of everyone's way.[5]

The Candle-Glo Inn hummed with activity. The days flew quickly by, and on Friday night, the eve of the wedding, the phone rang. It was Rarey. He had been restricted to the base for the weekend because his navigation marks were low. The wedding would have to be postponed. Hodge wept, someone called the minister, and who knows what went on in the Candle-Glo kitchen. The next morning, the phone rang again. The top brass had had a change of heart and would allow Rarey to come to town to get married—as long as he returned to base by seven that evening. Hodge and Rarey were married later that day in a church ceremony, surrounded by aviation cadets, flight instructors, and three camp wives. The bride wore a light blue, full skirt with a matching quilted top, an outfit she bought for five dollars after the Candle Glo Gang nixed the brown-and-white seersucker number she'd brought from New York. After the ceremony, the wedding party returned to the Candle-Glo Inn for the long-awaited celebration. Shortly before seven, the bride and groom reluctantly made their way to the town square, grabbed a taxi, and deposited Rarey at the base gate.

The newlyweds didn't see each other again for a full week; if the military had had its way, they wouldn't have met again until after the war. The service provided neither housing nor work for service wives of noncommissioned officers. If the wives chose to follow their husbands, they were on their own. "I was deeply in love and wasn't going to leave Rarey, no matter what," said Betty Lou. "And that was the smartest decision I ever made."[6] For the first eight weeks in Florida, Betty Lou scraped by on Rarey's military pay of $50 a month, wedding gift money, and the few dollars she had saved from her job back in New York City. But after Florida, reason dawned: The newlyweds were flat broke. There wasn't even enough money for Betty Lou to rent a room with other women in Greenville, Mississippi, the next military town on Rarey's training itinerary. A sodden mess, Betty Lou was certain she'd have to go home. But Lady Luck intervened. Rarey was talking to a civilian at the bus stop who mentioned that he needed a secretary for two weeks. Needless to say, he got a secretary. Then a group of Greenville ladies got together and decided that the aviation cadets should have a club. Word of Rarey's talents as an artist had gotten around, and he was offered $100 and free weekend meals in exchange for painting murals in the club ballroom.

> I can still see him in that ballroom, paint brush in one hand, bottle of beer in the other, rocking back on his heels as he surveyed his work, always surrounded by a crowd of cadet onlookers. In three corners of the big room he painted formations of the basic trainer the cadets were then flying. In the fourth corner, behind the slightly raised bandstand, he painted a Dixieland band playing its heart out. The two months in Mississippi were as close to idyllic as possible in wartime.[7]

"MOTHERHOOD'S BACK IN STYLE"

Wartime for service wives who chose to follow their men was described in the August 30, 1943, issue of *Time* as a "strange, unorganized home-front battle being fought by a vast, unorganized army of women" whose "enemies" included "the painfully crowded transportation system, soaring prices and low military pay, appalling housing shortages and brutal rent gouges, plus the thousand and one exasperating accidents of fortune.[8] With no official traveling status, service wives were at the bottom of the priority heap. They often wound up in train coaches overnight, sitting on a suitcase in the middle of the aisle. Many had never traveled before and had no idea what to expect, away from home for the first time. Women traveling with small children ran into landlords who were dead set against renting to them. An ad taken out by a service wife with small children in the New Orleans *Times-Picayune* decried the virtual embargo:

WANTED BY A NAVAL OFFICER'S WIFE—
whose husband is serving overseas—and
THREE MONSTERS in the form of my
little children—TO RENT—a 2-or3-bedroom house,
apartment, barn or cage or whatever is
supposed to serve as shelter when such
terrible creatures as children have to be
considered . . . [9]

Such difficulties didn't stop camp wives like Hazel Klauck from getting pregnant. Klauck vowed not to let the war interrupt her romance like it had her parents' during World War I. She joined her husband in June 1943, in Cookville, Tennessee, where she formed friendships with other camp wives, many of whom moved to the same base towns over a period of 16 months.

"It *was* an adventure!" she said. "There were a lot of other women just like me."

Klauck traveled light, never paid more than $7/week on rent, and never remembered being bored. She got pregnant on the road ("It was planned") because "my husband could have come back from the war without a leg or an arm or who knows what." Klauck went into labor on a Saturday when everyone in the small Alabama town where she had "settled" was at the football game. Thankfully, a doctor arrived less than 30 minutes before her son was born.

"It was a challenge being a young mother away from home," she said. "But the chance for the three of us to spend whatever time we could together was worth it." [10]

LOVE ON THE FLY

Jack Havener took Mary Alyce Janssen as his lawful wedded wife in a Christmas Eve ceremony in 1941. The newlyweds spent nine months together in their home town of Sterling, Illinois, before Jack entered the military, first in the army infantry, and later as a cadet in the army air corps. The Haveners agreed before Jack left that Mary Alyce should keep her job at the Green River Ordinance Center where rockets for the Bazooka rocket launcher were made. Once he was well settled into the aviation cadet routine, she would join him on the road and stay with him as long as she could. Havener kept a diary and letters written during the war, and his entries from July 1943 until January 12, 1944 detail the joys of having his wandering service wife with him during the heady days of training and waiting to go to war:

I love everybody! Yes, even my instructor! When I told him my wife was arriving, he said: "I can see your head is in the clouds, so I'm not going to dampen your spirits. Get in all the solo flying time you can."[11]

This passage dated June 20, 1943, says it all: After almost nine months apart, Jack's wife, Mary Alyce, joined him in Waco, Texas—a long way from Sterling, Illinois. Mary Alyce and some of the other service wives settled in at the Glenora Courts Motel. The rooms each had a double bed, a shower, and a tiny kitchenette, the latter consisting of a small floor cabinet on which rested an electric hot plate, sufficient for cooking most of their meals. Neither Jack nor the other girls' husbands wanted their wives to work, so, in many ways, their time in Waco was like an extended vacation filled with sleeping late, window shopping, and swimming. But with only one double bed shared by two wives, Saturday night visits—the only time the husbands were allowed off base overnight—became an exercise in logistics. As Havener described in his diary, after dinner the rest of the night was divided into two segments of two hours each.

> We drew straws to see which couple would use the room during the first time period. The losing pairs (or winning, depending upon how you looked at the situation) would then await their turn in their respective automobiles parked out front. It was seldom that the first shift occupants had to be routed out by a knock on the door, but it happened with the second shift lovers. More often than not, the first shifters would grope their way to the cars in a euphoric state of half undress. . . . Living on love during the weekends, in spite of the obstacles, became a reality for us.[12]

The men had to be back at the base by 18:30 Sunday evening. Their wives were allowed to bring them into the base but had to park at the edge of the cadet parade ground. They could go no further. As the entire squadron gathered for what was called the retreat parade, the women stayed to watch the marching ceremony that eventually led back to the barracks for the evening mess formation and the study hour to follow. The cadets were strictly forbidden from waving at their wives (or other women who had gathered). But just as they marched past the line of cars, the Cadet Squadron Commander would give the "eyes right" command so the cadets had one last look at the women, a look that would have to last until the following weekend.

After eight weeks of basic flight training, Havener's squadron was transferred to Houston's Ellington Field. Mary Alyce and the other service wives put up at a local motel until they could find a better place to stay. On base, Lieutenant Colonel Charles D. Chitty, Jr., delivered the usual "this is what we expect" routine and then dropped a bombshell. There was a polio epidemic in the Bombardier Squadron, and all pilot cadets would be under quarantine indefinitely and restricted to the base. The scramble for the telephones, with men pushing and shoving to get in line, undermined any semblance of military protocol. Havener was fourth in line, and *he* had to stand and wait for almost an hour. By the time he got through to Mary Alyce to tell her about the quarantine, she and another service wife had already found a three-bedroom brick house whose owner, Mrs. Howard, a widow, had a room with kitchen privileges to rent. Housing for many service wives crisscrossing the country, however, was often appalling. A reporter discovered young women, some with babies, paying up to $50 a month to live in a warren of sheds, converted chicken coops and ramshackle barns in Leesville, Louisiana, a stagnant backwater near Camp Polk. The places were broken up into cubicles, and three people slept in a bed. There was one toilet for 35 people. Sophie Holbrook, a service wife who took a train across the country from Akron, Ohio, to join her husband, Bill, in Santa Ana, California, found a room and found a problem. "It was a house of prostitution!" she said. "There were men always walking through the hallways . . . constant noise and motion. I was scared to death in there."[13]

Havener's wife was one of the lucky ones, and she lived in Mrs. Howard's house until her husband's squadron was transferred once again. With the housing problem solved, there was the quarantine to worry about. Refusing to be denied human contact with their wives for however long the forced "jail sentence" lasted, Havener and two other married buddies dreamed up a little scheme. There was a wide shoulder off the Houston to Galveston highway that ran right by the main entrance of the base. The wives could park the car there, walk about 20 feet, and be at the fence that surrounded Ellington Field. At the appointed time, Havener and the two other cadets waited anxiously at the fence. "Surprisingly," the wives were on schedule. And what followed were two hours of the "most unusual antics passing motorists had seen in a long time":

Here we were hanging on the fence like monkeys in a zoo with our wives outside peering through at us. Occasionally, we'd touch fingers through the mesh . . . Trying to kiss one another through a three-inch opening required an unusual amount of pucker and dexterity. The old Dutch saying, "Apple pie without cheese is like a kiss without a squeeze" had a reverse connotation in this situation . . . This Sunday ritual went on for as long as we were quarantined . . . Six weeks! Each week the group of lovers, married and unmarried, increased until toward the end the traffic hazard became acute . . . It was easy to recognize anyone who had been at the fence. The tell-tale streaks of chain link metal oxidation across the bridge of the nose and the cleft of the chin were dead giveaways . . . We did learn later that the polio epidemic had been successfully quelled, and that no new cases were reported.[14]

It was with mixed emotions that the Haveners rang in 1943, knowing that it would be the last formal event before his squadron departed for England. Nine days later, movement orders for the fifteen aircraft of the 497th Squadron were issued, along with instructions for all wives and children to return home. Mary Alyce and another service wife loaded up the Zephyr and, with a supplemental coupon book of 17 ten-gallon ration tickets, the wives had more than enough gas to drive home to Illinois. It would be a year and two months before Jack and Mary Alyce would see each other again. They enjoyed a long marriage of nearly 30 years before Mary Alyce succumbed to cancer in October 1971.

MAKING ENDS MEET

Jobs in small military towns were hard to come by, particularly when employers realized that service wives would be moving on every eight weeks or so as their husbands' squadrons were transferred to another base. Many of the training bases for all branches of the service were located in small, out-of-the-way towns, often long distances from a major city. The plethora of available factory and government jobs in large urban centers were inaccessible to most service wives. If they needed to augment their husband's paltry military pay that began at $50 a month, they had to find work in small towns where employment opportunities were few and far between. Florence Dennis managed to land a job in a stationery store in Columbus, Georgia. On her first day, the owner's son handed her a broom and told her to sweep the entrance to the store. Insulted, the well-dressed young service wife who had held an excellent office job before the war said, "I wasn't hired to be a janitor." Somehow, she wasn't fired. On military payday weekend, the store was filled with soldiers buying greeting cards for family and friends back home. Among the many customers on a particular payday was a black soldier who bought a very expensive pen and pencil set. Dennis was in the process of wrapping the set for mailing when the owner's son noticed and yelled across the store, "What do you think you're doing?" He was furious that she deigned to take the time to wrap an item for a black man. Flustered, the soldier grabbed his half-wrapped package, apologized to Dennis, hoping that he hadn't caused her to get fired, and hurriedly left the store. Once outside, he bumped into a cadet and told him what had just happened. Ironically, the cadet was Dennis's husband, who was waiting for her to get off of work. "Don't worry," he said, doing his best to ease the soldier's guilt. "She's perfectly capable of finding another job, if it comes to that." Dennis was too good of an employee to fire, even if her northern sensibilities clashed with prevailing racist attitudes in the south. She worked eight hours a day, six days a week for $2.00 a day, until her husband was transferred to another military base.[15]

Blanche Kishner followed her husband, Harry, from their home in Chicago to the sweltering Florida Everglades, where the temperature often topped 120 degrees. An officer by this time, Harry was allowed to live off base with his wife. The young couple rented a room with a $25 down payment ("a lot of money then"), deposited their belongings, and went out to get a cheap bite to eat. They returned to their new "home," turned on the lights, and watched in horror as roaches roamed every surface of the room. "I was quietly hysterical," said Blanche. "I sat up all night with my clothes on and my feet on the bed. The next day, we gave up the room. The landlady, obviously not pleased, said it was the soldiers from the North who brought all the bugs."[16] The Kishners found another place to rent without roaches, and Harry was up every morning at 3 A.M. in order to take a bus to the base in time for revelry. The suffocating heat and mandated blackouts at night made life miserable. "We couldn't keep any lights on because of the blackouts and couldn't keep the windows closed with the shades down because we couldn't breathe," Blanche said. "It was hotter than hell, and I cooked dinner in my bathing suit!" Even on an officer's pay, there wasn't enough money. So, Blanche, who had a civil service rank, got a job writing technical manuals on subjects about which she knew absolutely nothing. "How we won the war beats me," she said. "I had no idea what I was doing." In the four years she was on the road, Blanche traveled about 25,000 miles. "Back and forth . . . Life on those trains. All those women with crying babies and having to change diapers in the toilets. And the mice running around on the floor! I remember one ride when my husband was going to Harvard to study Chinese as part of the specialized army language program. I tried to pay the train conductor to let the wives share sleeping berths with their husbands. Only around midnight was I allowed to join Harry in an upper berth with two soldiers down below. Those guys teased me forever." They arrived in Cambridge, Massachusetts, and were put in a house. The landlady was an eccentric older woman who didn't believe in turning on the heat. She wore long underwear and sweaters day and night. The thermometer in the hall read 42 degrees. "First the heat in Florida. Later, the cold in Massachusetts. Harry and I got into bed, fully clothed, covered with every item we had. Still, my teeth chattered, and I ended up with a very severe cough. Only then did the landlady turn on a little heat."

During her time on the road, Blanche worked at a base PX selling perfume, as a secretary for a man who owned a large farm, and as a secretary in a small defense plant that made a piece of equipment for submarines. "I remember thinking at the time how tough those days were and how I'd never be able to forget the experiences we had. There was no way I wanted to have children while Harry was in the service. The additional pay for men with children wasn't enough to change my mind."

In 1942, Congress passed the Servicemen's Dependence Allowance Act, which raised the pay of enlisted men with dependents by providing an additional $28 monthly for a wife, $40 for a wife and child, $10 for each additional child. But for many traveling service wives, the extra money wasn't enough to make ends meet. Landlords often raised rents, particularly for service wives. The cost of food—whether the wives cooked or ate out—put a hole in monthly budgets. Transportation from military town to military town could be costly. And with most evenings to themselves, there was a desire to get out, see a movie, go bowling, or grab an ice cream at a local creamery. Service wife Barbara Higby grew up during the Depression and knew what it was like to struggle to put food on the table. Her father had owned a successful grocery store and meat market but drove his profits into the ground by insisting on carrying his customers on credit. He eventually lost his store and his home to the bank. Even though he later got a job as a night watchman, he was unable to support his large family of 12: Everyone in the house had to contribute in some way to help make ends meet. Higby and her mother embroidered samplers for Woolworth five-and-dime stores and made five cents for each one. One of her older brothers got a job as an accountant in Detroit. Though she graduated from high school with honors, Higby's dreams of attending college were shattered by the hard times. She did manage to attend business school at night while working during the day in the materiel control office of the Willow Run bomber plant in Ypsilanti, Michigan. At the tender age of 18, not really ready to marry her high school boyfriend but finally persuaded by his "touching" letters, Higby left Michigan for St. Louis to get married. "When young people are in love," she said, "the important thing is to be together." Higby did some photographic modeling for a while and then worked for an abstract and title company. When her husband, an army air corps cadet, was assigned to Ellington Field near Houston, she found a room there near some of her family who had relocated and then found a job with a different abstract and title company. Though her family thought it was a crazy thing to do, she quit that job and followed her husband to Laredo, Texas, where he trained to be a bombardier:

On the train from Houston to Laredo, Texas, I met a fruit importer who had a friend in the chicle business. An invitation to join him for breakfast the next day resulted in a typing job for me that started immediately. When the typing was completed, I became the office manager because the previous manager resigned. The wages were very good, and my boss treated me well even though he knew that I would leave at the end of my husband's training. When the boss went away on business, he gave me the use of his Cadillac limousine. When Paul had a weekend off I drove out to the base to get him. All the cadets saluted the car assuming that the driver was at least a General! Paul's next assignment was at Midland, Texas. My boss offered all kinds of inducements to get me to stay, even offered to double my salary and the loan of his car on weekends, but love prevailed.[17]

Higby discovered she was pregnant not long after arriving in Midland and returned to Michigan to live with her husband's parents. For the first time in her married life, money was not a constant concern—nor was finding a job. She settled down in her in-laws' home to wait for the birth of her first child and the eventual return of her husband.

WEDDING BLISS

> *Love was epidemic at Fort Bliss . . . By the time Lent drew to a close, a first Lieutenant, five sergeants, a corporal, two privates and a Medical Corps technician had confided to chaplains that they wanted to be married on Easter Sunday. Faced with this nuptial problem, Fort Bliss did not quail. Instead it provided the remarkable ceremony shown on these pages . . . When the ceremony actually began, only seven couples appeared before the five chaplains, for three, impatient of delay, had eloped.*
>
> —*Life*, May 4, 1942

Of the seven couples who wed on April 5, 1942, in what was dubbed a "Mass Marriage Ceremony" at Fort Bliss in El Paso, Texas, only two brides and one groom are thought to still be alive. Bessie Stroud, 88, now living in a retirement facility in Texas, recalled how she was fixed up with her future husband. Her brother and cousin ran a service station in El Paso. One hot afternoon, two soldiers who bought gas there all the time confided in the other men that they'd like to meet some nice girls. Stroud, then 23, and her girlfriend, Madge, fit the bill and doubled on a blind date with the two soldiers the very next night. The four drove around El Paso and took in a movie. On that first double date, Bessie paired off with Dan Pettuse. On the second date, the couples switched, and Bessie and Harold Stroud became a fast item. "Harold was a decent man . . . real quiet. . . . didn't drink," said Stroud. "They say opposites attract, and we fell in love."[18] Bessie was three years older than her new beau. But age, said Bessie, didn't mean a darn thing to them. The new lovers "did some smoochin'" but that was it. "Back then," said Stroud, "couples didn't live together before they were married, and they didn't have sex." Stroud can't recall Harold actually proposing to her. They just heard about the mass wedding ceremony and thought it was a good idea. Madge and Dan decided it was a good idea, too, and made plans to join them. Memories of the actual ceremony are a bit vague in Bessie's mind. But the photographs in *Life* picture Corporal Harold H. Stroud locked in a kiss with his new bride and then, moments later, the newlyweds smiling broadly. The noticeable gap between Corporal Stroud's front teeth accents a round, boyish face with his hair trimmed close on the sides and slicked back on top. He stands a good head-and-a-half taller than his bride, whose dark dress with a light collar is graced by a large corsage. She is wearing a small white hat that nestles amid tight brown curls. The newlyweds had known each other for three months. The new Mrs. Madge Pettuse wore a wide-brimmed white hat that arched away from her face, a white corsage to match, and a grin as wide as the hat. She and Sergeant Daniel Pettuse almost pass for siblings, though Madge's hair and complexion are much lighter than that of her groom's.

Following the ceremony, Bessie, Madge, and their husbands shared a small, two-bedroom house in town. (The men were now officers and allowed to live off base with their wives.) When Harold was shipped to a training camp in Medford, Oregon, Bessie followed. She was pregnant. ("To tell you the truth, getting pregnant was an accident. But that's all right.") For the next year or so, she moved back and forth between Medford and El Paso. When Harold went overseas, Bessie worked for the railroad as a clerk. "I wrote to him every day," she said. "But then I didn't hear a word from him for almost three months. Everybody told me to cheer up . . . that if he'd been critically wounded, I would have known about it. As it turned out, he got shot through the shoulder and was evacuated behind the lines in France. My mail finally caught up with him, and he said he'd never seen so many letters in his whole life!"

Private Manuel Solis, born in 1915, and his childhood sweetheart from Morenzie, Arizona, were also married in the mass wedding ceremony at Fort Bliss. Trinidad Loya and Solis had shared the same locker and used the same books. "We shared some of the homework, too," said Solis, laughing. The fact that Trinidad had "messed around with someone else" and gotten pregnant somewhere along the line didn't bother him. "Back then, I was busy playing sports and had little time for her. Sports were more important to me than running around with the girls."[19] But by the ripe old age of 27, Private Solis was ready to tie the knot before being shipped overseas. The two *Time* photographs of this second of seven couples who were married in the mass wedding ceremony capture the bride and groom sealing their marriage vows with a kiss and warm embrace and then standing side-by-side, smiling for the camera. Trinidad wears her long curly hair with the bangs rolled back, as was the style. Her finely arched eyebrows set off dark brown eyes, a delicate nose, and rather thin lips that perfectly suit her small features. It would seem that Private Solis enjoyed military food, his belt stretched around an ample middle and a round face, accentuated by the short military hair cut. The Solises had known each other for 10 years, longer than any of the other couples who were married that day. Once pronounced husband and wife, the newlyweds rented a little room, and Solis rode a bus for 10 cents back and forth to the base every day. He ate most of his meals on base, and Trinidad usually joined him for lunch. Solis was shipped to France in 1943, where he traveled two days behind the infantry, carrying food and other supplies for the troops. He never fired a shot. Trinidad stayed in Texas and worked in a defense factory. "I was overseas for three years," Solis said. "I wrote her every day. Well, almost. . . . I made copies of my letters and, when I didn't feel like writing, I just mailed a duplicate." Apparently, Trinidad never knew the difference.

HARD LESSONS ON THE ROAD

Historically, soldiers went off to war to fight, leaving their wives and sweethearts to "keep the home fires burning until the boys came home." World War II, to a far greater extent than World War I, broke this traditional pattern. For the "army" of service wives that chose to follow their husbands from one military base to another—picking up whatever roots they could put down in eight weeks and moving on to put them down somewhere else—there were inflated rents to pay, strange neighbors, and often lousy living conditions. Lila Saulson recalls a string of "horrors": fleas from a downstairs neighbor's dog crawling all over the hair on her husband Bill's chest; roaches running rampant in a landlord's refrigerator; summer heat so bad that she had to sit with towels wrapped around her neck to catch the sweat; and requisite blackouts that made the heat even more unbearable. But she was young, in love, and with her husband. Saulson was Jewish but never personally experienced blatant anti-Semitism. That was not the case with one young newlywed, Doris Levine, who was all of 18 years old when she moved into a rooming house in Seabring, Florida, where four other service wives had already settled. The newcomer was initially welcomed with open arms. But on the second day of her stay, she was asked to verify her last name. "Levine?" "Yes," she said. In the days ahead, it became clear that she was being ostracized because she was Jewish. "They ignored me as if I never existed," she said. "I had never encountered anti-Semitism before, and that was tough."[20] Another service wife, Ruth Berns, heard more than her share of anti-Semitic slurs as she traveled with her husband. Because her last name is not "necessarily Jewish," people who met her casually said things like, "Have you noticed that there aren't many Jewish boys in the army?"[21] Statements like this were personally offensive and factually untrue. Approximately 550,000 Jewish men and women served in the U.S. armed forces during World War II, the equivalent of 37 divisions. The participation of 11 percent of the U.S. Jewish population in the service, 50 percent of the men ages 18–44 years, ensured that most Jewish families had a close relative in uniform.[22] To test the level of anti-Semitism, Berns and her husband, Bob, tried to register at a Santa Barbara, California, hotel under the name Bernstein. They were told there were no vacancies. Later, they returned, spoke to a different person at the front desk, and used their real name. They got a room right away. The irony that America had gone to war against Hitler's Germany and that anti-Semitism was alive and well at home was not lost on her or on many other Jews who, along with the rest of the country, sacrificed and fought in the name of democracy and freedom.

Historian David M. Kennedy writes in his Pulitzer Prize–winning book, *Freedom from Fear,* about Americans' ignorance of and inability to comprehend Hitler's campaign of genocide against Europe's Jews: "They knew some facts, but facts did not necessarily mean understanding, especially for a people so mercifully sheltered from the war's harshest suffering."[23] Kennedy goes on to detail the skepticism of the American government when first informed of the mass exterminations of Jews under Nazi control. The report, thought to have had the "earmarks of a war rumor inspired by fear," was later confirmed, however, by further evidence. "No one as yet grasped the degree to which the killing was going on systematically in purpose-built death camps," Kennedy writes. "But it was now clear that the question facing Washington was not a matter of providing asylum to refugees but of rescuing prisoners trapped in a death-machine."[24] American Jewish leaders publicized what they knew, the mainstream press reported what scant news of the Holocaust it had, and Roosevelt eventually established the War Refugee Board (WRB) to do what it could. In March 1944 when Adolf Eichmann arrived in Budapest to impose the Final Solution on the Jews of Hungary, the WRB sent an emissary who, through any means possible, saved thousands of Jews. But, in the end, America's efforts to stop the mass exterminations—and some would say those efforts were too late and too few—failed, and six million Jews were exterminated.

Many service wives, especially those from the North, witnessed segregation up front instead of reading about it in magazines and newspapers. "It was the very first time I went through the South," said Doris Levine. Sensitive now to the hurt and dangers of anti-Semitism, the reality of racism hit her head on. "And that first time I noticed Negroes, . . . colored . . . water fountains and washrooms. There was tremendous separation between Negroes and whites, and that became very apparent. It was terrible."[25] The wives of the Tuskegee Airmen who chose to follow their husbands lived at Tuskegee Institute, an oasis in the midst of the town of Tuskegee, Alabama. Lois Marchbanks drew a vivid picture of a southern town that wanted absolutely nothing to do with their "kind." "We didn't go downtown," Marchbanks said. "It wasn't safe. We mainly stayed at the institute. There were very few blacks who lived in Tuskegee, and they were not treated well."[26] The citizens of Tuskegee, Alabama, were dead set against the government's decision to train the country's first class of black flyers in the midst of their town and fought the decision tooth and nail. Motivated by fear that the presence of the black cadets would drive down real estate prices and wreak havoc on the social structure of the town, townspeople signed petitions in an attempt to sway the government and force it to move the black airmen somewhere else. Their efforts failed, yet they continued to make life uncomfortable for the cadets and their wives. (Ironically, today the town celebrates the history and accomplishments of the Tuskegee Airmen with store after store selling memorabilia.) It would take more than a war to begin to curb racial discrimination and lay the groundwork for civil equality in the United States and in the U.S. armed forces.

SAYING GOOD-BYE

During the war, nearly one family of every five—18.1 percent—contributed one or more family members to the armed forces. Statistics do not exist to tell precisely how many wives suffered from the absence of a husband, but the best estimate puts that number at four million. For wives with children, there was no end of advice as to the "right" way to say good-bye. Men worried about the final good-bye and whether the emotional anxiety of the last few moments together was worth the happiness of the leave. The experts consistently proffered one piece of advice: Say good-bye at home, rather than in a crowded train station. *Parents' Magazine* told mothers not to take children out of school in order to have a final good-bye ceremony. One concession, however, was to let Daddy call for the children at school: "To have their classmates see their Daddy in uniform will set the children up tremendously. . . .

And don't," the magazine insisted, "end Daddy's leave with tears and dramatic farewells."[27] Of course, many farewells did not follow this prepared script. Many service wives like Marion Yetter faced dramatic farewells when their husbands shipped overseas. Yetter, a self-described "small-town gal" from Hill, New Hampshire, who was a nurse, followed her husband for months before hearing through the grapevine that he was embarking from either New York or California. (Military rules dictated that servicemen leaving for overseas not divulge their time or point of departure.) Intent on saying good-bye in person, Yetter and another military wife bet on New York and drove all the way from Virginia with a bazooka rocket in the back seat for protection. When asked what in the world they would do with a bazooka rocket, the women said they'd use it to hit an intruder over the head! Once in New York, staying in a predetermined hotel, they waited nervously for a phone call. Chances were fifty-fifty that they'd be able to see their husbands. After two days of waiting that seemed like an eternity, the call came. "We hope to see the Bowers (a code for we're leaving from New York), and we have twenty-four hours." Once the couples were reunited, the time flew by. Twenty-four hours together and then a very uncertain future dictated by the whims of war. Yetter clung to her husband's reassurances that he'd return safely and in one piece. She had no other choice than to believe him or to fall apart.[28] Yetter became one of the estimated four million waiting wives of World War II.

NOTES

1. Betty Lou Kratoville, World War II service wife. Interview by author. May 29, 2002.

2. Damon Frantz Rarey, ed., *Laughter and Tears: A Combat Pilot's Sketchbooks of World War II Squadron Life* (Santa Rosa, CA: Vision Books International 1996), p. 4.

3. Ibid., p. 8.

4. Ibid., p. 24.

5. Ibid., p. 25.

6. Kratoville.

7. Rarey, p. 28.

8. "Whither Thou Goest . . . ," *Time,* August 30, 1943, pp. 65–68.

9. Ibid., p. 68.

10. Hazel Klauck, World War II service wife. Interview by author. December 29, 2001.

11. Jack Havener, *Marauders in the Midst* (unpublished), p. 53.

12. Ibid., p. 57.

13. Sophie Holbrook, service wife. Interview by author. September 10, 2002.

14. Havener, pp. 62–63.

15. Florence Dennis, World War II service wife. Interview by author. November 13, 2002.

16. Blanche Kishner, World War II service wife. Interview by author. July 23, 2002.

17. George L. McDermott, ed., *Women Recall the War Years: Memories of World War II* (Chapel Hill, NC: Professional Press), pp. 192–93.

18. Bessie Stroud, bride in Fort Bliss Mass Wedding Ceremony. Interview by author. March 22, 2004.

19. Manuel Solis, World War II army supply, groom in Fort Bliss Mass Wedding Ceremony. Interview by author. March 17, 2004.

20. Doris Levine, World War II service wife. Interview by author. May 26, 2002.

21. Ruth Berns, World War II service wife. Interview by author. July 18, 2002.

22. "When Jews Were GIs: World War II and the Remaking of American Jewry," University of Michigan, http://www.fathom.com/course/21701756/session2.html.

23. David M. Kennedy, *Freedom from Fear: The American People in Depression and War, 1929–1945* (New York: Oxford University Press, 1999), p. 794.

24. Ibid.

25. Levine.

26. Lois Marchbanks, wife of a Tuskegee Airman. Interview by author. April 14, 2005.

27. William M. Tuttle, Jr., *Daddy's Gone to War: The Second World War in the Lives of America's Children* (New York: Oxford University Press, 1993), p. 55.

28. Marion Yetter, World War II nurse and service wife. Interview by author. February 13, 2002.

Six

WAITING WIVES AND HOME
FRONT POPULAR CULTURE

With a peak of 15 million men overseas during World War II, life on the home front took on a very feminine quality. Women, both single and married, flooded the workplace in record numbers. Female film stars rose to the fore with so many male actors off fighting the war. Female singing groups like the Andrews Sisters sang their hearts out over the radio and in USO shows across the country. And pinup photos of Betty Grable, Rita Hayworth, and Jane Russell, among others, appeared in popular magazines like *Life*, and pinup drawings by Alberto Vargas graced the pages of *Esquire*. Despite all of their visibility and responsibility during the war, women continued to be regarded as morale boosters, sex symbols, and temporary workers for the "duration." Few sociologists, psychologists, and historians imagined that women's full participation in both home and work would encourage the depth of self-confidence and independence that would sustain many of these women for the rest of their lives and ultimately force a restructuring of the place of women in American society.

For the women whose husbands were overseas, the challenges were many. They had to carry on, dreading bad news from the front with every knock on the front door. As Jan Williamson put it, "If I could have foreseen what life would have been like, I don't think I could have handled it. But my love was deep enough, and I barreled on ahead." Williamson's husband, Oscar, a B17 pilot, left for a base near London, and she moved back into her old bedroom in her parents' home, terrified and pregnant. "It was terrible," she said. "I was the loneliest girl in the world." Williamson's wait was rendered even more difficult when, after not hearing from Oscar for weeks, she received a missing-in-action telegram. Shortly after, she was told by ham radio operators on the East Coast who'd been listening to German radio propaganda that her husband was being held as a prisoner of war (POW). Williamson would learn later that Oscar's plane had been shot down over Germany. He and the rest of his crew bailed out, pulled the ripcords on their parachutes, dodged enemy artillery fire, and miraculously landed in one piece on the main street of a small town near Nuremberg. But the moment he "landed," there were enemy hands all over him, and Oscar was certain that he would be killed by townspeople right then and there. But a kind German woman grabbed him and somehow managed to get him to her house, where she kept him until the German military arrived. After several days of interrogation, Oscar was sent to a POW camp. "There were meetings for POW wives back here in the States, but I didn't go," Williamson said. "What I *did* do was go to work as a secretary in a factory that made amphibious ducks." After the birth of a healthy baby girl, Williamson went back to work at General Motors as a "Rosie the Riveter," helping to build military buses. She liked the work but hated the guys who hadn't gone into service. "I wore bib overalls and a sweater," she said. "And certain guys would say, 'Hey, Blondie, why don't you just wear your sweater?' There was a lot of sarcasm." Williamson knew her job was temporary and that, as soon as the men came back, she'd be let go. Sure enough, she got laid off. All the women got laid off. "I wanted to keep working because the time went so slowly with Oscar gone." After almost two years, Oscar made it home, physically and apparently psychologically unscathed from his POW experience. According to Williamson, he just accepted what had happened to him and picked up his life where he left off. Williamson wasn't so laissez faire. "Waiting was hell. It was the worst time of my life. I've had sickness in my life and trouble with my children, but nothing ever as bad as that!" In 1947, Williamson had twin boys and, until they were teenagers, she was a full-time mother. "I didn't really like being a homemaker, but that was my job. Everything revolved around the family." Still, she looks back on the war years and marvels. "I learned I could be independent. I never imagined that I could do what I did. I would tackle anything. I think if it hadn't been for that experience and if I hadn't developed those skills, I would have been a real mess."[1]

For many waiting wives, the shared experience of having husbands overseas cemented friendships, some of which have lasted a lifetime. "Our friendships blossomed very quickly," said Ruth Berns. "And they meant a lot." Estherose

Bachrach was pregnant when her husband, an army air corps officer who enlisted immediately after the attack on Pearl Harbor, shipped out. "It was unplanned," said Bachrach. "I was so young and didn't even have enough sense to be real concerned that my child might not have a father." Bachrach had trudged around the country, moving 16 times in 18 months, just so she could be with her husband before he was sent to India to service planes that were flying "The Hump," a route across the forbidding Himalayan mountain range in western China that connected Allied supply bases in India to China's combat forces. "No wonder my mother was upset," Bachrach said. "If it had been my daughter running all over the country, I would have been hysterical!" Bachrach lived at home with her parents in Gary, Indiana, and spent a lot of time with other women, many of whom she'd known before the war. "As I look back, I don't think I could do anything like that again. But you're in it, so you go on. I was very lonesome and unhappy but I was busy. There were other women in my situation, so we spent a lot of time together and tried to make the best of a lousy situation. I matured very quickly, and the experience allowed me to appreciate all the good we've had in our lives since the war."[2] The United Service Organizations (USO) also served as a meeting place for wives whose husbands marched off to war. From the Nyack, New York, USO "Chins Up!" Club to the "Foreign Legion" group in the South to the "Ladies-in-Waiting Club" of Albuquerque, New Mexico, and the "Heirborne Division" of the Rockingham, North Carolina, USO, young wives found companionship and courage in the company of other wives living under the same strained and temporary conditions of wartime. "I'd be just lost without the USO," said a young wife in Dover, Delaware, attending an Army wives luncheon. Her companions echoed her statement. This group, one of many throughout the country, prepared a weekly get-together luncheon. While they congregated in the dining room, their babies slept in a row of perambulators in the club lobby.

LETTERS . . . WE GET LETTERS

Louise Chase was not to see her husband for two years and two months. Most wives like Chase wrote their husbands every day and substituted the intimacies shared in letters for those shared when living together. "I lived for his letters," wrote Chase. "And he lived for mine." Lewie Chase was stationed in the China, Burma, and India theaters and spent most of his time deep in the jungles. Mail delivery was irregular at best. At one point, Lewie hadn't received any mail for several months. When his mail was finally delivered, the event made headlines in the Boston newspapers: "A Monsoon of Mail Hits Yank in India!" The delighted soldier was presented with a sack of mail containing 207 letters—over 180 from Louise! "I wrote at least twice a day, often three times. Writing and working and praying helped me somehow get through the day." Separations are not pleasant, writes Chase, but they can be survived. "I don't mean to minimize the trauma and loneliness of the military wives of today when their husbands are deployed, but they do have good housing and are treated with some kind of dignity—dignity that was not given to service wives in World War II."[3]

Jeanne Isaac, Nebraska born and raised, spent two years waiting for her husband to return home from the Pacific, where he served as a radioman on board a U.S. navy destroyer. Isaac wanted desperately to work on the assembly line at the Glenn L. Martin Company plant in Omaha during her husband's tour of duty, but her eyesight wasn't good enough and she had to settle for a job as a private secretary. Each evening after work, Isaac faithfully wrote and numbered a letter to her husband. That way, he'd be sure to eventually read the letters in chronological order, even if they arrived—as they often did—out of sequence. "I worried about him an awful lot," Isaac said. "But I don't think we thought much about the future. It was the here and the now." The Martin Company where Isaac worked built B-29 Superfortress bombers, the single most complicated and expensive weapon produced by the United States during World War II. There were almost 4,000 B-29s built for combat in the Pacific theater, including the Enola Gay, the plane that dropped the first atomic bomb over Hiroshima, Japan, on August 6, 1945. "The Enola Gay was built at Martin, but we weren't real proud of that fact," Isaac said.[4] On the one hand, the bombing successfully ended World War II; on the other hand, it wreaked horrible carnage on the civilian population of a country on the verge of surrender and inaugurated a nuclear arms race and the Cold War.

In sequence or out, letters from fighter pilot George Rarey to his pregnant wife, Betty Lou, brimmed over with joy about the birth of their baby and the wonderful life that lay ahead:

> I want to live with you, Betty Lou, with you and our boy or girl. I want to live with you and love you for the next forty-three-thousand years. . . . I usually refer to our little stranger (who isn't a stranger) as a boy. This is not wishful thinking. Betty Lou— a little girl would be fine. I do it as a matter of convenience. I will *not* refer to our child as an "it" or a "little thing." Even though the sex is undetermined, I'll wager the personality that will later make him or her the toast of the new generation is in full flower—a very remarkable child. How's that for a preview of true paternal understatement—just practicing.

Happy New Year, Mama—1944 will go down in history as the year in which Betty Lou and Rarey's first child saw the light of day. I hope it will also be marked by the destruction of Fascism in Germany and the rest of Europe. I hope our child has a chance to contribute his two cents' worth of light and color to this battered old world without being swept up in one of these mechanized free-for-alls. . . .

Is it time for the expectant father to start getting panicky? Maybe I'm premature but, pal, I get weak as hell when I think of the time approaching. I'm there with you, darling, every minute. It's probably a good thing I'm not there in person, because I'd be an awful bother—I'm a sissy where such things are concerned. When I get home you must spare me no details of the phenomenon of the birth of a baby. I think it's the most wonderful thing in the world. . . . You are the official Madonna of the 379th and our child has the finest bunch of uncles that ever rolled an airplane.

God, I wish I could be with you. I know everything will be fine but this being so far away is oppressing. I must remember that I'm only the kid's father and that I'd only snarl things up anyway. Father—gee, I really hadn't thought of the word—father—father—it's wonderful.

The self-portrait that Rarey drew the day he learned of his child's birth captures a relieved fighter pilot, his bomber jacket unzipped, an opened envelope in his hand. A thought bubble over his head shows a smiling Betty Lou with a little tike tucked in bed next to her. He wrote:

This happiness is unbearable. Got back from a mission at 4:00 this afternoon and came up to the hut for a quick shave before chow. What did I see the Deacon waving at me as I walked up the road to the shack? A small yellow envelope! I thought it was a little early but I quit breathing completely until the wonderful news was unfolded. A son! Darling, Betty Lou! How did you do it? I'm so proud I'm beside myself! All of the boys in the squadron went wild. I had saved my tobacco ration for the last two weeks and had obtained a box of good American cigars. Old Doc Finn trotted out two quarts of Black and White from his medicine chest, and we all toasted the fine son and his beautiful mother. What a ridiculous and worthless thing a war is in the light of such a wonderful event. That there will be no war for Damon![5]

Damon Frantz Rarey, all 8 pounds, 6 ounces, of the "little brute," was one of 3,104,000 babies born in the United States in 1943, the greatest birth rate in United States history until after the war.[6] World War II ushered in a baby boom in the United States, and this after a decade in which Americans had delayed having children because of the uncertainties of the Depression. Birth rates in the 1930s were lower than in any previous period in American history. In 1940, the year before Pearl Harbor, fewer than 25 percent of Americans were below age 15 years. At the same time, the population of Americans age 65 years and over was growing. Most experts agreed that an overall population decline was imminent. The 1940 White House Conference on Children in a Democracy concluded that the number of children in 1940 was smaller than in 1930, and there would be "still fewer in 1950, if recent trends continue." But then came the war and, with it, the escalating number of babies born. Not coincidentally, peaks in the birth rate followed by nine or ten months to a year the peaks in the marriage rate. The year 1942 was the top wartime year for marriages, and so a year later, in 1943, the fertility rate for American women aged 15–44 years peaked at 22 births per every 1,000 women. The passage of the Emergency Maternity and Infant Care (EMIC) program in March 1943, provided free maternity care and medical treatment during an infant's first year for the wives and children of military personnel in the four lowest enlisted pay grades—those who, up to this time, had often suffered substandard conditions, often in the "badly congested areas surrounding the military camps." The EMIC program was wildly successful, with an estimated 85 percent of the prospective mothers eligible having applied for aid.[7] For many Americans, the baby boom underscored the importance of family and home and helped to bolster a vision of a strong America in which women played traditional roles of mother and homemaker. "Patriotic domesticity" became a popular theme that ran through films, songs, and popular magazines.

In his essay about World War II films, Larry May, associate professor of American studies and history at the University of Minnesota, discusses *Since You Went Away,* which won the Academy Award for best picture in 1944, and how its female lead played by Claudette Colbert experiences a conversion and ultimately becomes an icon for "patriotic domesticity." The epilogue of *Since You Went Away* explains that it is the story of that "unconquerable American fortress, the American Home." Colbert, who plays the wife of a GI off to war, suppresses her desire for romance and the old world of nightclubs and dance. She rejects a naval officer who wants to take her out and condemns as subversive a friend who sees prosperity as the chance to have a good time. As Colbert's character explains, "I have a husband who went off to fight for this home and for me. I have children who have shown courage and intelligence while their mother lived in a dream world. Well, believe me I've come out of it. . . . I want to do something more." As an expression of her patriotism and new identity as mother and wife, Colbert does her part in the war effort and takes a job in a munitions factory—not because it's pleasurable or an expression of her independence but because it's her duty as the ideal American woman who makes guns during the day and dreams of her husband's safe return at night.[8]

PATRIOTISM HAS ITS LIMITS

By the end of 1942, rationing cut through every aspect of American life. Each man, woman, and child in the United States was given a book of stamps worth 48 points and good for six months. The stamps could be spent on any combination of goods from meat, butter, and canned vegetables to sugar and shoes. By and large, American housewives accepted the system cheerfully. When butter became scarce, they added a yellow dye to margarine. When sugar was cut back, they substituted corn syrup and saccharin in cakes and cookies. Women planted Victory Gardens of fresh vegetables in their back-yards. They saved fats and exchanged them at the butcher shop for points. For a premium, almost anything could be bought—nylon hose for five dollars a pair, cigarettes for 30 cents a pack, boneless ham for twice the ceiling price. But nothing cut so deeply as rationing of gasoline and tires. (By December 1942, Japan had moved toward the rubber-rich islands of Malaya and Indonesia.) Although gasoline was not in short supply, government officials believed that gas rationing was the only way to save rubber. The majority of drivers were limited to five gallons a week. Shortages of iron and steel prohibited the manufacture of a wide variety of consumer goods—electric refrigerators, vacuum cleaners, sewing machines, washing machines, electric ranges, radios and phonographs, lawn mowers, waffle irons, and toasters. Shoe companies were ordered to avoid double soles and overlapping tips. Lingerie makers were limited to styles without ruffles, pleating, or full sleeves. But as Doris Kearns Goodwin describes in *No Ordinary Time,* women drew the line when it came to the rubber shortage threatening the manufacture of girdles. Although the government sources tried to suggest that "women grow their own muscular girdles by exercising," the women would hear none of it. With-out "proper support from well-fitted foundation garments," argued journal-ist Marion Dixon, there was no way a woman past 30 years could keep her posture erect and do physical work without tiring. "Certainly," Dixon wrote, "Uncle Sam does not want American women to wear garments that would menace their health or hamper their efficiency, especially during wartime, when every ounce of energy and effort is needed." In the end, the government bowed to the women's outcry and announced that foundation garments were an essential part of a woman's wardrobe.[9]

SLEEPING AROUND

Traditionally, wives waved their husbands off to war, trying not to acknowledge that strict fidelity was incompatible with soldiering. They may not have talked about the real possibilities of their husbands being unfaithful. Certainly, their husbands did not. But one only had to hear bits and pieces of talk among returning GIs at the local barber shop or town tavern to know that there was plenty of sleeping around. What made World War II different from previous wars were the new choices and opportunities presented to wives back home. Out in the work world, perhaps living far away from their home community and family, the waiting wives of World War II, lonely and needy for love, could just as easily fall into the arms of another man as their husbands could succumb to the temptations of another woman. Given the uncertainties of war and the disruption of everyday life, brief love affairs escalated. Twenty-five-year-old Lorraine Bodnar, wearing a navy wool gabardine suit made by her mother, a white silk blouse, small navy straw hat and low-heeled navy pumps, repeated her marriage vows in a Baptist church in the outskirts of Washington, D.C., with 25 or 30 friends in attendance. By the time her husband left for a two-year stint in the army's Quartermaster Corps in Trinidad, Bodnar was head of the stenographers' pool in a division of the navy. Her husband hadn't been gone for more than a week when the commander of the division approached her in the hall. "You must be lonely without your husband," he said. "Why don't I take you out for dinner after work?" Bodnar was curious about the never-married, 39-year-old who had spent most of his career working overseas as a reporter and decided to accept his invitation. The commander picked her up after work in his Chrysler convertible and surprised her right off the bat: "Lorraine, Lorraine, for two years I've wanted to do this." Instead of driving to a restaurant, he made a beeline for his apartment, just a few blocks away from where Bodnar had lived with several other women before she married. Driven by her curiosity, she agreed to going in for a drink before going out to dinner. "I felt mature," she said, "and felt I could handle any situation." She refused the offer of rum in her Coca-Cola and, once seated, was reminded by the commander of the no-fraternization rule between officers and their staff. But with her husband gone for two years, he couldn't resist. He had, he said, fallen in love with her the first time they met. Bodnar was stunned and "stupidly flattered." In autobiographical notes she titled "Lorraine Remembers," Bodnar shared her life experiences for her grandchildren. She wrote a chapter for each decade, ending at her eightieth birthday. The chapter about life in her 20s during World War II described the temptation to be with another man while her husband was away:

Yes, we went to a fine restaurant for dinner. We were ready to leave when the commander saw two men from the office. The Commander asked me not to move. It was nearing midnight before the other men left and we could leave . . . I had noticed that he was drinking quite a bit of alcohol. . . . I was too naïve to realize that he shouldn't be driving . . . I gave him directions to my apartment. He asked me to let him come in and fix him some coffee, so I did. But I made it clear that I never wanted to go out with him again . . . Finally, I forced him to leave but let him give me a long kiss . . . The next afternoon, he called me on the office phone. He wanted to apologize for keeping me up so late and said he was more convinced of his love and wanted to take me for an early dinner. I told him no and hung up.

One cool Sunday in November I saw all the colored leaves and got a yearning for a ride into the countryside. When I met the commander in the hall and he asked me to call him by his first name and told me how patient he was waiting for me, I told him he could take me for a ride in the countryside after work. I recall seeing the beauty of the colors and then it was dark, and we stopped to eat at a crowded roadside restaurant. Then back to D.C. and in front of his apartment house. I asked him to take me home. He just stood there. By this time, I was thoroughly chilled. Finally, I agreed to go in but on the condition that he drive me home when I asked. I remember how he immediately ran water in his bathtub for me to soak my feet to get warm while he fixed hot cocoa. Then he got down on his knees and sang 'Oh, Lady Be Good to Me.' I must admit that I liked that, fascinated that my sophisticated boss wanted me so. He did take me home telling me he would never force himself on me. He said we could see each other secretly and that he felt eventually I would fall in love with him. Right now, I'm feeling a bit guilty for remembering this so well. Certainly I had a weakness. But I knew he only wanted me for his mistress, and I also knew that he could ruin my marriage and my life. Why was I so fascinated with him?

Bodnar knew she was headed for trouble. Help arrived in a letter from her husband who had found a job opening for her in Trinidad. It took several months and some doing, but Bodnar's travel orders finally arrived. In the interim, the commander had "disappeared." Bodnar wanted to be subtle about asking where he had gone. Someone said no one knew what had happened to him. Someone else said that he had accepted an appointment in Cairo, Egypt. Wherever his destination, Bodnar never saw or heard from him again.[10]

Wives like Bodnar managed to escape temptation and remain faithful. Others did not. Jane Fitzke tells the story of her roommate, Alberta, from Georgia. The two women met near Camp Roberts in Camp Roberts, California, where their husbands had been in training. Alberta was a little older than Fitzke and, in Fitzke's mind, a role model of what an army wife should be. After three months of sharing an apartment, Fitzke came home from her $1.50-an-hour job at the Rexall drugstore and found Alberta in the room with her "boyfriend." "It wasn't nice," recalled Fitzke. "I kicked her out right there and then. She didn't even have time to get her stuff out. And you know . . . she left me holding the bag for three months' rent. I couldn't possibly pay, so my landlady came knocking on my door and offered me a room in her house." Fitzke's landlady wasn't a bit surprised by what had happened. She'd seen it all before. "I don't care if it's Camp Roberts or Camp Fort. It doesn't matter if it's the army, navy, air force, or marines. They all have camp tramps. She saw a sucker in you. You were nice, agreeable, and she took advantage." As Fitzke looks back, she is sure her landlady was right. That kind of woman had always been around. "I was burned but learned," Fitzke said. "I grew up. . . . I grew up quick!"[11]

The issue of marital fidelity on the part of servicemen's wives preoccupied servicemen who anxiously awaited letters from home. Whereas infidelity on the part of the fighting husbands was considered "natural" and "inevitable," unfaithful wives were vilified as unpatriotic and unsavory. A column by Army Chaplain Captain H. A. Robinson in the *Baltimore Afro-American* warned that servicemen's wives who were unfaithful could have their allotments stopped or be divorced by their husbands. Yet as Karen Anderson discusses in *Wartime Women: Sex Roles, Family Relations, and the Status of Women during World War II,* many wives, especially those who married hastily at a young age, found remaining faithful to their husbands so far away very difficult. "For many of these young war brides," writes Anderson, "marital bonds were tenuous, and the desire for companionship, social activities, male approval, and sexual experience which had contributed to their hasty marriages persisted even in their husbands' absence."[12] Anderson goes on to talk about the countless letters sent to advice columnists from such women. One sent to Dorothy Dix pointed out that "married servicemen could participate in the same social activities as single men while their wives could not seek the company of men in any way. She complained that such a double standard was "unfair, intolerable, and lousy." According to the Kinsey survey, *Sexual Behavior in the Human Female,* first published in 1953, infidelity among very young married women increased to some extent during the 1940s, making them the only group to experience such a change.[13] How well the bonds of a wartime marriage held usually depended more on mutual affection and respect than on a solemn nuptial oath. "To this old woman today, this young woman and young man seem like people in a storybook," wrote Harriet Bloom, now 84, in an introduction to her World War II letters. "They are not the people—and yet they are—that I recall today. Living is a changing experience, and I am not the woman I was fifty years ago. But they loved one another wholeheartedly, and they remained faithful to one another despite temptations then and throughout their life together. It is a love story with a happy ending."[14]

FILM AND POPULAR CULTURE

World War II popular culture—films, music, magazines, and the ubiquitous pinups—reflected and captured a country consumed by war and by a shift in relations between the sexes. Media images of women were initially expansive, widening the range of acceptable female behavior, providing positive examples of unconventional women, and blurring the traditional gender distinctions. Yet, underneath it all, women were consistently reminded of their domestic and familial responsibilities and their "duty" to appeal to men.[15] Magazines like *Vogue* vigorously expressed the opinion that the ideal woman's role was to "maintain the good spirits of the fighting man," and this should be done by maintaining her "looks." "Rosie the Riveter," despite her participation in the unromantic world of industrial life, wore red lipstick and red nail polish, along with her overalls and bandanna. Apparently, that wasn't enough on the sex appeal meter when Paramount made *Rosie the Riveter,* a 1944 musical that told the "inspiring" tale of a pretty girl who delayed marriage so that she could take a job in an aircraft factory. The movie was a complete bomb with American GIs, who did not take kindly to women coping with the war by fulfilling traditional male roles. This film and other wartime "women are coping" films like *So Proudly We Hail* (1943) about a group of army nurses or *Since You Went Away* (1944) about war widows did not play well to the American male audience, either. Films in this category showed women reversing the traditional gender-typing in the workplace and in the armed forces and aroused in American men the "fear that World War II might be banishing forever the traditional values of home and hearth that many GIs believed they were fighting for." Still, the clamoring for films continued. "Without movies we'd go nuts," wrote a GI from the Pacific. During the war years of 1942, 1943, and 1944, Hollywood turned out a total of 1,313 features, 28 percent of which were about the war. Hollywood reached its peak production year in 1943, when one-third of feature films dealt directly or indirectly with the war.[16] Movie attendance on the home front skyrocketed. With bigger paychecks than most workers had ever earned, people flocked to the movies, often several times a week. Weekly attendance in 1942 was an estimated 100 million—at a time when the national population stood at 135 million. The previous high had been 90 million tickets sold per week in 1930. Responding to double features and new films every Sunday, box office receipts soared during the war, doubling from $735 million in 1940 to $1.45 billion in 1945.[17]

While it was the Motion Picture Production Code (the Hays Code) that oversaw the film industry during the Depression with a focus on eliminating nudity and profanity, it was the *Government Information Manual for the Motion Picture* created by the Bureau of Motion Pictures (BMP) that established official guidelines for filmmakers during World War II. Most important among the manual's "suggestions" was the casual insertion of a constructive "war message" in a film whenever possible:

> At every opportunity, naturally and inconspicuously, show people making small sacrifices for victory—making them voluntarily, cheerfully, and because of the people's own sense of responsibility, not because of any laws. For example, show people bringing their own sugar when invited out to dinner, carrying their own parcels when shopping, traveling on planes or trains with light luggage, uncomplainingly giving up seats for servicemen or others traveling on war priorities; show persons accepting dimout restrictions, tire and gas rationing cheerfully, show well-dressed persons, obviously car owners riding in crowded buses and streetcars.[18]

To bring home the grim realities of war, the manual advised: "In crowds unostentatiously show a few wounded men. Prepare people but do not alarm them against the casualties to come." And show them this is a democratic war: "Show colored soldiers in crowd scenes; occasionally colored officers. Stress our national unity by using names of foreign extraction, showing foreign types in the services." The Bureau of Motion Pictures also suggested that filmmakers ask themselves seven questions before beginning a movie, the most "soul-searching" of which was this: "Will this picture help win the war?" Other caveats suggested to filmmakers included the following:

- Contribute something new to our understanding of the world conflict
- Don't make use of the war purely as a basis for a profitable picture
- Make sure the film will not be outdated by current conditions when it is released
- Don't create a false picture of America, her allies or the world we live in, if you are making an "escape" film

And, finally, filmmakers were asked to consider their film as an historical document: "Does the picture tell the truth or will the young people of today scorn it a few years hence, when they are running the world, and say they were misled by propaganda?" By December 1942, a letter from the BMP requested that as a "routine procedure" studio treatment and synopses be sent to the BMP for review. Though anxious about censorship and the possible disruption of its profits through too much government interference, studio heads agreed to cooperate. Many directors could agree that our "primary responsibility was not to the box office, nor to our paychecks. It was a special responsibility . . . to the men who wore the uniform" of the armed forces.[19]

President Roosevelt's statement that the "American motion picture is one of our most effective mediums in informing and entertaining our citizens" set the tone for films made during the war. In film after film, the United States was portrayed as a great "melting pot" of many races and creeds, all living and working together in a world free of fear and want. No matter what the genre, previously outcast Americans were shown taking their rightful place in American society, contributing to the war effort. In musicals like *This Is the Army* (1943), *Star Spangled Rhythm* (1942), and *Yankee Doodle Dandy* (1942), ethnic showmen and black boxers like Joe Louis were featured. Racially balanced military units and platoons, comprised of Texans, Jews, Italians, and African Americans, appeared in films like *Airforce* (1943), *Life Boat* (1944), *Bataan and Back to Bataan* (1945), and *Sahara* (1943). Spy films and movies about subversion were made by all the major film studios. And as the war labored on, more and more films showed women who had gone to work now focusing their energies on making the home the ideal that the men would return to when the war was over.[20] Of all the film genres, romantic films remained the staple ingredient in wartime films because, as the trailer for a B-movie called *China Girl* put it, "An American will fight for only three things—for a woman, for himself, and for a better world."[21] Hollywood boy-meets-girl musicals like *Yankee Doodle Dandy* (1942) and *This Is the Army* (1943) played to sold-out theaters. These wartime musicals not only served as respites from the horrors of war but as preludes to a hopeful future in which couples would reunite and singles would find the partner of their dreams.

OOH, THOSE LEGS!

The American public may not have embraced film starlets in their roles as independent, working women who seemed to do just fine, thank you, in a "man's world," but they couldn't get enough of the Hollywood publicity stills featuring film stars in various stages of dress and poses. The World War II photos known as pinups were hailed by a public that, for the most part, perceived pinup girls as patriots who boosted the morale of soldiers. Betty Grable, with her "million dollar legs," was the undisputed leader of the wartime pinup parade. The photo of her wearing a one-piece bathing suit, high heels, an ankle bracelet, and that all-American-girl smile adorned the tents, duffle bags, and vehicles of GIs stationed all over the world. Even women thought she was cute and accepted her muted sex appeal for the good of the troops. Other pinups like the sultry Jane Russell, Rita Hayworth, Paulette Goddard, and Ann Sheridan, whose chest profile left no doubt about why she was known by her fans as the "Oomph Girl," and more erotic pinups including Veronica Lake, "the peek-a-boo girl," and Lana Turner seemed to pass muster. It was wartime, and pinups reminded men of personal ties back home and all they were fighting for. The flattered female wartime home audience was apparently thrilled as well.[22]

By the 1930s, scantily clad women were ubiquitous in American popular culture. Even middle-class magazines like *Life* featured photos of women posing in swimwear. During World War II, Hollywood studios and popular magazines accelerated the distribution when they sent pinups to soldiers overseas. Not everyone was pleased: Protesters voiced fears that sex in the mass media had undermined moral order and that the exposed female body, whether arms and legs in a swimsuit or much more, should not be on public display. This position may have gained more traction if not for the outbreak of the war. Still, local protests persisted and, in the wake of these protests, Postmaster General Frank C. Walker began to deny discount postal rates to dozens of girlie, detective, and adventure magazines. He questioned their contribution to the public good, classifying them as borderline material. By September 1943, Walker revoked the second-class mailing privilege of *Esquire,* a GI favorite, claiming that the magazine included matters of "obscene, lewd, and lascivious character."[23] The claim objected especially to the "Varga girls," the popular pinups created by illustrator Alberto Vargas, who was hired in 1939 as a replacement for George Petty, the magazine's first pinup artist. Agreeing to drop the "s" from his last name in all his work for *Esquire,* "Varga's" debut painting titled "1st Love" appeared in the October 1940 issue. "1st Love" pictured a lanky, curvaceous blonde ostensibly lying on a bed while talking on the phone to her first love. While her nipples show through her skin-tight slip, a bent right leg conceals all that lies beneath it. Her "come hither" look, punctuated by ruby-red lipstick and toenail polish to match, did more than tickle a man's fancy. Over the next five years, Vargas became known worldwide, and his work, both in *Esquire* and in the yearly calendar, was eagerly awaited. Eagerly awaited, that is, by many GIs overseas—but not by the Postmaster General.

Postmaster General Walker held hearings in October and November 1943, to allow *Esquire* to "show cause" as to why the second-class mailing privilege should not be revoked. In her article titled "Women, Cheesecake, and Borderline Material: Responses to Girlie Pictures in the Mid-Twentieth-Century U.S.," Joanne Meyerowitz, Professor of History and American Studies at Yale University, details how *Esquire* pulled out all the stops to win its case. There was a three-quarter page ad in the *Washington Post* proclaiming the magazine's morale-boosting benefits to U.S. troops, a long "respondent's memorandum" to refute obscenity charges, and well-known witnesses like H. L. Mencken, the most prominent newspaperman, book reviewer, and commentator of his day. Rae Weissman, the second woman to testify on behalf of *Esquire,* spoke to the "Varga Girl" and "the type of physical perfection that . . . few, if any, women are fortunate to possess." Weissman found the Varga pinups "pleasing to the eye," claiming that "most women would derive a deep sense of gratification in the thought that the female form is so beautifully portrayed." Under questioning, she denied that normal boys or men would find "the picture of a nude woman" particularly stimulating. Only the abnormal man, with "extreme erotic needs," she said, would "derive unusual or extreme satisfaction from looking at a picture."[24] Spokespeople for the U.S. Post Office Department's side included feminist Anna Kelton Wiley, a longtime Washington, D.C., activist in the National Woman's Party and other women's organizations, who couldn't have disagreed more. Wiley found *Esquire* "degrading and depressing to women":

> I have spent my life in trying to build up the dignity of women. I have been thirty years in this movement to secure . . . equal rights for men and women . . . and all of this is contrary to the campaign that we women have . . . sacrificed so much to carry on.[25]

The lawyer for *Esquire* took Wiley to task, casting her as the "prudish Victorian matriarch." As Meyerowitz reports, Wiley anticipated the attack, and the newspaper coverage of the following day proved her right. The *Washington Daily News* poked fun at her, and the *Washington Post* called her "grim" and mocked her in a cartoon. Neither men nor most women saw the pinups in *Esquire* as anything but wholesome cheesecake that was "modern," "healthy," and "admired by both sexes." Wiley's vision of erotic images of the female body as harmful to all women and her concept that a woman's power should emanate from her "mental and spiritual capacities," not from her body, fell on blinded eyes and deaf ears. For some, pictures or drawings of seminude women represented a welcome change from a repressive past—a past when everything was kept under cover. For others, the pinups served as tributes to female beauty and only corrupted the abnormal mind. At the conclusion of the hearings, the Post Office board voted two-to-one in *Esquire*'s favor, but Postmaster General Walker ignored the vote and upheld his original decision.

The case was appealed and went all the way to the U.S. Supreme Court where, in a unanimous 1946 decision in *Hannegan v. Esquire,* the court struck down Walker's ability to exercise "a power of censorship . . . abhorrent to our traditions." Although the decision came too late for the millions of GIs who had already returned home, it did, however, narrow the federal power to control the flood of girlie magazines like *Playboy* that surged in the 1950s following the war.[26]

The pinup craze reached new heights with nose art—pinups on the noses of airplanes. Interestingly, before the idea of painting an image on the skin of an airplane arose, crews of the army air corps pasted pages from *Esquire, Men Only,* and sometimes *Look* on the nose section, fuselage, and tail sections of the B-17 bombers known as "Flying Fortresses."[27] Almost every squadron in the army air corps (restrictions had been placed on the navy and marines) had somebody who could paint—some more talented than others—and the images ranged from innocent to lewd, from cartoons to realistic renderings. At one point, nose art became an issue with the wife of the Secretary of War, Mrs. Henry Stimson. Mrs. Stimson wanted the army air corps to remove all suggestive nose art from its planes. When one anonymous pilot heard her complaints, he said, "The only way that art is coming off my plane is if it's shot down!" Mrs. Stimson's complaints aside, the army air corps tolerated the nose art, recognizing that the stresses of war merited creative outlets and visions of what awaited the men after the war. At one point, the air corps tried to restore a sense of decorum and in August 1944 issued AAF Regulation 35–22. The regulation allowed nose art but with a "sense of decency." But this was one battle the army could not win; airmen refused to follow the regulation that had come much too late in the war. The heavily sexualized images of women splayed across the noses of some fighting planes affirmed the men's virility and, perhaps unexpectedly, carved out a permanent place for what some considered the exploitation of women in "lewd and lascivious" pictures, one of many issues that would galvanize women in the second wave of the women's liberation movement of the 1960s and 1970s.

"SWING GOES TO WAR"

It's hard to find a member of the World War II generation who can't remember the lyrics or hum the tune of his favorite wartime song. For men who fought overseas, perhaps "The Boogie-Woogie Bugle Boy of Company B," made famous by the Andrews Sisters, or Irving Berlin's more sentimental song, "I'll Be Home for Christmas," is what takes them down memory lane. For those sweethearts who waited for their boyfriends or fiancés to return home, "Don't Get Around Much Anymore," in which the girl in the song has been invited on dates but always declines, or "I'll Walk Alone" about the lonely wait until her loved one comes home is the song that best captures their sentiments. The songs that got Americans through World War II reflected the full range of emotions of a country at war and men and women separated for long periods of time. With 90 percent of American families owning at least one radio set to which they listened an average of three to four hours a day, the power of song cannot be underestimated. "Popular music took on an extra emotional weight during the war," said Lewis A. Erenberg, professor of history at Loyola University, Chicago, and author of *Swinging the Dream: Big Band Jazz and the Reorientation of American Culture*. "People had been forced apart, and they listened to music that reminded them of better times when they were together. The music, certainly at the beginning of the war, also took on a patriotic overtone."[28] There were patriotic songs—like "Anchors Aweigh," "There's a Star Spangled Banner Waving Somewhere," and "Me and Uncle Sam"—that captured the Americans' spirit and their fight for democracy and freedom. After 1942, Tin Pan Alley patriotism gave way to more sentimental songs with a love interest, with titles such as "I Left My Heart at the Stage Door Canteen," "He Wears a Pair of Silver Wings," "A Boy in Khaki, A Girl in Lace," and the biggest selling hit of the war, Irving Berlin's "White Christmas." Berlin's song went on to sell more than one million copies in sheet music alone and to top the Hit Parade nine times.[29]

Swing, the jazzy, big band sound that from 1935 on had become the most popular music in America, kept on swinging throughout the war. In fact, swing's best-known band leader, Glenn Miller, went to war along with the music. In 1942, Miller enlisted in the army and came to embody the "wartime ideal of sacrifice for a nation that allowed individuals to succeed and prosper."[30] Miller's version of swing emphasized neat, orderly patterns and a group harmony that was emotional as well as musical. The team spirit of Miller's and most other swing bands mirrored a society in which it was assumed that every able-bodied man would gladly serve his country or risk being socially ostracized. Miller's military band, like his civilian band, was not integrated. The band leader supposedly tried to get a few of his black music arrangers into his military band, but that fell through. "Miller was no mold breaker," Erenberg said. "And I'm not sure how serious he was about that."[31] However, other big bands like those of Count Basie, Benny Goodman, Artie Shaw, and Charlie Barnet did hold out a more inclusive vision of American culture. And Miller did use his orchestra and a series of propaganda radio broadcasts overseas to provide an idealized vision of a pluralistic America at war and at home. The six one-half hour radio programs called "Sustain the

Wings" were beamed toward German troops. All announcements and most lyrics were translated into German. Songs ranged from the patriotic to the romantic to the sentimental, and as part of the propaganda, Miller made no bones about claiming swing music as America's own and touting the virtues of free expression in America.

Swing was highly danceable, and the jitterbug (also known as the "Lindy Hop," named after Charles Lindberg and his flight—or hop—across the Atlantic) became the basic American dance. Though highly athletic, the jitterbug was a partner dance and easily served as a "romantic backdrop for dating." "If the young woman was wearing a short skirt and turning rapidly or being tossed over her male partner, there was always the chance of her skirt coming up and possible visions of heaven," said Erenberg. And to do the jitterbug right, dancers had to swivel their hips—a movement some older folks found quite "lewd" but that younger men and women found quite sexy.[32] An RAF pilot remembered listening to Miller's band in a smoke-hazed airplane hangar in England, a hangar crowded to "capacity with uniformed boys and girls swaying gently or 'jiving' wildly." As the band wove its spell, they "were conscious of the music . . . the exhilarating rhythm and of course, the girl in our arms . . . she was Alice Faye, Betty Grable, Rita Hayworth or whoever our 'pin up' of that particular week may have been."[33]

While young men and women at home and overseas continued to cram into dance halls, USO clubs, and local drug stores to jitterbug the night away throughout the war, there was an addition to popular music as the war wore on: Female singers crooning sentimental ballads that oozed with the pain of waiting for their men to return or for the normal life of boys and dating rose to the top of the music charts. Women made up the majority of the home front audiences, and they wanted to hear ballads that expressed their longing. Singers like Helen Forrest and Peggy Lee sang of loss and parting and lovers separated by the war. Women vowed to wait in songs like "If That's the Way You Want It Baby" and "Saturday Night Is the Loneliest Night of the Week." They pledged their faithfulness in songs like "I'll Walk Alone" and "I Don't Want to Walk without You." But when the lonely girls had had "enough of stiff-upper-lip renunciation and V-mail passion," a wave of dream songs was recorded. Richard Lingeman, author of *Don't You Know There's a War On?*, points out that these songs had a simple plot: "Love (or happiness) denied by the real or waking world is achieved in a dream."[34] "I Had the Craziest Dream," "Thanks for the Dream, "I Dream of You," "I'll Buy that Dream," "Sweet Dreams, Sweetheart," "My Dreams Are Getting' Better All the Time," "Linda," and "Laura" were all songs in which young women and men could escape into the arms of their sweethearts or into a world in which things were never as bad as they seemed.

Throughout the war, the American woman served as a symbol of home and all that the GIs were fighting for. The image of women keeping the home fires burning and staying true to their men, expressed in song and in movies, helped sustain the troops and the promise of an unchanged home front to which the men would return. But as Erenberg discusses, songs of home front devotion contained "deep anxieties about sexuality." A song like "Don't Sit under the Apple Tree" with anyone else but me expressed jealousy and fears about women's sexual activity. What is *she* doing when she goes out dancing? Who *is* sleeping in my bed? GIs were well aware of their own or other soldiers' infidelities with women "over there." How could they be certain that their sweetheart or young wife back home wasn't unfaithful as well? As the war wore on, the limits of faithfulness stretched even thinner. The mass hysteria surrounding Frank Sinatra, the bobbysoxers' idol who made adolescent girls scream and swoon with sexual fervor, further exacerbated GIs' insecurities. Here was this frail-looking man, classified 4-F (rejected for military service because of a punctured eardrum), who "challenged wartime images of male toughness." His sex appeal for women of all ages was strong. As one girl told *Time*, "My sister saw him twice and she was afraid to go again because she's engaged."[35]

In the fall of 1944, the Glenn Miller band was scheduled to be sent on a six-week tour of Europe with Paris as the band's station. Miller decided to go ahead, in order to make the proper arrangements for the group's arrival. On December 15, 1944, Glenn Miller boarded a transport plane to Paris, never to be seen again. The plane disappeared over the English Channel and was never recovered. The band, without Miller, performed a scheduled Christmas concert and continued to play until November 13, 1945, when they played their last concert at the National Press Club dinner for President Truman in Washington, D.C. The death and ultimate breakup of the Glenn Miller Orchestra, as well as the end of World War II, signaled the end of swing music's popularity. Most of the major swing bands—Count Basie and Benny Goodman—followed suit and disbanded. Peacetime and Americans' desire to cling and hold and be close led to music that was "sweeter," less "jumpy," and more "melodic"—at least for a brief moment. Modern jazz, bebop, and regional music like country and western would eventually compete for America's musical soul.

NOTES

1. Jan Williamson, World War II service wife. Interview by author. October 2, 2002.

2. Estherose Bachrach, waiting wife. Interview by author. June 17, 2002.

3. Louise Chase, "Separated but Still One" (unpublished), February 26, 1988.

4. Jeanne Isaac, waiting wife. Interview by author, July 23, 2002.

5. Damon Frantz Rarey, ed., *Laughter and Tears: A Combat Pilot's Sketchbooks of World War II Squadron Life* (Santa Rosa, CA: Vision Books International 1996), pp. 78, 86, 132, 136.

6. William M. Tuttle, Jr., *Daddy's Gone to War: The Second World War in the Lives of America's Children,* (New York: Oxford University Press 1993), p. 25.

7. Ibid., p. 26.

8. Larry May, "Making the American Consensus: The Narrative of Conversion and Subversion in World War II Films," in *The War in American Culture: Society and Consciousness during World War II,* ed. Lewis A. Erenberg and Susan E. Hirsch (Chicago and London: The Chicago University Press), pp. 89–90.

9. Doris Kearns Goodwin, *No Ordinary Times: Franklin and Eleanor Roosevelt: The Home Front in World War II* (New York: Touchstone Books, 1994), pp. 355–56.

10. Lorraine Bodnar, "Lorraine Remembers" (unpublished), pp. 50–52.

11. Jane Fitzke, service wife. Interview by author. October 18, 2002.

12. Karen Anderson, *Wartime Women: Sex Roles, Family Relations, and the Status of Women during World War II* (Westport, CT: Greenwood Press, 1981), pp. 80–81.

13. Ibid., p. 81.

14. Harriet Bloom, "Preface to World War II Letters" (unpublished).

15. Susan M. Hartmann, *The Home Front and Beyond: American Women in the 1940s* (Boston: Twayne Publishers, 1982), p. 189.

16. Tuttle, p. 154.

17. Ibid.

18. Richard Lingeman*, Don't You Know There's a War On? The American Home Front 1941–1945* (New York: Thunder's Mouth Press/Nation Books, 2003), pp. 183–84.

19. Lester Koenig, "Back from the Wars," *Screenwriter* 1 (1945), pp. 23–25.

20. May, p. 76, 91.

21. John Costello, *Love, Sex and War: Changing Values 1939–45* (London: Collins, 1985), p. 179.

22. Ibid., pp. 188–89.

23. Ibid., p. 190.

24. Joanne Meyerowitz, "Women, Cheesecake, and Borderline Material: Responses to Girlie Pictures in the Mid-Twentieth-Century U.S." *Journal of Women's History* 8, No. 3 (Fall 1996): p. 16.

25. Ibid., p. 17.

26. Ibid., p. 18.

27. "Military Aircraft Nose Art: An American Tradition," University of Arizona Library, http://dizzy.library.arizona.edu/noseart/ww2–3.htm.

28. Lewis A. Erenberg, history professor and author. Interview by author. December 12, 2005.

29. Lingeman, pp. 213–14.

30. Lewis A. Erenberg, "Swing Goes to War: Glenn Miller and the Popular Music of World War II," in *The War in American Culture: Society And Consciousness During World War II,* ed. Lewis A. Erenberg and Susan E. Hirsch (Chicago and London: The Chicago University Press), p. 144.

31. Erenberg interview.

32. Ibid.

33. Costello, p. 110.

34. Lingeman, p. 218.

35. Erenberg, pp. 157–58.

Seven

"OVER SEXED, OVER FED, OVER PAID, OVER THERE"

The fiction that five million perfectly normal, young energetic and concu-piscent men and boys had for the period of the war effort put aside their ha-bitual preoccupation, girls, underscored the hypocrisy of public opinion. The fact that they carried pictures of nude girls, called pin-ups, did not occur to anyone as a paradox. The convention was the law. When the Army supply ordered millions of rubber contraceptives and disease-preventing items, it had to be explained that they were used to keep moisture out of machine gun barrels—and perhaps they did.

—John Steinbeck, *Once There Was a War*

A good number of the 250,000 American soldiers on British soil by the end of 1942 fell into the arms of lonely British women who were either single or whose husbands may have already been killed or hadn't been heard from for months, if not years. Morale among many British women was understandably low, and the arrival of the Americans warmed many a woman's bed, sometimes even her heart. "There was a heck of a lot more sex than there was romance," said Ken Hechler, one of the newly designated combat historians sent to capture in-depth stories of front-line units. Hechler, a 30-year-old virgin with a girlfriend back home, realized the opportunities during his first trip to London's Hyde Park. Among the many "ladies," there was a woman sporting captain bars on her blouse. Hechler figured she hadn't come by those bars without earning them, so he approached her, started a conversation, and eventually ended up at the woman's flat. "Do you have a condom?" she asked the naïve American. "I'm not that kind of person!" Hechler said, insulted and hurt that she'd taken him for some kind of sexual predator. But it didn't take long for Hechler to come to his senses, and the next time he saw the woman with the captain's bars, he came prepared. The 91-year-old former United States Congressman and author of *The Bridge at Remagen* and *Working with Truman: A Personal Memoir of the White House Years (Give 'em Hell Harry Series)*, laughed when recalling another incident that occurred on London's underground, or "tube." He sat down across from an attractive young woman. He swears all he did was smile. Without hesitation, the woman pulled a "prepared script" out of her purse with her name, address, and phone number. Hechler followed up on that invitation as well.

The opportunity to have sex virtually at will during time away from the front lines without fear of repercussions from family, neighbors, even wives, found young men and their officers moving from one bed to another. Condoms had to be rationed to American forces at four per man per month, and medical officers considered this "entirely inadequate." Hechler tells the story of a man in the army air corps with whom he roomed while in Ireland, where he followed the training of U.S. troops. This roommate constantly bragged about his sexual exploits. What shocked even the now emboldened Hechler were the seven fake diamond rings the GI pulled out of his duffle bag, rings that he promised to countless unsuspecting women in exchange for sex. "The guy was so brazen," said Hechler. "He'd run into a likely prospect and tell her he wanted to sleep with her. Sometimes, he'd get slapped in the face. More often, he'd end up in the sack."[1] A 1945 U.S. Army survey "revealed that the level of promiscuity among the troops was far higher than officially admitted, and rates rose in direct proportion to the amount of time the men had spent overseas." Eighty percent of GIs away from home for two years or more admitted to regular sexual intercourse. Nearly a third of these men had wives at home, and almost half indicated they intended to marry their girlfriend waiting back in the States.[2]

Although most GIs in Britain were stationed in the countryside, the mecca for sex was London's Piccadilly Circus. The good-time girls of London—dubbed "Piccadilly commandos" because of the speed with which they serviced their customers—set the stage for the women who were to greet American GIs wherever they landed. Don Hyde, an army weatherman stationed in Cornwall, England, wrote in *Notes for His Children*, an unpublished memoir:

On June 16, 1944, I was in London transferring to another station. I was in the Red Cross building for the night and decided to walk to Piccadilly Circus.

During this walk, I was propositioned eighteen times. All the girls wore short fur coats and looked very desirable and very sexy. I stopped and talked to all eighteen of them. Twenty pounds was the going rate, with the pound being around $4 American. That alone was enough to discourage one. Anyway, I had a gal back home and wanted no other. But there were plenty of guys who paid the going rate. When I walked back to the Red Cross around midnight, the rate had dropped to five pounds, and some of the girls said it was for the whole night.[3]

Even though it was pitch dark because of the nightly blackouts, a GI like Hyde could make out several couples "going at it" against a wall. Rumor held that a woman couldn't get pregnant if she had sex standing up; thus the genesis of the term "wall job" and its popularity.

Hyde may have resisted temptation that night, but he wasn't so strong later in his overseas service when, months later, he read a bulletin board notice inviting the troops to "Come to Bakers Folly." The place was at the end of town and down a hill to the water. A swimming pool filled with water every day at high tide looked inviting:

I knocked, and a girl let me in. I assumed she was a maid. She showed me where to go to some changing rooms, where I put on my bathing trunks. I stuck a toe in the water and decided it was too cold for a swim. . . . The next thing I knew, somebody grabbed me and threw me in. It was the girl who had opened the door for me. . . . By the time I finished helping her clean up the place, I had missed my curfew. She invited me to stay at her house. . . . Then I kissed her not once but several times. And when I learned she was engaged like me, everything was fine. We could cheat and then go back to our true loves. . . . We could satisfy our desires, and nobody would get hurt.[4]

Hyde cheated but did not lose his virginity. That waited until his wedding night after the war. Still, he enjoyed a "loving relationship" that lasted from June to December 1944, when he left England and moved with his company to Marignane, France, to take over from the 10th Weather Squadron. Just before departing England, he wrote his fiancée, Grace, a "Dear Jane" letter. He can't say what made him write the letter. Maybe it was the nagging guilt over his affair. Or maybe it was the influence of his English girlfriend's mother, who felt it unfair to keep his fiancée waiting. "It took many a start to write that letter because my tears kept wetting the paper," Hyde recorded. But write the letter he did. Hyde then spent time in France and in Germany before his service ended. On December 12, 1945, he shipped out of Marseille, France, en route back to the United States. Grace married another man one week later. Shaken, Hyde started dating other women, but none lived up to his memories of the fiancée he let get away. Forty-seven years later, married for the second time after the death of his first wife, Hyde still carried a torch for Grace. When her husband passed away, Hyde sent her a sympathy card and a letter. She threw them away, unopened. "That sort of irked me," Hyde wrote, "so I started sending her letters through other people. . . . I even sent her pictures of herself. I don't know if she ever got them. She is eighty-eight now and may be dead. I will keep trying. . . . Maybe she will get so mad she will write." Hyde loved both of his wives ("I knew the minute I met each, in turn, that they were the one") but makes no bones about still caring for Grace after all this time. He has so many questions he'd like to ask and clings to the possibility that he may still get them answered.[5]

For other GIs like Sidney Forman, author of *D-Day to Victory,* sexual escapades overseas never interfered with relationships back home. Forman, who was drafted into the army immediately following his eighteenth birthday, describes in his book his first sexual encounter with a woman in London named Marjorie. She was a "stately built" and "well endowed" woman whom he met at the ballroom in Covent Gardens, where she was a hostess. Marjorie attended such ballroom dances regularly as her "contribution" to the war effort. The newly acquainted couple danced until nearly closing time, when Forman asked if he could walk Marjorie home. Rules dictated that a hostess not leave the Gardens with any of the visitors. Marjorie quietly suggested that she meet Forman under the lamp post on the corner right after closing. Forman waited for "15-draggy minutes," when a soft voice of a woman whispered his name. The two walked and talked, ending up in the shadow of an arched walkway down a narrow lane. A virgin, Forman's inexperience didn't seem to matter. Marjorie took the lead and guided him through his first lovemaking adventure. "For the first time since my arrival in England," Forman writes, "I understood why the British Tommies were so enthusiastic when they sang their song, 'Underneath the Arches.'"[6] Forman saw his "lady love" several more times before he returned to his base outside of London. From there, the young soldier's overseas duty took him to France, Belgium, and then on to Germany. During his 13 months at war, he experienced the heat of battle and the steamy sexual encounters with a bevy of women. He and a buddy named Billy always managed to "score." In Germany, he described Hilda, "a beautiful German maiden who was starved for affection for they had not seen their soldiers or anything but old men for longer than they wanted to remember. Even the Americans were welcome and we had already endeared ourselves to them through the food that we had brought and shared."[7]

Forman's romp in the sack with Hilda was simply a side dish for the main entrée, another luscious German woman with whom he had taken up earlier. The 18-year-old virgin inducted into the army returned home after the war both a decorated soldier and a grown man, experienced in the ways of romance and sex.

THE TAN YANKS

Some 115,000 American/British romances ended in marriage, and numerous others led to a sky-high number of illegitimate births. Of the 5.3 million British infants born between 1939 and 1945, more than a third were illegitimate. The rate peaked in 1945 with 16.1 illegitimate births per 1,000.[8] (Of course, not all of these births were a result of GI/British couplings, and those before 1942 did not involve American troops.) Complicating matters even further was the arrival of some 130,000 black GIs during the war. White British society initially welcomed the "Tan Yanks," as they were fondly called, showing them warm hospitality and eventually respect. However, the "luggage of racism" followed them overseas, with the U.S. Congress passing the United States of America Visiting Forces Act in August 1942. The act stipulated that black soldiers abroad were to be subjected to the same restrictions and racial segregation that they were back home. Black GIs were not allowed to marry white British women without permission from their commanding officer, permission that was almost always denied. They were forbidden to enter official whites-only areas in public places established by U.S. forces. And these men, viewed by the British as fighting for European liberty like all other soldiers, suffered a host of other racist restrictions, including the inability to bring children they fathered back to the United States.[9] There were an estimated 2,000 illegitimate mixed-race babies born in England during World War II. Not only were these children illegitimate, but they were also "coffee-coloured," making their absorption into society even more complicated. Harold Moody, the black doctor who founded the League of Coloured Peoples in England in the 1930s, summed up the situation: "When what public opinion regards as the taint of illegitimacy is added to the disadvantage of mixed race, the chances of these children having a fair opportunity for development and service are much reduced."[10] Three possible solutions to the "brown baby" problem were floated: The mothers could keep their babies; the children could be put into homes with, hopefully, some of them ultimately being adopted; or the babies could be sent to the United States to either live with their fathers or with adoptive black families. Some mothers—almost all of them single—kept their babies but under great pressure. One such young mother described how she was shunned by her whole village: "The inspector for the National Society for the Prevention of Cruelty to Children told my friend to keep her children away from my house . . . as didn't she know that I had two coloured illegitimate babies? Isn't there anywhere I can go where my children will not get pushed around?"[11] For married women, the price of reconciliation with their returning husbands—if there was to be a reconciliation at all—was painful: They almost always had to give up their children. And for the few women who did marry a black GI, their marriages were deemed illegal in many American states because of anti-miscegenation laws, and under British law, children were not allowed to be sent abroad to live with British subjects. With no viable solution, many of the "brown babies" were slated for years spent in children's homes or being pushed from one foster home to the next. The struggles of mixed-race children remain one of the hush-hush and distasteful stories of World War II.

D-DAY AND BEYOND

London, Tuesday, June 6, 1944:
Under command of General Eisenhower, Allied naval forces, supported by strong air forces, began landing Allied armies this morning on the northern coast of France.

The world caught its breath. Not since 1688 had an invading army crossed the English Channel, but now it was happening—Operation Overlord, D-Day, the all-out attack on Hitler's fortress, Europe. The first assault wave hit the beaches of Normandy at 6:30 A.M. A total of 150,000 American and British soldiers waded to shore in an operation that changed the course of World War II by beginning to loosen Germany's grip on France. Despite their ultimate triumph, 10,000 Americans died that day. For many of the survivors, it marked the beginning of horrific combat *and* unimagined sexual exploits. After four years of Nazi occupation, French women were thrilled to see Americans and grateful that they'd saved their lives. "The French girls were ready to have fun," said Seymour Simon, who swept waters for mines as part of his assignment in the navy. "That's when I learned that there were respectable girls who wanted to know everything about making love. They trained for sex like our girls trained for . . . playing bridge or something like that. It was marvelous. I had a gal there, and that was an experience. That was my graduate school in sex."[12] Long lines of soldiers formed outside the French military brothels. According to dictates, officers' brothels were indicated by blue lights and other ranks' by red lamps. Within hours of the American capture of Cherbourg, two houses of prostitution were doing a land mine business, with one brothel for whites and a second for blacks.[13] For those who preferred to risk contracting a venereal disease rather than copulate under military supervision, there was always a willing "mademoiselle" to be found.

Alarmed by the more than warm reception by French women and the degree to which the strength of the Allied armies in Italy had been sapped by venereal disease (VD), American troops were warned: "You will go there as liberating heroes and those women will be eager and urgent in the solicitation of you. Now bear these facts in mind. The women who will be soliciting your attentions are prostitutes of the most promiscuous type."[14] A fleet of mobile VD treatment centers staffed by two medical officers and six orderlies was mounted on trucks "to treat as far forward as possible all cases of primary and recurrent venereal disease." With thousands of high-strength doses of penicillin on board, the medical staff were charged with providing a quick treatment in order to maintain the strength of the troops. In 1943, clinical trials proved penicillin to be the most effective antibacterial agent to date. Labeled a "wonder drug," its production was quickly increased, and the drug was made available in large quantities to treat Allied soldiers wounded on D-Day and to control VDs like syphilis and gonorrhea. Some experts were against using penicillin as a fast cure for VD because its use would remove the threat of illness as a restraint on sexual activities. But the dire need to have as many GIs in good health outweighed any moral objections. Paris, like London before it, was the mecca for GIs for "rest and relaxation" during the final months of the war in Europe. Every Yank seemed to speak just enough French to get by: "*Voulez-vous couchez avec moi?*" Not surprisingly, the number of VD cases skyrocketed, increasing sixfold after the Allied troops liberated France. It would seem many of the GIs were liberated as well.

THE BELLES OF SHANGRI-LA

We cannot ring the noses of our men and tie them up in compounds or corrals at night . . . I should like to ask him (the moralist) to remember that fighting men cannot be herded about like steers and capons.[15]

The story of Task Force 5889, one of the army's few integrated units, and its assignment in a North African jungle outpost during World War II boggles even the hedonist's mind. George "Doc" Abraham, author of *The Belles of Shangri-La and Other Stories of Sex, Snakes, and Survival from World War II,* documents how 76 white men and 2,000 black infantrymen survived together in hot, rain-soaked Liberia, suffering from malaria, boredom, and absolutely no morale-building front-line action. It didn't take long for the GIs to discover that the best way to relieve their homesickness and ennui was a trip into the fog-bound jungles, where native women offered cheap "jig-jig," or promiscuous sex. The friendly intercourse sent the VD rate soaring and sidelined scores of troops with malaria. Panicked, the army determined that the soldiers would have to be forced to ration their jig-jig, just as food and gas were being rationed back home. But the army's wishes didn't stop the young Liberian girls from answering the call of the war boom and flocking to the base from sometimes hundreds of miles away, hoping to cash in on the war windfall. "The border of the military reservation soon came alive with half-nude, fancifully mud-painted females who wore, at most, bright beaded G-strings," Abraham writes. ". . . Stories spread by black panderers—namely that the Americans were wealthy and paid fabulous prices—caused hordes of female safaris."[16] The young girls brought with them dreams of getting "rich," as well as the organisms that caused chancroid, syphilis, and gonorrhea. It didn't take long before seven out of every ten soldiers were infected with one form of sexually transmitted disease or another.

As the army feared, the high number of days lost to the effects of VD and malaria created a severe manpower shortage. A few days after the troops came ashore, the VD rate was only 60 per 1,000 men. In one month it rose to 215 per 1,000 and, by August, it was 580 per 1,000.[17] The army did all it could to control the clandestine prostitution. Still, almost 20 percent of the force was hospitalized in one week due to malaria, presumably acquired while carrying on in the bush at night when mosquitoes are out in full force. The drastic situation called for drastic measures. And as in Hawaii, where the army tacitly approved of regulated prostitution, supervised bordellos were established. The two "villages," comprised of one-room huts built of bamboo sticks, were to be operated by an army-inspected native prostitute who was prevented from catering to native males or white soldiers. One village was named "Shangri-La" and housed around 300 girls who became known as "The Belles of Shangri-La." The other village, "Paradise," held about the same number of girls. After a visit, every GI needed a ticket to get out of the village, a ticket certifying that he had taken a chemical prophylactic before leaving. The prostitutes were inspected weekly, as physicians quickly checked for signs of disease. When it was discovered that weekly inspections of the girls were not enough to keep VD in check, daily clinics were held at a nearby plantation. Any girl who did not pass the physical inspection was confined to a "resting area" called "Idylewilde," an area guarded by military police. Medical leaders had long ago found such inspections ineffective. On June 9, 1942, the House of Delegates of the American Medical Association said "medical inspection of prostitutes is untrustworthy, inefficient, gives a false sense of security and fails to prevent the spread of infection." Still, the army forged ahead with the flawed system, apparently from a lack of any alternative, more effective means of curbing the spread of VD.

As Sergeant George Abraham points out in *The Belles of Shangri-La,* the prostitutes were allowed to keep all of the money they took in. Some of the girl's incomes were "fantastically high." Abraham writes that one army officer kept track of the money he spent on his native "mistress," noting that her earnings in one six-month period were $1,000—an exorbitant amount of money in Liberia at the time. Another girl earned $200 in just one week and bought a sewing machine that one of her customers had promised but failed to produce. The girls were not only industrious but showed a real knack for learning to speak English. They were also witty and didn't hesitate to stand up for themselves. When one of the GIs approached a prostitute and said, "Hey, you—pull up your dress for us," she barked back, "Go to hell, you fish head. I don't ask you to pull down your pants."[18] Throughout the war—no matter where it was fought—the military's emphasis on "safe sex" was never intended as a deterrent against unwanted pregnancies. Its sole focus was the prevention of VD. But wherever GIs fought, there were illegitimate children left in their wake. The brothels in Liberia were no exception. An editorial in the *African Nationalist* on August 14, 1943, titled "Large Numbers of Expectant Mothers in Army Prostitution Camp: Social Problem for Liberian Government," underscored the problem, decrying the more than 30 expectant mothers at Roberts Field, base of the American fighting force, all of whom would bear children without fathers and place a serious burden on the Liberian government. Abraham was never able to find out what happened to these babies after birth. He writes that it was too much of a "hush-hush" affair. Whenever a health officer was asked about these babies, he would "cough, turn red, and walk off. No one wanted to be heard talking about it."

HERE COME THE WAR BRIDES

The girl back home writes her boyfriend overseas and asks, "What do those foreign women have that I don't?" Answer: "Nothin', honey, but they got it over here."[19]

Bob Dinda jumped out of the plane at about 200 feet and landed in a grove of trees, some 30 feet up. With bullets from German gunners whizzing all around him, he attempted to slide down a tree branch, only to get the harness of his parachute caught under his helmet. Suspended in midair with his arms tangled, pointing skyward, Dinda muttered his "good-byes," convinced that a German bullet had his name on it. Amidst the barrage of bullets, he could hear other GIs down below talking about what to do with him and, after what felt like forever and a day, a brave GI shimmied up the tree, cut the tangled lines of the parachute, and released Dinda from his unintended trap. Without time to prepare for the 30-foot fall, Dinda hit the ground with a thud, dislocating his shoulder, suffering scrapes and bruises. His shoulder was put in a temporary sling and, a few days later, the young army paratrooper was carted off to a Belgian hospital to recuperate. Once healed, Dinda was assigned to the Ruhr Valley, the "Pittsburgh of Germany." The American army air corps had blasted the place. Roofs were blown off; most houses had no windows. There was little food, no electricity, and barely running water. A spider web of rivers, canals, and bridges—almost all of which had been destroyed—made it very difficult to get around. Dinda was ordered to guard one of the bombed-out bridges, not sure exactly what he was guarding against.

In the face of near starvation for many of the townspeople, the young American soldier meted out what gum and chocolate he had saved, thus attracting kids like the Pied Piper. He spoke "high school" German and tried his language skills whenever he had the chance. One of the children, a young girl, took a liking to Dinda and felt compelled to play matchmaker. She knew, she said, just the right German girl for him. Several days later, while he sat on his helmet, reading, he looked up and saw the "brightest eyes he'd ever seen." Margit Bedrunka, 17 at the time, was on her way to take what passed as soup to a sick woman on the other side of the bridge. The German girl and the American GI did their best to exchange pleasantries and, before he helped her across the bridge, Dinda suggested that she come back the same way. She came back. But when Bedrunka excitedly told her mother about the American, she was forbidden to return. Undeterred, Dinda sent a note to Bedrunka in care of the little matchmaker, asking to see her again. Margit's mother relented but only if the American GI visited her daughter at their home. And so began frequent visits to the Bedrunka household, with either Margit's mother or father in the room to chaperone at all times. When his unit was moved to the other side of town, Dinda snuck out at night and, with a loaded rifle over his shoulder, felt his way through all the debris, crawling across bombed-out bridges, holding on to the remaining girders that protruded from the water. Hardened by war but naïve in the ways of love, Bedrunka said there were no thoughts of romance running through her head; she saw the relationship as a potentially long-lasting friendship. Then, as suddenly as the two had met, Dinda's unit was transferred to the 82nd Airborne to aid in the occupation of Berlin. There were plenty of available women in Berlin, and many of Dinda's fellow GIs ignored the orders not to fraternize with the enemy. Dinda didn't bend the rules. He spent three months in Berlin and, with the war winding down in Europe and enough points to return home, he happily boarded a train en route to South Hampton, England, where he would embark for the United States on the *Queen Mary.* The train made a quick stop at the station in Bedrunka's hometown. Dinda jumped off the train, knowing he had only a few minutes. He noticed a woman standing by the tracks and approached her. Would she be willing to deliver a letter to Margit Bedrunka? She agreed.[20]

Six months passed before Bedrunka received a second letter from Dinda, who was by then living in Cleveland, attending Case Western University on the GI Bill. Bedrunka wrote back, and so a three-year correspondence that progressed slowly but steadily from friendship to love commenced. Still, there was little hope that the two would see one another again, let alone share a life together. Bedrunka had no desire to leave her elderly parents, and Dinda's life was set in America. The American War Brides Act passed by Congress in December 1945 allowed alien spouses (and children) to enter the United States outside the respective quotas of their country of origin. Additions to the act in 1946, then dubbed the "Sweethearts' Law," expanded the welcome mat to include alien fiancées and fiancés—fiancées and fiancés from everywhere except Germany. That changed in January 1947, when the law was amended again, this time to include Germans. But the amended act came with a deadline of December 1948, and when Dinda heard the law was going to expire, he proposed marriage in a letter. Twenty-year-old Bedrunka accepted. The application process to enter the United States was grueling, with authorities interviewing Bedrunka's neighbors, a physical exam, form after form to be filled out and, eventually, a several-day quarantine before boarding a ship to New York City. "Yes, there was some trepidation," said Bedrunka. "I really felt that I was in love but didn't know if I would measure up to his intellect. I had gotten to know his parents who wrote me beautiful letters in German, their native language. I felt very close to them, and that would help my transition to marriage with a man I hadn't seen in three years and to a foreign country."[21]

The day the bride-to-be's ship was scheduled to dock in New York, Dinda arrived on time, only to have to wait for what seemed as long as the three years he and his fiancée had known one another. Nervous as a skittish cat, he paced up and down the waiting area. The corsage he had bought faded with every passing minute. Maybe he'd made a mistake. But the moment he laid eyes on his fiancée, still the woman with the brightest eyes he'd ever seen, he knew his life was blessed. The newly reunited couple stayed in a hotel that night. It was their first night of love. "It was wonderful . . . gentle . . . beautiful," said Margit Dinda. "We were both innocent and learned together how to please each other." They were married on June 11, 1948, and have shared 58 years together. Margit got the education she so desperately wanted and, ultimately, became a teacher. Dinda went on to a successful career in engineering. When they discovered that their chances of having children were dim, they adopted a boy, now a humanities professor and organist, and a little girl who chose medicine as a career. "You know," said Dinda, "Margit went through all of these terrible experiences . . . being sprayed by spit fire, having to scavenge for food. And yet she is very positive, always smiling, always trying to find the good things in life. For us, World War II was, in some ways, a blessing. If it hadn't been for the war, we wouldn't have found each other."

A HARDY LOT

Margit Dinda was one of approximately one million brides and soon-to-be brides who followed their men to the United States from 1942 to 1952. They came from Europe, Australia, New Zealand, and as far away as Japan. Most had lived through ration books and blackout drapes, air-raid sirens and whistling bombs, whirlwind courtships, ocean crossings, and baffled neighbors who asked the newcomers, "Did you speak American before you came to this country?" They'd run for bomb shelters, went hungry, and often had to go to work in their teens. Many of the war brides saw family and friends die and witnessed the destruction of their neighborhoods and cities. They tried their best to live normal lives in abnormal times, and most, hardened by the realities of war, were hardy, brave, and up for new adventures.[22]

The largest number of war brides, estimated at some 115,000 strong, came from England—not surprising when one considers that, of the 4.5 million GIs that served in World War II, 3 million of them passed through or served in Britain. The average GI was, depending on the branch of the service, 22, 23, or 26 years old and had finished one year of high school. The "Yanks" (or "Yankees") as they were called—a name first recorded in 1765 as a name for an inhabitant of New Britain—were seen by some English as a friendly, generous lot. But as the December 1943 issue of *Time* described them, they could also be "free-spending," "free-loving," and "free-speaking," drinking too much, consorting with prostitutes, and necking in doorways.[23] It was precisely that no-holds-barred attitude that attracted many British women to the more assertive American GIs. Between 1940 and 1944, fifty-two percent of British men had served in the armed forces, with the majority seeing overseas duty at some point during their tour of duty.[24] Single and married women were starved for love and attention and, with the anonymity of war also came an explosion of sexual encounters, romances, and marriages. As might be expected, the rate of venereal infection among both British women and GIs continued to rise. In early 1943, understanding the need to attack the problem, the British government launched a massive education campaign that brought sex into the open. By the spring of 1944, the effort paid off with a dramatic drop in the rate of VD. However, the education campaign, as in the United States, focused its energy on preventing disease, not on preventing pregnancies. The percentage of illegitimate births rose from 5.5 percent during 1939–1940 to 10.4 percent during 1944–1955.[25] Understandably, a British soldier returning from overseas who found his wife either pregnant or already caring for a baby that was not his own found it difficult, if not impossible, to forgive his wife. A whopping 58 percent of divorce petitions were filed by husbands, 75 percent of whom filed for adultery.[26]

Sixteen-year-old Lilian VanVoorem didn't have to worry about the anger of a betrayed husband. She was still single when she met her GI in Northhampton, England, close to where he served in the 203rd Army Ordinance Battalion and where she and her family had settled after escaping the bombings in London. VanVoorem was a waitress at the Geisha Café when this "handsome, charming" American came in and started to flirt. He eventually asked her out, and the two became a couple, going to dances, double dating with friends. VanVoorem's mother supported the love affair, but her father was dead set against it. GIs had a bad reputation, as far as he was concerned, and he didn't want his daughter to have anything to do with them. But love trumped her father's issues and, when the then-21-year-old GI proposed, VanVoorem accepted. Unlike many war marriages, theirs took place in England in November 1945, not back in the States. It was a simple church wedding. The bride's father did not attend. A month later, on Christmas Day, the groom left for home in Moline, Illinois, leaving his bride behind. It would be another six months before she boarded the *Queen Mary* for New York City. The newlyweds settled in Moline, where the GI who never saw any front-line action went back to his job as a machinist at John Deere and Company and the newcomer to the United States adjusted. "I was awfully scared," she said. "Things were so different. . . . But we lived in a beautiful house—a palace in comparison to what I came from—and my husband was such a wonderful guy."[27] The citizens of Moline treated the war bride well, and she assimilated easily into American life. She remembers one woman who said, "Well, you've got two eyes, two ears, and a nose. . . . You're just like us!" The couple had three daughters, ages two, seven, and ten, when VanVoorem's 37-year-old husband died from stomach cancer. The young widow's mother pleaded with her to return to England but, by then, VanVoorem was an American citizen, sold on the United States. She married again 12 years later and ran a household with her three children and her second husband's four. It was a good marriage but again too short. Her second husband died at the age of 67 years. "I'm living alone," the 81-year-old said. "And I don't like it one bit. I wouldn't marry again because of social security and benefits but I'd certainly like to find a good man for a companion."[28]

A TOUGH ROAD

Neither the British nor American government nor the American military made it easy for British women to marry GIs. The military viewed these liaisons as "distractions," not to mention monetary strains. The need for sex was acknowledged; the need to form lasting relationships was not. The approximate 115,000 British war brides had a tough road to follow before they could leave for the United States. There were issues of immigration and transportation. How would the thousands of brides get to America? How could they expect transportation before all of the servicemen had returned home? Shipping space to New York was limited, and public opinion seemed to favor bringing the GIs home over reuniting servicemen with their brides or brides-to-be. The wait to straighten out these roadblocks could be months, if not years. Before December 28, 1945, wives and fiancées of GIs had to enter the United States as quota emigrants from their respective countries. That was a major problem for women who lived in areas with small quota numbers. One way to get around the quota issue was to come to the U.S. on a visitor's visa, get married, return home, and apply for reentry as a non–quota immigrant. For the vast majority of women, the expense of such a trek loomed much too high. They not only had to pay for transportation, if they could get it, but post a $500 deportation fee, in the event the marriage did not work out or never occurred and they had to be deported. By October 1945, war brides had begun to protest the delays. They were driven by money problems, concern for their unborn babies, and, of course, a desire to reunite with their husbands. Relief for war brides in all countries except Germany came in December 1945 with the passage of the War Brides Act, which waived visa and exclusion requirements. Public Law 471 passed by Congress in June of the following year opened the same opportunity for brides-to-be.

The majority of media coverage about war brides back in the States was very positive. Their arrival led to intense curiosity and publicity, with newspaper headlines like "Here Come the Brides" and "Stork Ship Brings GI Wives and Babies." Prime Minister Thomas Breuner, of the New Zealand Counsul in New York City, reflected the mainly favorable attitude toward American-Aussie marriages when he told a *New York Times* reporter: "It's a jolly good thing. It brings us all closer together. There's nothing like a baby or two to break down international barriers."[29] But following the Americans' liberation of France on August 25, 1944, stories of GIs marrying French women by the hundreds and then reports of American troops fraternizing with German women propelled wives in the United States to send a flood of letters to their husbands. "Bring Back Daddy" clubs and American wives appealed to then General Dwight D. Eisenhower to return their husbands as soon as possible. Married women were suddenly aware of what was going on "over there" and worried about their husbands' potential infidelities. Single women, concerned that these women had "stolen our young men" fretted that the pool of eligible GIs would be seriously drained, diminishing their chances of finding a husband.

French war bride Alice Rose Brozak ran smack-dab into some of that fear when she worked at a furniture factory in Streeter, Illinois, after the war. None of the women would speak to her, and she had no idea why. One of the male factory workers filled her in: "They're mad at you because they think you stole one of their guys."[30] Brozak, 16 years younger than her husband, met him after the Americans liberated France. She was back home after having spent a good part of the war in southern France, where she and her brother had been sent out of harm's way. Michael Brozak was an army cook for "lieutenants who liked to eat well." When he discovered that Alice Rose's family had somehow managed to maintain their vegetable garden, he traded the young French girl's family vegetables for staples like peanut butter and orange jelly. Brozak soon liked more than the fresh vegetables and started coming around on a regular basis. Alice Rose didn't like him at first, but, like the vegetables in her garden, he "grew" on her and, after a six-month courtship of sorts, he asked her to marry him. She agreed, but his officers refused to give their permission. They simply didn't like their "boys" marrying the foreign "girls." Brozak persevered and eventually found an officer from close to his hometown back in Illinois who was at least willing to have the girl and her family checked out. The officer assigned a GI to virtually follow Alice Rose everywhere she went for three days straight. "Maybe they were trying to find out if I was a Nazi or something," Alice Rose said. "But after three days, we were given permission to get married." The couple shared two days together after the simple wedding ceremony before Brozak had to return to Germany, where his unit was then stationed. It would be almost a year before Alice Rose would follow him to Streeter, Illinois. Like many other war brides, Alice Rose didn't recognize her husband when he came to meet her train in Chicago. She'd never seen him in civilian clothes, and he was wearing a hat. Adjusting to a new country, a new language (Alice Rose spoke no English), and new customs took some doing. A neighbor brought over some fresh country corn, and Alice Rose was furious. She'd never eaten a kernel of corn in her life. Corn was for cows, not humans. But with two boys born a year apart, neighbors who helped her learn English, and a loving husband, Alice Rose made the transition. Her parents and brothers eventually immigrated to the United States and, surrounded by family, Alice Rose, the war bride, became an American citizen, got her GED, worked for 30 years in a glass factory after her sons were in school, and is now enjoying life with her 92-year-old husband, who recently had a full checkup and received a clean bill of health.

The successful transition of one million war brides to their new lives in America might have been a harbinger for a relatively smooth homecoming for American troops. Many had been away from home for years, and dreams of picking up their lives where they left off motivated them to fight the good fight and return home safely. They dreamed of holding their wife or sweetheart in their arms once again. They dreamed of a good job and a house in the suburbs. The women who had gone to work to keep the war machine rolling would gladly give up their jobs, return to the home, and be the good wives and caring mothers they were intended to be. Sure, things had gotten a bit whacky with the passion of war and the uncertainty of the future. The sexy pinups, the nose art, the sometimes bawdy USO shows. And, yes, the affairs with the women "over there." But those would be experiences to share with the boys at the barber shop or in a bar and would not change their desire to settle down with a "good" girl. The servicemen could hardly be blamed for their traditional views and sense of normalcy. After all, their reference point was the home front as they knew it before the war. They couldn't anticipate that many of the women had also strayed in their absence. It was impossible to imagine that millions of women would want to keep their jobs. There was no way of knowing that, left on their own, women had had to pick up the pieces and fend for themselves and, in the process, realized how much they could handle and the satisfaction that came with being independent. The married men whose wives had given birth in their absence couldn't have comprehended how quickly their children grew and how living without a father in the house changed the dynamics between mother and child. Still, the men counted the days until their discharge and their long-awaited homecoming.

NOTES

1. Ken Hechler, World War II combat historian. Interview by author. September 30, 2005.

2. John Costello, *Love, Sex and War: Changing Values 1939–45* (London: Collins, 1985), p. 351.

3. Donald Hyde, *Notes for His Children* (unpublished), 1988.

4. Ibid.

5. Donald Hyde, World War II weatherman. Interview by author. February 22, 2005.

6. Sidney Forman, *"D" Day to Victory* (Tinicum, PA: Xlibris, 2000), pp. 42–51.

7. Ibid., p. 401.

8. Costello, pp. 276–77.

9. "Untold—Black History Season," www.channel4.com/history/microsites/U/untold/programs/babies/page2.html

10. Ibid.

11. Ibid.

12. Seymour Simon, World War II veteran. Interview by author. April 14, 2004.

13. Costello, p. 335.

14. Ibid.

15. George "Doc" Abraham, *The Belles of Shangri-La and Other Stories of Sex, Snakes, and Survival from World War II* (New York: Vantage Press, 2000), p. 79.

16. Ibid., pp. 81–82.

17. Ibid., p. 84.

18. Ibid., p. 93.

19. Elfreida Shukert and Barbara Scibetta, *War Brides of World War II* (Novato, CA: Presidio, 1988), p. 31.

20. Bob Dinda, World War II army paratrooper. Interview by author. December 12, 2004.

21. Margit Bedrunka Dinda, World War II war bride. Interview by author. December 12, 2004.

22. M. L. Lyke, "In a World War, They Found Love—and Marriage," *The Seattle Post Intelligencer,* August 11, 2005, p. B1.

23. Jenel Virden, *Good-bye, Piccadilly: British War Brides in America* (Urbana and Chicago: University of Illinois Press, 1996), p. 19.

24. Ibid., p. 29.

25. Ibid., p. 27.

26. Ibid., p. 27.

27. Lilian Van Voorem, British war bride. Interview by author. September 21, 2005.

28. Ibid.

29. Shukert and Scibetta, p. 20.

30. Alice Rose Brozak, French war bride. Interview by author. September 23, 2005.

Eight

"YOU'D BE SO NICE TO COME HOME TO"

The moment she heard the CBS announcer say, "We interrupt this program," Jan Klein clutched her six-month-old baby girl in her arms and turned up the volume on the radio that had become her lifeline during the war. She could barely breathe as Emperor Hirohito's message of surrender was read paragraph by paragraph, with alternate translations and additional paragraphs coming in by the minute. Americans had been fooled and disappointed by false reports before, and no piece of information was too insignificant, no word too minor. But this time, on August 14, 1945, the rumors of Japan's surrender were true, and World War II, the most devastating world war in history, had come to a fiery end. After more than three-and-a-half years of anxiety and sacrifice on the home front and injury and death on the battlefield, Americans enthusiastically embraced the prospect of peace and dared imagine a bright future of unlimited possibilities.

The sweet news of Japan's surrender spread like soft butter on a warm piece of raisin toast from New York to California. Jubilant crowds poured in to Times Square to celebrate as if it were midnight on New Year's Eve. NBC's radio announcer, Ben Grauer, reported live from a mobile unit in the midst of the celebration. "It's a seething mass of faces," he said, with loud cheering in the background. "It's a pulsing focus of a joyous nation . . . with every type of person in the country represented here!" In Washington, D.C., the mood was similarly joyous as a reporter marveled at the throng of people that seemed to have "sprung out of the ground," appearing like "a great river of humanity." Reporter Tom McCarthy of WKRC, Cincinnati, held his microphone to the window so listeners there could here the bells ringing and the factory whistles blowing. "This is it, friends," McCarthy said. "The victory has been won. The sounds of guns have been stilled. The job has been done!"

Like their counterparts, roving reporters on the street at Hollywood and Vine painted a scene of "Hollywood going absolutely mad" with traffic at a standstill, horns blaring, and a mix of soldiers, sailors, and civilians whooping it up. One sailor talked about how he couldn't wait to get out of his uniform and back into a "nice tweed suit with a loud tie." A marine from Iowa City, Iowa, contemplated the end of the war and gushed, "Oh, what a life I'm going to lead!" And the reporter, having lost all notion of propriety, commented gleefully, "I'm loving the kissing and I'm loving the lipstick impressions as souvenirs of the place. I'm doing very well . . . very well, indeed!" Just then a convertible with "thirty people piled on top" passed by, and a band could be heard marching up the street.

"I'll never forget that day!" said Klein, now 84. "My husband and I walked into the house, my mother took our daughter in her arms, and said, 'Bye, kids. I'm leaving.' We hadn't been together in *so* long! We couldn't wait." But just as they walked into the bedroom, the doorbell rang.

"We knew immediately it was my mother-in-law," Klein said. Perturbed, her husband refused to answer the bell. But Klein, who hadn't been let to forget that her mother-in-law never approved of her, *knew* this woman wasn't going to give up until she could see her precious son. Relentless, she sat on the doorbell like a rodeo contestant clinging to a bucking bronco. The shrill distraction made lovemaking impossible. Finally, with no other choice, the mother-in-law had her way, and Klein's husband answered the door.

"Our reunion had to wait just a while longer," Klein said.[1]

Eight million mothers had a son (or daughter) in the war and, between 1942 and 1945, eight percent of American wives had a husband overseas.[2] Nearly one-fifth of the country's families had suffered wartime separation from sons, husbands, or fathers.

Now, all across the country in railroad stations, bus depots, and in private homes, GIs reunited with their families and friends. It was a homecoming of major proportions. Historian and author William Chafe summed up the expectant massive reunion this way: "Anxious soldiers wondered if the war had permanently changed their wives and whether they'd get their old jobs back. Parents waited to see if their daughters would come back home and settle down nearby. And social scientists speculated on the war's impact on marriage, family, and morals."[3] As the public held its collective breath, GIs continued their exit from the military and return to civilian life. For many married couples, the long-awaited reunions went off without a hitch. "I was thrilled to death to see him!" said Peggy Werkman, who was separated from her husband for almost three years. "He's a quiet person and just acted like we'd seen each other the day before. . . . He was so fortunate. He'd been in the Battle of the Bulge and other terrible battles and came out without a scratch." For other returning GIs, homecoming meant seeing a child for the first time or rekindling a relationship that had been interrupted for months, often years. Each family, commented sociologist and author Reuben Hill, had "missed its man in terms of his special role in the home." [4] During the war, the published cases on the impact of a father's absence on a child's identity focused almost exclusively on boys. In his book *Daddy's Gone to War,* William Tuttle, Jr., discusses the "particularly galling" void in the literature about father-absence and girls and suggests that the solution to discovering how the war affected girls is to explore the recollections of home front girls as well as boys, which is what he does in his personal study. Tuttle found that the mother's response to her husband's absence, as well as that of the grandparents', mattered more than any other variables.[5] The way mothers responded to news about the war, the answers they were willing to give to their children's questions, the courage and assertiveness they showed, and the amount of tears and anxiety they displayed all contributed to how the children adjusted to their father being away at war and to his return.

For those children old enough, there was worry that their fathers might not accept them or even recognize them. Younger children worried that it would be *they* who would not recognize their fathers. And for children too young to understand on a verbal level who this "stranger" was in their home, the adjustment was often the wife's, who had developed an effective solo parenting style that was thrown up for grabs. For fathers coming home after spending years in a military environment in which they either gave orders or obeyed them, they saw their role as disciplinarian and enforcer of "appropriate" sex-role behavior. Young boys were to follow in the stalwart steps of their fathers—to be assertive, athletic, and ready for any bully that crossed their path—and young girls were to be primed to be little ladies who good-naturedly accepted a more passive, gracious role. Relationships between fathers and their children could quickly become a test of wills, particularly if, during their father's absence, the children had been raised as "half orphans" who were doted upon, even spoiled. *Parents' Magazine,* anticipating postwar difficulties, sent free issues to fathers serving overseas whose children had been born in their absence. Psychologist Lois Meek Stolz explained that there was greater peace and harmony in the household while the father was away than when he returned. Home life, Stolz wrote, had been "quieter and less punitive with mother in charge of decorum and discipline" and that these children showed "less tendency to aggression than the children whose fathers were at home."[6] Many mothers had trouble adjusting to having a father in the picture at all, let alone a man whose ideas about decorum and discipline were different from her own.

ALL WAS NOT JUBILATION

The painful story of veterans who suffered war wounds, severe emotional scars, alcoholism, and depression was virtually unspoken of after the war. (Though one film, *The Best Years of Our Lives,* dealt openly and realistically with the problems.) Yet the 670,846 Americans who suffered physical wounds, losing a leg, an arm, an eye—and the 83,000 men so severely wounded that they were placed in Veterans Administration hospitals—were constant reminders of the ravages of war. For those veterans who suffered psychologically, the stigma of being labeled a man with a nervous or emotional problem prevented them from seeking treatment. It was not until 1980, in response to the Vietnam veterans' experiences, that the American Psychiatric Association officially diagnosed the serious psychological disorder afflicting combat veterans as Post-Traumatic Stress Disorder (PTSD). But in the years immediately following World War II, the disorder was often misdiagnosed; labeled "combat fatigue," with a call for rest and recuperation; or ignored.[7]

"He had a mental breakdown upon his return," said one waiting wife, talking about her husband. "He had been an easy-going man who made everyone else feel good about themselves. But the horrors of war . . . he served in the medical corps in the Pacific . . . were too much for him. While hospitalized, he was given electric shock therapy, a procedure that was in many ways quite barbaric in 1946. The therapy did manage to draw him out of his severe depression but left him 'less than whole' for the rest of his life. Although he continued to be a loving husband, he would have outbursts, often inappropriate, that tore me apart. Some of the connections in his brain never fired properly again."[8] Another wife talked about the night her recently-returned husband almost killed her. "We were living at his mother's, and his sister happened to be there. Fortunately! She heard a lot of noise in our bedroom and thought, 'Oh, man! They're really having sex!' But when the noise continued, she came in the bedroom, and my husband was evidently having a bad dream and had his hands around my throat. Of course, his sister hit him and knocked him back into reality. I think he probably would have killed me. I'm sure he had no intentions, but he thought he was in battle."[9]

From corroboration in interviews with wives and husbands, it is evident that many of America's returning veterans suffered from PTSD after World War II. Jack Havener had slept "like a baby" for his first week back home. Then a "delayed reaction" set in, and he began waking up each morning between 4:30 A.M. and 5:30 A.M., waiting for the duty officer to route him out for a briefing. Once he realized that he was not in France but home in his own bed with his beloved wife, Mary Alyce, he would heave a sigh of relief, roll over, and fall back into a sleep so deep that persistent efforts by Mary Alyce were required to wake him. But Havener couldn't shake what he called the "combat jitters." He explained that the entry to his second floor apartment was off the stairs into the living room. From there, a door opened into the bedroom and, on through the bedroom, there was a door to the kitchen. At night, he would close the doors and open the bedroom window for cool, fresh air. For lack of storage space, the ironing board stood upright behind the kitchen door. In the middle of one night, Havener was tossing and turning in the throes of yet another nightmare. Mary Alyce was about to wake him when the ironing board fell flat on the floor next to the bed with a resounding whack. In his dream, Havener had been flying a rough mission, and his plane was catching a lot of enemy flak. One shot caught the plane right in the bomb bay and flipped the plane over on its back. He managed to right the plane but, no sooner had he leveled out again, another loud burst tore off the right wing. Havener hit the bail-out alarm button. He clawed at the plane's canopy hatch in a desperate attempt to push it open, but somebody kept pulling him away from it. The plane was diving fast. When he awoke from the nightmare, Havener saw that he'd clawed a hole in the bedroom window screen while trying to remove it so he could jump. He was hanging half out the window with Mary Alyce's arms clutched around his waist, desperately trying to pull him in. Havener's sense of humor downplays the event: "Only my wife's strength saved me from diving out the window into the bed of irises below as I tried to escape that ironing board flak burst!"[10]

Havener was one of the lucky ones: His nightmares lasted for only a month or so after the war. He picked up his life where he'd left off, going back to work as a shipping clerk at International Harvester and eventually assuming a managerial position as materials controller. Mary Alyce, who had worked in an ordinance plant during the war and been laid off like the majority of women, found work at a credit union. She loved the life of a working woman, and Jack was unaffected by the general consensus that wives should stay at home. When the Haveners adopted a "forty-five-minute-old" baby boy, Mary Alyce left work to raise him. As soon as he was old enough to go to school, she went back to work as a secretary at his school. Havener's job eventually took the family to Canton, Illinois, and then on to Memphis, Tennessee. In 1969, Mary Alyce had what was to have been a routine hysterectomy. The doctors found cancer in her ovaries, and, after a valiant struggle, she died in October 1971. Havener, now 85, past Vice President of the B-26 Marauder Historical Society (the only historical society for an aircraft), remarried not quite two years after Mary Alyce's death and is again tending to an ill wife who is riddled with all sorts of maladies. Yet his spirit remains strong, his attitude toward life positive, and his memories of the war sharp. "That war taught me to live every day to the fullest," he said. "And as far as my first marriage . . . it counter sunk it . . . made it even stronger. The separation from the woman I loved helped me appreciate her even more."[11]

Many men, separated from wives, sweethearts, or family, turned to alcohol to dull the pain of distance, death, and the daily grind of war. Alcoholism was rampant among the returning men. In fact, alcohol abuse throughout the postwar population was a significant, though largely unacknowledged, characteristic of American family life.[12] Jane Fitzke was a young war bride whose husband fought in North Africa. Fitzke lived at home with her parents and was raising two children. As the months passed, she could, she said, see through the tone in her husband's letters that things were beginning to change. He was cheating on her, at least that's what she suspected. Thousands of miles away, she was unable to know for sure. "He came back so mixed up and he was drinking," she said. "He'd never been a drinker before. It was not good. He was a different person. And he was not happy being a father, especially with our daughter. But I loved my home and my children. *He* was the one who wanted to leave." She and her husband divorced about a year after the war, becoming part of the wartime divorce phenomenon.[13] In 1942, the first year of American involvement in the war, 321,000 couples were divorced. By 1945, that total had reached 485,000; and in 1946, the first full year of peace, the number soared to 610,000. By 1950, a million veterans had been divorced.[14] Drinking, extramarital affairs, hasty war time marriages, postwar trauma, and the growing independence of wives all contributed to the postwar stampede to the nearest divorce lawyer. Some men even admitted to filing for divorce because their wives had aged and could no longer compete with the glamorous Hollywood pinups who appeared forever young.[15] And women, reluctant to give up their freedom and authority within the family, often decided they were happier without their husbands. On the other hand, those marriages based on personal compatibility, support, and understanding often withstood the pressures and stresses of war. In an informal study of service couples in which the wife followed her husband during stateside military training, more than 90 percent were celebrating fifty-five, even sixty-year wedding anniversaries. World War II, they said, had cemented their marriages and proved that they could survive just about anything.[16]

"I'LL BE SEEING YOU"

Betty Lou,

Every night I crawl into my little sack and light up the last cigarette of the day and there in the dark with the wind whippin' around the tent flaps I think of you—of your hair and eyes and pretty face—of your lovely young body—of your warmth and sweetness. It isn't in the spirit of frustration but of fulfillment. I've known these things and knowing them and having them once, I have them forever. That wonderful look in your eyes when we'd meet after being apart for a few hours—or a few weeks—always the same—full of love. Ah, Betty Lou, you're the perfect girl for me—I love ya', Mama![17]

This letter was written around June 11, 1945, when Rarey added yet another sketch to his sketchbook journal. In it, Rarey sits in bed, smoking his last cigarette of the day. The smoke from his cigarette rises into a "thought" bubble with sketches of Betty Lou, the skyline of New York City, an outline of the United States, and what looks to be a martini jigger being poured into a glass. There is no doubt what he's thinking of and where he wants to be.

On June 26, 1945, Rarey wrote to Betty Lou again. Though he confided to the 362nd's Information Officer, Paul Mitchell, that he had a strong conviction that he "wasn't going to make it," Rarey's letters were just as lighthearted and upbeat as ever.

Dear Betty Lou,

. . . Lord, Betty Lou, it seems like an eternity since I've seen you—since last November in that fine little world of ours. I hated to leave it. I don't care for this war—I want you and Damon and the life of our choosing. I want to worry about the bills—Ho! Ho!—and mow the lawn and make kites and stuff for the Damon and his friends. I want to see you and kiss you every day of my life. . . . I've got all these things to do and time's awastin'—I ain't getting any younger neither! So let's get the war over—okay? "Until that happy day you know darned well, I can't give you anything but love letters, baby." Silly isn't it? You just keep that old light in your eyes and the one in the window and we'll be fat. Ah, I love you, my sweet Betty Lou.

Love,

Rarey[18]

That was George Rarey's last letter to his beloved wife, Betty Lou. On July 13, 1944, Betty Lou was with friends when her father called to say she'd "had a telegram." Her dear "Rarey," a fighter pilot, had been shot down over central France on his sixty-third bombing mission. One of the other fighter pilots on the same search and destroy mission saw Rarey's plane take a direct hit and watched in horror as the plane disintegrated. Later, he assured Betty Lou that Rarey "never felt a thing." Betty Lou was suddenly a widow and single parent of a three-month-old boy, Damon, who was one of about 183,000 American children who lost their fathers in World War II. "I would have hated myself if I hadn't spent those months with Rarey on the road during his training," said Betty Lou. "And I always felt I could look Damon in the eye because I stuck with his dad to the very last moment."[19] To this day, at age 85, Betty Lou has no idea how she dealt with the news of her husband's death. All she remembers is grabbing Damon and wrapping her arms around him, holding on tight. She shudders to think what her life would have been like without him. An old school friend asked her what she was going to do. "I don't know," the young widow said. "Just go crazy, I guess." During that same conversation, another friend mentioned that her office needed a secretary. Betty Lou jumped at the chance to keep herself occupied and got the job. Her mother cared for Damon during the day, and the young widow and her infant son somehow made it through the long, lonely nights.

Before he died, Rarey had asked his best friend overseas and eventually his commanding officer to be Damon's godfather. Sometime after the war ended, Bill Flavin came to visit Betty Lou and to meet his godson. The young widow and the officer spent hours reminiscing about Rarey and sharing the sketchbook he'd left behind. Damon grew attached to the only father figure he'd ever known and, two years after Rarey's death, Betty Lou married Bill Flavin. They had a daughter and enjoyed eight years of marriage until Flavin died in an airplane crash caused by an assembly-line error at North American Aviation, where he was a test pilot. The cruel irony of losing two husbands in plane crashes would be enough to sink even the strongest woman. But Betty Lou isn't the type of person who "craters." "I learned to cope with a certain amount of strength," she said. And because she liked being married, she married one last time. She had three more children, twin boys and a girl. But the third marriage didn't last. "All of a sudden," she said, "we went down a different path." Betty

Lou was a stay-at-home mom until she and her husband separated. With three young children, she had to hustle to make a living. She taught special education and eventually landed a "great" job as a special education editor at a California-based publishing house, where she worked full-time for 22 years. Despite her active, full life, the memories of Rarey, dead now for more than 62 years, remain clear and precious. "You never get over a loss like that," she said. "There is never a day that goes by that I don't think of the war and my dear Rarey. What a high penalty we sometimes have to pay for living and loving!"[20]

A "FIRST FATHER"

Damon Rarey grew up with a stepfather, the only dad he'd ever known. But he remembered a day when he was around four and somebody from the war days came to visit. His mother and "daddy" had brought out some of Rarey's drawings, and there was much reminiscing about the war and talk of "Damon's first father." At one point, his younger sister tugged on his mother's sleeve, "Do I have a 'first father,' too?" "It was a very positive thing to have a 'first father,'" Damon said. "I felt special because my father had been killed in the war. . . . Actually, it was a plus for me. I had no sense of grieving or loss. . . . It was just part of the landscape." (That, of course, was not the case with many children, particularly those who had known their fathers before they went to war.) He remembers looking at his father's drawings at a very early age, finding them strange, hard to understand, wonderful but mysterious. Once in school, he continually received recognition for his own drawings, filled with cartoon-like illustrations. A self-described Disney freak, he watched Heckyl and Jeckyl at the movies and found them "kinda' scary because they were so world-wise, so flippant . . . way beyond his consciousness. But he was bowled over just the same. When Damon was nine, his "daddy" was killed in a plane accident. Too young to comprehend the depth of his mother's pain and not in touch with his own, he stood in the front hall of their home, watching his mother refuse to let in a minister who had come to offer his condolences. She wanted nothing to do with religious compassion. The nine-year-old who had lost his first and now his second father felt a "great sadness" well up inside, then felt nothing at all.

The self-imposed but understandable pressure to live up to the memory of Rarey, the war hero, the talented cartoonist, propelled Damon to search for things about his father that were *not* so positive. He needed to deconstruct the romanticized memories that had unintentionally created self-doubts about his own character and abilities. If only there had been a chance to have a "settled" relationship with a real person, that would have made things so much easier. As an adult, when he and his mother were writing *Laughter and Tears: A Combat Pilot's Sketchbook of World War II Squadron Life,* a compilation of Rarey's drawings, many of his wartime letters, along with remembrances of his war buddies and Betty Lou, Damon discovered that his father loved to drink. And the man was a "slob." "If you want to throw something away," he would say, "just throw it on the floor." And Rarey struggled against being improvident. One time, before they married, he bought Betty Lou a ring on time, intending to pay it off. But he forgot about the payments, and the bills were eventually sent to Betty Lou. But Damon also discovered that Rarey was the love of his mother's life, and that the two young people whose dreams of a long future together were blown to bits during an instant that day in France were as committed to one another as any couple could ever be.

Damon became a commercial artist just like his father. And he understood on some very deep level the value of marriage and the strong, strong sense of persevering. He eventually had three children of his own and was keenly aware of men's relationships with their fathers. He had almost a sixth sense for recognizing—it was hard to put his finger on it—a father who was at ease with himself, the world, and with his son. "I feel my dad's presence quite a lot," he said. "Sometimes as a system of values; sometimes if I'm having trouble sorting things out. When people talk about my dad's legacy of such wonderful art and memories, I say, 'I'd trade all of it just to have 15 minutes to sit down and shoot the shit with him.' "[21] Damon died in 2003 of the "mad cow" variant of Creutzfeldt-Jacob disease. Only cynics would wager that he hasn't had his 15 minutes and many, many more.

FACING DEATH THE AMERICAN WAY

The advice to mothers whose husbands were killed in the war was to set a good example for their children. If they could make it through the grieving process without falling apart, so could their kids. In some ways, war widows without children faced a more difficult challenge. They were alone in their grief, unable to lose themselves in the day-to-day responsibilities of parenting. Geraldine Greene met her husband, Jack Brooke, on a bus in March 1942. She was on her way home from work as a waitress when a group of army recruits hopped on the bus she was riding. Greene and Brooke dated for just three weeks and were married in a small ceremony presided over by an Episcopalian minister. "I just fell in love right quick." Greene said. The newlyweds had no honeymoon; in fact, they didn't share the same bed for over a week. Like all other enlistees, Brooke had to live on base with limited off-base privileges. But Greene didn't let that stop her.

She made a "home" for her husband and then, when he was transferred first to California, then to Florida, she followed him as a "wandering service wife." "We had a wonderful marriage," Greene said. "We were very much in love with each other. Jack would get out of camp as often as he could, and, in all the time we were separated, I became a very independent woman." Brooke was wounded in the landing on Omaha Beach in Normandy, France (nurses said it was his big chin that saved him) and then killed on December 18, 1944, in the Battle of the Bulge. "I absolutely fell apart at the seams," Greene said. She desperately wanted her husband's body brought back to the States. Initially, the U.S. government offered her a trip to Belgium to visit the cemetery where he'd been buried. "I wasn't willing then and haven't been willing in the 60-plus years since to make a trip to Europe," she said adamantly. "I knew the first time I'd see a German that I'd go up and kick him you know where!" It took 4 years of wrangling with the military and U.S. government, but Greene persevered and had her husband's body returned home, where he was laid to rest a second time in a little cemetery in Douglasville, Texas, close to his family. Greene led a parade down the town's main street. One of the onlookers was Brooke's father who sat in a wheelchair, as his son's casket passed him by.

Greene struggled to pull herself together. She went back to school and earned a Masters in Education from the University of Miami. She taught elementary school and then middle school civics and government. Greene remarried, only to lose her second husband prematurely at the age of 42. Life had thrown Greene some curve balls, but the independence and self-sufficiency she cultivated during her wartime days served her well once again. She went back to school, this time earning accreditation in guidance and counseling and then landing on her feet as a counselor at Coral Shores High School on Plantation Key, Florida. She took a stab at love one more time, marrying Lou Greene in 1968. The two enjoyed a good marriage until Lou's death in 1994. "I have three burial plots in Miami Memorial Cemetery," she said. "My aunt Gertie is buried in one. I buried my second husband in the second plot, and my last husband, Lou, in the third. I asked them to dig the hole deeper, so I could be buried on top of Lou." She laughed heartily. "How many ladies do you know who send a check to one cemetery in Texas for the care of their first husband's grave and then are going to be buried with two others?"[22]

DOWN THE AISLE IN DROVES

While war widows like Greene and Rarey struggled to put their lives back together after the deaths of their husbands, scores of single women were intent on finding a man and settling down. Two out of three men who returned from the war were still single, and most were anxious to marry a wholesome girl back home and create for themselves the "ideal" life they'd dreamed about during their time overseas. The marriage rate jumped by nearly 50 percent in 1946—118 per 1,000 women 15 years and older—and stayed over 20 percent above prewar levels throughout the remainder of the decade.[23] Couples lost no time in starting a family. As author Betty Friedan said, "We were all vulnerable, homesick, lonely, frightened. A pent-up hunger for marriage, home, and children was felt simultaneously by several different generations; a hunger which, in the prosperity of postwar America, everyone could suddenly satisfy."[24] The postwar baby boom officially got under way in 1946, with some 50 million babies born in the 15 years after the war. For the first time since the desperation of the Great Depression and the subsequent horrors of World War II, the infinite possibilities for financial and personal security appeared within reach. There was, said historian and author Elaine Tyler May, a massive push back to domesticity. "It was as if Americans caught the family fever. . . . The home became a kind of container for a lot of postwar aspirations. Homemaking became professionalized. Marriage became eroticized in new ways. Motherhood was glorified. Initially, a powerful belief in togetherness with men as the breadwinners and women tending to home and family."[25]

In the years immediately following the war, the baby boom posed a problem. For 15 years, there had been virtually no new housing built in the United States. To solve the pent-up demand for new homes, a housing boom to end all housing booms got off the ground. Nationwide, housing starts soared from a low of only 1 per 1,000 people in 1944 to a high of 12 per 1,000 in 1950. The majority of these new homes were built outside of major cities in what would become known as the suburbs. A family didn't have to be wealthy to get a piece of the American dream, but they did have to be white. Despite the contributions of African Americans to the war effort, Jim Crow laws held fast. The "Double V" campaign for victory abroad and victory at home fell mostly on deaf ears. While the social and economic upheavals of wartime laid the groundwork for the civil rights movement, it would be another 15 years or so before the movement marched forward. African American women were not likely to avoid full-time domestic work, but they were more than likely to do it in someone else's home. By 1950, forty-one percent of all employed black women worked in private homes. Whereas white women faced pressure to become full-time homemakers and were often stigmatized if they held jobs, black women had a long history of combining paid work with their own domestic responsibilities.[26]

"THEY'D GOTTEN OUT OF HAND"

With the return of peace and the homecoming of millions of GIs, American men and women entered into a period of testing and adjustments. The society that fighting men left behind had changed on a dime, with 6 million first-time female workers flooding the workplace. Millions more participated in public life, volunteering for organizations like the Red Cross. Young wives handled the family finances, made all of the household decisions, and often raised a child alone. Still, once the war ended, a substantial number of Americans, including women, believed a woman's place was in the home. In a 1945 *Fortune* poll, 65 percent of men and 57 percent of women felt that married women should not work. Willard Waller, a Barnard sociologist, charged that during the war, women had gotten "out of hand," with the result that children were neglected and the very survival of the home was endangered. A Southern senator went a step further and urged Congress to force wives and mothers back to the kitchen. In part, the desire to restore old patterns of economic responsibility was motivated by fear of a recession, with memories of the grueling Great Depression still fresh enough in people's minds. Just as persistent was the hostility toward the idea of women participating as equals in an economic world. If a husband could support her, a woman should not work. It didn't matter that four out of five industrial female workers preferred to keep their jobs.[27] The desire to continue working crossed all age groups but was the strongest among women aged 45 years and older. But under the Selective Service Act, veterans took priority over wartime workers. Women were the last to be hired and the first to be fired.

Delana Close had a girlfriend from her hometown of Emery, Utah, who had moved to California and found a "good" job in a shipyard there. When Close graduated from high school, she "took a chance" and joined her friend in search of work and wartime excitement. Close had absolutely no manual labor experience—she'd wanted a career in the theatre—but decided to try her luck. She took a train from Utah to Venice, California ("The train was full of troops!") and landed a job as a machinist second class. "They gave me all these aptitude tests," Close said, "and I was hired. My company made the 23-foot-long barrels for the 155 millimeter Howitzers. Imagine, my machine was 35 feet long, but I did very well." Close made $1.31 an hour—a lot of money at the time, particularly for a woman—and was able to buy a home. She can't remember how much of a down payment she made but, by renting two of the bedrooms to friends, she was able to more than cover her monthly mortgage payments. On the morning of May 9, 1945, the day after Americans and their Allies celebrated Germany's surrender and the end of the war in Europe, Close showed up at the factory where she'd worked for more than two years and found it locked shut. With the war winding down, there was no longer any need to produce more guns. While Close and the others rejoiced that the war had officially ended in Europe, none of them was pleased about losing their job without any warning or severance pay. "I was always aware that I was taking a man's place at the plant and always felt that I'd be willing to give the job up once the war ended," Close said. But I wasn't ready to give it up quite so soon."[28]

After the war, the majority of the 700,000 women who had swapped aprons and oven mitts for welding torches and drills wanted to keep their factory or shipyard jobs. A female shipbuilder, for example, had taken home an average of $37 a week, a far better wage than the $14 a week typically earned as a waitress.[29] These Rosie the Riveters who had become a national icon of the strong working woman had heeded the call and given "the boys the support they needed." They had ignored the often poor treatment from male workers ("Some of the men treated us pretty badly because when a woman walked in, it meant another man went to war.") and accepted the reality that their paychecks were less than those of their male counterparts. For those women with children, they often made the ultimate sacrifice, leaving them alone at home or sending them to live with relatives, often in another state. Yet these hardy women persevered despite the lack of respect for their lives outside of work. But, as they would be reminded over and over again, they had been hired for the "duration," and now that the men were home, they were forced to quit.

For the four Rosies interviewed in Connie Field's documentary film, *The Life and Times of Rosie the Riveter,* the end of the war marked, in many ways, the end of a dream. Gladys Belcher, a welder, worked an eight-hour shift and then attended welding school for four hours every weekday. She anticipated stiff competition when the men came home and intended on being prepared in all phases of welding. Like most female welders, she was laid off almost as soon as peace was declared. Undaunted, she approached another company and put her papers down on the recruiter's desk. He looked them over and said, "If you were a man, we'd hire you. But we can't. You're a woman." Belcher was heartbroken but didn't have time to pine. She'd purchased a small house during the war and had mortgage payments and other bills to pay. She had to get a job somewhere and ended up working in a restaurant kitchen for the next 17 years. "It was hot, a lot harder work than welding, and a lot less pay," she said.[30]

As far as welder Lola Weikel, saw it, women had been "sold a bill of goods." "They trained us, and we did what we set out to do. But there were never any plans to keep us." Weikel pounded the pavement postwar looking for a welding job. There were none. "As a woman," she said, "it was over for us." Just like that, the men they had supported as comrades had become competitors. But Weikel was a self-described "working" person who always felt she'd accomplished something at the end of a day. "All I wanted to do was make a beautiful ornamental gate. Was that so much to want?"[31]

The government and industry propaganda that had done such a brilliant job of wooing women to work now turned its attention to the returning GIs. In a War Department short newsreel, the narrator asks, "Now that he returns, what does he want?" He wants the "longest sleep in the softest feather bed in the world. He wants a platoon of bathing beauties who only have eyes for him." And, more than anything, he wants a "job." The military training and skills gained from fighting a war could be adapted to an "amazing variety of civilian jobs." These seasoned veterans represented the potential to become the most capable group of workers the nation had ever known—once again, the best of America.

For black Rosies like Wanda Allen and Margaret Wright, the end of World War II marked the end of their brief taste of a more equitable job market, job self-esteem, and a salary that lifted them out of the financial basement. Wright had a daughter to feed and returned to her prewar job as a domestic. "It was defeating—very defeating," she said.[32] Belcher, who didn't have a "guy who's got a diamond mine" but was a "welder on the old assembly line," loved to buy nice things for herself like the fictional Minnie in the song, "Minnie's in the Money." But once she got bumped from her welding job, there was no extra dough for shopping. She went out to a nearby airport and got a job in the cafeteria. "Those were jobs blacks could always get," she said.[33]

"We believed we were new women," said Weikel. "Largely, we were a big joke to most of America. . . . Women quivering for their man to come home so we could go back to the kitchen."

Historian and author Sara Evans was asked whether it was so obvious to women that jobs during the war were for the duration and no longer. On the one hand, she said, ads in the paper were very clear. And the term "for the duration" showed up over and over again. But for the women who actually went to work and enjoyed the challenge, the income, and the independence, Evans doesn't think it was so obvious at all. "Some saw this as an aberration in their lives . . . doing their patriotic duty . . . eager to go back to the home," Evans said. "But there was a whole group of women who maybe didn't take the job thinking they would care whether it lasted or not but who changed their minds once they moved in to the work place. There is good opinion poll data at the end of the war supporting the feeling that a large proportion of these women would have preferred to stay in the labor force at the level where they were. But they were forced out." Surveys of thousands of female factory workers found that 61 to 85 percent of them wanted to continue their employment in peacetime, and that more than half of all married women wanted to keep their jobs and newfound economic prosperity. Evans was quick to point out, however, that this is a "double story," that a lot of women went home voluntarily, to have their babies, eager for something "normal." "In the end," she said, "women were left with only two options: leave the work place completely or downgrade their jobs significantly. Women were fired from the higher-paying, skilled jobs but were able to reenter the work place in traditionally female areas, the 'pink collar' jobs like clerical, education and service."[34] Between September 1945 and November 1946, there were 2.25 million women who left work and another million who were laid off. But in the same period, 2.75 million women were hired. By 1950, just five years after the end of World War II, the female labor force had increased by more than 5.25 million, substantially more than the expected increase without the war.[35]

THE BEST YEARS OF OUR LIVES

No film better captures the difficult, often traumatic adjustments following World War II than William Wyler's 1946 Oscar-winning movie, *The Best Years of Our Lives*. Film buffs and general audience members alike point to the film as a particularly realistic portrayal of the struggle many soldiers faced, a struggle sometimes almost as great as the one they fought overseas. *The Best Years of Our Lives* tells the story of three American servicemen returning home to the fictional Boone City. Not only had they, like most servicemen, changed dramatically during their time as soldiers, but so had the home front they had left behind. The world these men had known—the country for which they fought so valiantly—could look almost as foreign as the countries "over there."

From the air on board a soon-to-be-retired air force bomber, the three veterans fly over their home town. Their excitement is palpable.

"Boy, oh boy, hey, look at that," says Homer Parrish, a young sailor who lost both of his hands in a torpedo explosion. "Look at those automobiles down there. You can see them so plain, you can even see the people in them."

Fred Derry, the much-decorated air force bombardier/captain who married during basic training only a few weeks before becoming a bomber pilot, points out the local golf course and the normalcy of it all. "There's the golf course, people playing golf just as if nothing ever happened."

"Hey, there's Jackson High football field," says Homer. "Boy, I sure would like to have a dollar for every forward pass I threw down there. Good ol' Jackson High."

The cruel irony that Homer will never throw another football is not lost on the three men—or on the audience.

Al Stephenson, the third veteran on board, a middle-aged, married banker who fought in the infantry, spots an airfield graveyard with a slew of parked war bombers.

"And they're junking them," says Fred. "Boy, oh boy, what we could have done with those in '43! . . . Some of 'em look brand new, factory to the scrap heap. That's all they're good for now."[36]

The plane carrying the three men lands in Boone City, and the veterans share the back seat of a taxicab to their separate hometown addresses. Along the way, signs of normality and civilian life are everywhere: Butch Engle's place with a new neon sign, a five-and-ten Woolworth's department store, and a used car lot. But the men feel uncomfortably out of place, behind the times. One by one, the taxi driver drops them off. Homer, the first to arrive home, stands alone on his parents' front lawn. The moment he's been dreading for months has arrived: How will his girl, Wilma, who lives next door, react when she sees the hooks he now has for hands? She's only a "kid" who has never seen anything like this. Will it be pity or disgust that pushes her away? Nervous, he stands there, wishing that he could go for a drink at his uncle's bar. But his younger sister spots him, and there is no time to escape. His pitying parents do their best to welcome their injured son home, but, when his mother sees the hooks for the first time, she makes a weak attempt at muffling a gasp and then sobs uncontrollably. And when Wilma rushes to greet him, Homer stands unresponsive with his hands glued to his side. The navy trained him to do everything from light a cigarette to open a can of beer but they couldn't, as Al observes later, "train him to put his arms around his girl to stroke her hair."

Al isn't any more comfortable about his homecoming, equating it to the feeling of "going to hit a beach." He enters his swanky apartment building and is immediately questioned by a suspicious front desk clerk. His uniform apparently doesn't count for anything. Al takes the elevator upstairs and, after a long pause, rings the bell. He wants to surprise his wife and, the moment he sees his two grown children, he cups his hands over their mouths and urges them not to say a word. His wife, who heard the bell ring, asks who is at the door. It takes a moment but, when she gets no answer, she seems to know intuitively that her husband has finally returned home. "In a long-held shot with Al's back to the camera, she appears at the end of the hallway corridor with arms half-outstretched. Both she and Al stand frozen to the ground and then silently, slowly move into each other's arms across the vast void. His children watch from afar as their parents share a long embrace."[37]

It doesn't take much time for questions, uncertainties, and regrets to surface. Al's children have grown up without him. "I should have stayed home," he says, "and found out what was really going on." His daughter, Peggy, has taken a course in Domestic Science and replaced the maid/cook. His son is less interested in talking about the role his father played in the war than in discussing the effects of nuclear warfare. When Milly, his wife, asks what he thinks of the children, he retorts, "Children? I don't recognize 'em. They've grown so old." "I tried to stop them," she says, "to keep them just as they were when you left, but they got away from me." And so it seems life has gotten away from Al. He asks for a drink, the first of many he will down that night and in the nights to come.

Fred, the last of the three veterans, is dropped off in front of his parents' home, a shack next to noisy railroad tracks. He rushes up the stairs, expecting to fall into the arms of his young bride, Marie, who had been installed there once he went overseas. Fred's father and stepmother are delighted to see him and awed by the "beautiful ribbons on his chest." But the homecoming turns sour the minute he's told that Marie has taken her own place at the Grandview Arms on Pine Street and that she's been working at "some nightclub" "'til all hours." Agitated, Fred can't sit still. He needs to kill some time before trying to find his wife and heads toward Butch's Place, a bar owned by Homer's uncle. By the end of the evening, Homer, then Al, accompanied by his wife and daughter, all end up at the bar for what becomes an impromptu "reunion." All three of the returning veterans have too much to drink and need to be escorted home. The Stephensons insist that Fred ride with them, with a promise that they'll drop him off at the Glenview Arms. But he can't gain entrance to Marie's apartment, and she is no where to be found. Disappointed and drunk, Fred is brought back to the Stephensons' apartment, where he is helped to bed in Peggy's bedroom. In the middle of the night, he suffers nightmares of a bombing mission gone terribly wrong over Germany. Peggy hears him from the living room where she is sleeping on a couch and goes to comfort him. "There's nothing to be afraid of. All you have to do is go to sleep and rest. Go to sleep. Go to sleep, Fred. Go to sleep and rest."

Director William Wyler has deftly set the scene and foreshadowed the challenges the three servicemen will face as they attempt to adjust to civilian life: alcoholism, recurring nightmares, infidelity, marital problems, divorce, the changing role of women, jobs or the lack of them, wartime injuries, and children who have grown since their fathers went away. The natural order of things—what the returning servicemen thought was natural—was in chaos. This wasn't the world they'd remembered and certainly not the women for whom they thought they had fought the war. As they sit in the living room surrounded by their family whom they no longer recognize, or cope with the lack of job opportunities, or try to accept a woman who has been unfaithful, could there be a certain nostalgia for the war, despite all of its horrors and death? Wyler's film title takes on an ironic twist, suggesting that perhaps the "best years" were not ahead but behind them now. *The Best Years of Our Lives,* released in 1946, so soon after the end of the war, made no attempt to whitewash the realities of the massive reassimilation of more than 16 million troops who had joined the military, excluding the 407,316 who never made it home—292,131 of whom were killed in action, and 115,185 who died from disease, accidents, or as prisoners of war.[38] In what David M. Kennedy calls the "mysterious zone where history mixes with memory to breed national myths," Americans remember World War II as the "good war," a just war waged by a peaceful people forced to fight only after intolerable provocation, a "war stoically endured by those at home and fought in far-away places by brave and wholesome young men with dedicated women standing behind them on the production lines . . . a war fought for democracy and freedom."[39] In that same "zone" where memories cloud the facts, the difficulties troops faced as they reentered civilian life and the response of the "dedicated" women who stood behind them are most often a footnote, if not ignored completely. Instead, it is the rush toward domesticity and the overwhelming desire to get back to "normal" that the country's collective memory chooses to recall.

But World War II had been a watershed moment for the country's young men and women and, no matter how hard revisionists try to fashion a postwar home front in which returning servicemen made the smoothest of transitions and women gladly exchanged their independence, nothing can change the many obstacles that often made the transition a difficult one.

In an October 1945 *Ladies' Home Journal* article titled "When Your Soldier Comes Home," a former front-line infantry man writes about the stumbling blocks to a seamless homecoming:

> If it is not the strain of combat, then what makes readjustment to normal life so difficult? The answer is: Having been a soldier, he finds it hard to be a civilian. Having missed you greatly, he has been forced to find ways of getting along without you. Having loved his fellow soldiers and hated the Army, he is lost when turned free as a civilian. Having looked forward so long and earnestly to civilian life, he finds it dull stuff compared with his dreams. . . . He has spent time in another world where men rule supreme and where women are marginal creatures at best. It will be difficult at first for him to yield to so many feminine influences. . . . He is not prepared to resume the close partnership with you as an equal. . . . Remember these things as he travels the slow road back to civilian life. As you love him, be patient with him in these trying times. . . . Remember—you were once a goddess.[40]

NOTES

1. Jan Klein, World War II service wife. Interview by author. July 2, 2002.

2. "Records of the Women's Bureau of the U.S. Department of Labor, 1918–1945," University Publications of America, 1997, www.lexisnexis.com/academic/guides/womens_studies/womlab.asp

3. William Chafe, *The Paradox of Change: American Women in the Twentieth Century* (New York: Oxford University Press, 1991), p. 154.

4. William M. Tuttle, Jr., *Daddy's Gone to War: The Second World War in the Lives of America's Children* (New York: Oxford University Press, 1993), p. 33.

5. Ibid., pp. 34–36.

6. Ibid., pp. 222–23.

7. Ibid., p. 217.

8. Eleanor Lieberman, wife of returning GI. Interview by author. June 11, 2002.

9. Betty Hart, Pentagon secretary. Interview by author. May 12, 2004.

10. Jack Havener, *Marauders in the Midst* (unpublished), p. 358.

11. Jack Havener, World War II veteran. Interview by author. August 14, 2002.

12. Tuttle, p. 218.

13. Jane Fitzke, World War II wife and mother. Interview by author. October 18, 2002.

14. Tuttle, p. 220.

15. John Costello, *Love, Sex and War: Changing Values 1939–45* (London: Collins, 1985) p. 274.

16. Informal study by author.

17. Betty Lou Kratoville, World War II service wife and widow. Interview by author. May 29, 2002.

18. Damon Frantz Rarey, ed., *Laughter and Tears: A Combat Pilot's Sketchbooks of World War II Squadron Life* (Santa Rosa, CA: Vision Books International 1996), p. 178.

19. Ibid., p. 182.

20. Kratoville.

21. Damon Rarey, son of World War II fighter pilot killed in war. Interview by author. July 18, 2002.

22. Geraldine Green, World War II widow. Interview by author. April 18, 2002.

23. Costello, pp. 369–70.

24. Betty Friedan, *The Feminine Mystique* (New York: W.W. Norton, 1963; New York: Dell, 1974), p. 174.

25. Elaine Tyler May, author and historian. Interview by author. November 20, 2002.

26. Elaine Tyler May, *Pushing the Limits: American Women 1940–1961* (Oxford University Press: New York), pp. 57–58.

27. Sara Evans, *Born for Liberty: A History of Women in America* (New York: The Free Press, 1989), p. 231.

28. Delana Close, World War II factory worker. Interview by author. June 7, 2004.

29. "Records of the Women's Bureau of the U.S. Department of Labor, 1918–1945," University Publications of America, 1997, www.lexisnexis.com/academic/guides/womens_studies

30. Connie Field, *The Life and Times of Rosie the Riveter,* VHS (Santa Monica, CA: Direct Cinema Limited, Inc., 1999).

31. Ibid.

32. Ibid.

33. Ibid.

34. Sara Evans, historian, author, professor. Interview by author. November 20, 2002.

35. William Chafe, *The Paradox of Change: American Women in the Twentieth Century* (New York: Oxford University Press, 1991), p. 161.

36. William Wyler, Director, *The Best Years of Our Lives* (Los Angeles: Samuel Goodwin Company), 1946.

37. Tim Dirks, Review of *The Best Years of Our Lives,* http://www.filmsite.org/besty2.html

38. "Statistical Summary: America's Greatest Wars," http://www.cwc.lsu.edu/cwc/other/stats/warcost.htm

39. David M. Kennedy, *Freedom from Fear: The American People in Depression and War, 1929–1945* (New York: Oxford University Press, 1999), p. 856.

40. "When Your Soldier Comes Home," *Ladies' Home Journal,* October 1945, p. 183.

This is one of the few World War II posters that pictures an African American, possibly a representative of the Tuskegee Airmen. Courtesy National Archives.

William Holton experienced segregation in the U.S. navy and, many years after the war, became the national historian for the Tuskegee Airmen.

Before they were married, Betty Lou Hodge and George Rarey posed on a rooftop in New York City.

Service wife Mary Alyce Havener is exhausted after packing her Zephyr for the trip back to Illinois from Savannah, Georgia, in mid-January 1944.

Jack Havener and his wife, Mary Alyce, pose for a photo in Havener's parents' back yard in October 1943, on leave from Twin Engine Flying School at Ellington Field in Houston, Texas.

A wife embraces her GI husband before he leaves for overseas, with their toddler looking on. Courtesy National Archives.

Betty Lou Rarey cuddles her new-born son, Damon, and waits for her husband to return home.

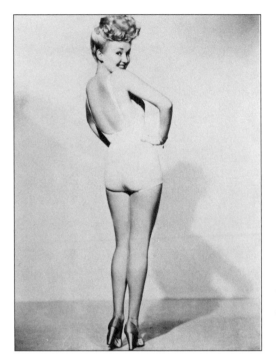

Betty Grable, with her million-dollar legs, was the most popular pinup of WWII. Courtesy National Archives.

Actress Rita Hayworth was one of the sexier Hollywood pinups whose photos were cherished by GIs overseas. Courtesy National Archives.

Members of the army air corps, some more talented than others, painted the noses of their airplanes.

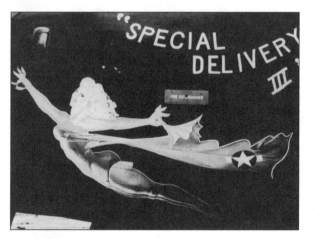

Almost every army air corps squadron had somebody who could paint.

The wife of the Secretary of War, Mrs. Henry Stimson, wanted all suggestive nose art to be removed.

Bob Dinda was transferred to the 82nd Airborne to aid in the occupation of Berlin, Germany, in 1945.

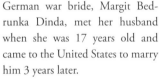

German war bride, Margit Bedrunka Dinda, met her husband when she was 17 years old and came to the United States to marry him 3 years later.

George Rarey drew himself sitting in the sack, dreaming of his wife, Betty Lou. Courtesy Betty Lou Kratoville.

This self-portrait drawn by George Rarey captures him writing another letter to his beloved Betty Lou. Courtesy Betty Lou Kratoville.

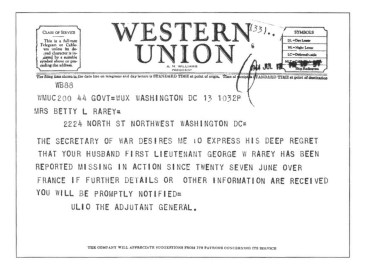

On July 13, 1944, Betty Lou received the dreaded telegram informing her that Rarey had been missing in action since June 27.

Jack Brooke (upper left) was wounded during the landing at Omaha Beach on June 6, 1944, taking a bullet in his overly long chin, which probably saved his life. Courtesy National Archives.

"Unconditional Surrender," standing 26 feet high in Sarasota, Florida, is artist J. Seward Johnson's tribute to *Life* magazine's famous photo known throughout the world as "The Kiss." Courtesy Alan Leder and The Sculpture Foundation.

Nine

BABIES, SUBURBIA, AND
THE SEEDS OF CHANGE

In the years after World War II, the collective consciousness of Americans revolved around the virtues of family, the good life, and the status quo. Whether it was getting married, moving to a new home in the suburbs, or raising children, American men and women appeared to be putting the horrors of war and the confusing changes on the home front behind them. Women left the workplace as quickly as they had entered it. There was no longer any room for the single, independent girl or the married career woman. Men reassumed their position as breadwinner, and prewar social and sexual mores prevailed. The double standard was still in full force, though women did begin to push against the taboo of premarital sex. The government, psychologists, and the media all hailed Americans' enthusiastic return to domesticity, and, on the surface, all was well.

Bella Gillaspie, the minister's daughter who had worked in a factory as the only woman with 400 men, returned to Iowa and raised a family of three boys. She enjoyed being a homemaker, singing in a church choir, and volunteering for various community activities.

Charles Collins, who enlisted in the army air corps right after high school graduation, went back to school on the GI Bill and studied engineering. He got married in 1947 and stayed in school until the GI Bill ran out in 1950.

Barbara Higby, the service wife who followed her husband stateside and worked everywhere she traveled, felt strongly that a mother's place was in the home. There would be plenty of time after her three children were grown to reenter the workplace.

"FAMILY FEVER"

Society as a whole was happy to get its women back in the home. Americans had never really gotten used to so many women going to work but had grudgingly accepted the phenomenon as a necessity of war. "There was no wholesale reversal of traditional notions that occurred as a result of the war."[1] Single men and women were marrying earlier than before the war and in huge numbers. The marriage rate rose by nearly 50 percent in 1946, the first full year after the war. The rate remained more than 20 percent above prewar levels throughout the next 10 years.[2] The flurry of "I dos" ushered in what is now referred to as the baby boom. In 1951 there were 3,845,000 babies born, which exceeded the Census Bureau's prediction by 450,000. In 1952 the birth rate reached 3,889,000, and by 1954, it reached more than 4 million. This rise continued to increase until, by the end of the 1950s, the overall number of babies born exceeded 40 million.[3] "It was as if Americans caught the family fever," said historian and author Elaine Tyler May. "The home became a kind of container for a lot of postwar aspirations."[4] May is quick to point out that, while everything was being couched in an air of normalcy, there was absolutely nothing normal about postwar domesticity. For the first time, the attempt was made to create a home that would fulfill virtually every family member's personal needs through an "energized and expressive personal life."

By war's end, unemployment was negligible. Americans commanded half of the entire planet's manufacturing capacity and generated more than half of the world's electricity. America owned two-thirds of the world's gold stocks and half of all its monetary reserves. The United States produced two times more petroleum than the rest of the world combined.[5] The war had richly delivered on its promises, and white, middle-class Americans rushed to enjoy the spoils of war. The idealized nuclear family owned a home in the new residential communities called suburbs that sprang up outside of major cities across the country. And, flush with good salaries—even if women no longer worked—consumer spending increased by 60 percent during the second half of the 1940s, and the amount spent on household furnishings and appliances increased 240 percent. The migration to the suburbs was accompanied by an increase in automobile ownership. At the beginning of the 1950s, just under 50 million cars were registered; by the end of the decade, there were nearly 74 million. One of the first shopping centers in a suburb of Detroit opened in 1954. Dorothy Thompson, a regular columnist for *Ladies' Home Journal*, compared it to the central marketplace of Greece and Europe.[6] Women funneled their energy and creativity into the home. Modern conveniences like ready-made clothing, nursery school, and prepackaged food made life easier for them. But between the new "labor-saving appliances" (which ultimately did not save any time at all), the time spent shopping, driving children to and from activities, and even doing the household accounting, the full-time homemaker still worked about 55 hours a week.[7] Homemaking had become "professionalized" in a big way, and married women took their domestic responsibilities as seriously as they'd taken Uncle Sam's campaign to keep the wartime industries moving.

FROM SOAP OPERAS TO PRIME TIME

As early as the late 1920s, market research suggested to advertisers the importance of the middle-class female consumer and her primary role in making decisions about family purchases. By the early 1930s, manufacturers of household products underwrote what we now call daytime "soap operas"—so called because of the household products that were the main advertisers. The narratives of these programs like *Betty and Bob, Just Plain Bill, The Romance of Helen Trent,* and *Ma Perkins* often revolved around central female characters, sure to capture the fan base of women listeners. The arrival of television in the American home in the 1950s was a new opportunity for soap-opera development. Some programs, like *Guiding Light,* simply moved from radio to television, whereas others—like *Search for Tomorrow, The Edge of Night,* and *As the World Turns*—were created for the new medium. The plots of these programs centered on the problems and complications of family life. Plots "twisted and turned around topics like the difficulty of finding and keeping love, affairs outside of marriage, and the troubles involved in raising children."[8] The situation comedy, which filled the early primetime hours from the early 1950s, was more of a "mixed bag" in terms of its portrayal of women and femininity. Because most of the shows focused on the family, women were mainly seen as wives, mothers, and daughters. Within that context, the programs might center on the value of the mother's nurturance and work, as in *Mama* or *The Goldbergs,* or marginalize her in decision making about the family's resources and children, as in *Leave It to Beaver.* Zany wives, who continually acted against their husband's wishes, were featured in *I Love Lucy, I Married Joan,* and *My Favorite Husband;* and *Private Secretary* and *Our Miss Brooks* represented single working women as only slightly less irrational. However, in programs like *Father Knows Best,* Jim Anderson's intelligent wife Margaret and ambitious daughter Betty deal with some of the polarizing choices that women faced in the 1950s. Similarly, Donna Stone of the *The Donna Reed Show* questions the connotations of the media's use of "housewife" in one episode, and Lucy Ricardo of *I Love Lucy* is probably the most ambitious and dissatisfied woman in all of television history.[9]

"THE HAPPY HOUSEWIFE"

Lucy Ricardo's ambition and dissatisfaction were couched in humor. Her screaming and posturing made audiences laugh, not think. If *I Love Lucy* had been a more serious, in-your-face drama rather than a comedy filled with laughs, chances are the program wouldn't have made it through its first season. Americans were much more comfortable with the image of the "happy housewife" who did whatever it took to keep her family healthy and content. Images of smiling women, often dressed in an apron and housedress, or of cheery-sounding women promoting refrigerators, recipes, and laundry detergents dominated the air waves and the print media. For example, a Fairmont Milk ad from October 3, 1950, displayed a picture of an attractive woman's smiling face with the quote, "My whole family loves this milk." An ad for Our Family Foods featured a woman saying, "Our family likes . . . " followed by a recipe.[10] A Singer advertisement from *Woman's Home Companion* in December 1956 shows a woman in a housedress, apron, and high heels smiling broadly as she effortlessly pushes the new Singer "Roll-a-Magic" vacuum cleaner with one hand. Her husband, dressed in a suit—perhaps just home from the office—stands at her side, focused on the apparent whirlwind suction that will "whisk up Christmas clutter instantly." A perfectly well-behaved child sits on the floor next to a Christmas tree, "reading" a book she's obviously received as a holiday gift.

This image of the "happy housewife" dominated women's magazines as well. Before the advent of television, video, and computers, magazines assumed even more importance than they do today in helping to both shape and reflect the values, habits, and aspirations of American women and their families. During World War II and after, the leading women's magazines boasted subscriber numbers from 2 million to 8 million, with actual readerships much higher.[11] (It was not until 1970, when *Essence* was launched, that there was a widely circulated magazine for African American women.) Women's magazines were a major force in their lives and, after the war, there was an "abrupt shift in the magazines' presentations of women's roles—from active participation in a national effort to containment in a private kitchen." In an article she wrote for the September 1951 issue of *Good Housekeeping* titled "Why I Quit Working," Jennifer Colton described the "guilt and despondency" she felt as a working mother with small children. Colton left her job and, in the year since departing, had time to "judge the advantages and disadvantages." She could no longer use her job as an alibi for not get- ting things done. She no longer had the pleasure of giving "showy" gifts. She missed the "special camaraderie and the common language" of working people, and acknowledged the adjustments she had to make moving from the workplace back to the home. "But," she wrote, "one day I realized that my office job was only a substitution for the real job I'd been 'hired' for: that of being purely a wife and mother." She continued, "At first I found it hard to believe that being a woman is something in itself. I had always thought that a woman had to do something more than manage a household to prove her worth. . . . Though I still wince a little at the phrase 'wife and mother,' I feel quite sure that these words soon will sound as satisfying to me as 'actress' or 'buyer' or 'secretary' or 'president.'"[12] Colton's struggle in 1951 to accept herself as the "happy housewife" mirrored the dilemma many middle-class married women faced at the time and foreshadowed the second wave of the women's liberation movement that would change so many lives a decade or so beyond.

THE HAPPY COED

Following the war, there was a national debate about the purpose and con- tent of women's education. A movement to change the curriculum in order to prepare coeds for home and family life took hold on the heels of a 1942 study that concluded women had not been prepared to adequately handle the problems they faced after graduation. Eighty-two percent of the women interviewed said they'd had difficulties with housekeeping "caused by a lack of skill, dislike of monotonous tasks, and inadequate opportunity for intellec- tual and creative pursuits." Based on the results, the study's lead investigators recommended courses that would give housekeeping a higher social status, while educating coeds in the ways of keeping a home. Colleges, they con- cluded, "had prepared her [the coed] well to follow her vocation, but neither college nor her parents had prepared her for *giving up* her vocation."[13] Edu- cators and psychologists emphasized the differences between the sexes and warned that women who sought intellectual and occupational pursuits like men were damaging themselves, their families, and society. A June 1948 *Good Housekeeping* article titled "Most Likely to Succeed" reinforced this popular postwar position by positing that success for a coed meant marriage and fam- ily, not brilliance. Therefore, a female college student with a "C" average was most likely to succeed.[14] The message to college coeds was loud and clear: Use college as a vehicle for finding a husband, not for intellectual stimulation or preparation for a career. Coeds were often said to be earning an MRS. degree, since so many met their husband in college and then dropped out—60 percent by the mid-fifties. "The times were different then," said Blanche Kishner. "I didn't finish college. I got married when I was 20 and dropped out. I'd probably kill my kids if they'd left school and gotten married so young." For those coeds who actually earned a degree, it was jokingly referred to as a "Ph. T," or "Putting Husband Through." Coed graduates would teach school, for example, but only as long as it took for their husbands to finish law, medical, or dental school. Once their husbands had attained their higher degree and entered the workforce, it was assumed that the women would quit working.

Even without the push to prepare for life as a homemaker, women's education was already different from that of men. Women concentrated on the humanities and social sciences and in preparing for jobs that were traditionally female such as teaching and social work. Mildred McAfee Horton, former Director of the WAVES who headed Wellesley College after the war, was upset to find that because women expected to marry they assumed they should be content with subordinate positions and felt that competition for higher-status jobs was unfeminine. Career counseling for women was based on the premise that most would get married and that their role as wife and homemaker would take precedence over any interest in a career. A bulletin at Indiana University did list "Earner" as one of four roles to which women should aspire but went on to diminish that role: "Those few years when she earned her way in the business or professional world would make her a good sport about the ups and downs of her husband's business." The bulletin discussed fields of study in terms of their compatibility with marriage.[15]

"THE MARRIED WOMAN GOES BACK TO WORK"

Ironically, by 1947 there were more women in the paid labor force than during the war and more working wives than ever before. Their average weekly pay had declined from $50 during the war to $37, and the opportunities were, for the most part, limited to clerical, sales, and service positions. Even more important was the impression that women went to work out of necessity. "If a woman had said she wanted to work for self-gratification or to prove her equality with men," writes William Chafe in *The Paradox of Change: American Women in the 20th Century,* "she would have come into conflict with the social norm that a wife should be happy to stay in the home." It's important to remember, Chafe adds, that the women most directly involved in the postwar expansion of the female labor force were wives over 35 years of age who had already finished their primary homemaking responsibility of raising children. "Women workers sought jobs, not careers."[16]

Bella Gillaspie's husband, Robert, owned a men's clothing store but had a rough time supporting Bella and their three children. Not wanting to leave her children full-time, Gillaspie went back to the classroom as a substitute teacher to help keep the family afloat financially. "It was hard for my husband at first to know that I had to work part-time to help out," Gillaspie said. "But he ultimately accepted my working and supported it." Unlike the first time she taught in the late 1930s, when married women were discouraged from teaching—if not, as in some states, actually barred from holding a job—working as a married teacher in the late 1950s was no longer viewed as a problem by a large majority of Americans. Over the years, Gillaspie went back to the university and earned two master's degrees; eventually, when her youngest son was in school, she started teaching full time.[17]

Like Gillaspie and millions of other women, Barbara Higby decided the time was right to continue her education. Still intent on being home with her children, she waited until the youngest was six and in school and then pursued her accreditation as a certified public accountant. It was 1956 and her decision, she says, was met with mixed reactions: Some felt that as a woman she should stay home, whereas others felt it was just as important for a woman as for a man to pursue an education and eventually a job.[18] It's no wonder that Higby's decision was met with opposing viewpoints. Books, women's magazines, and other media had taken up the "women's issue" with great vigor. Most championed the joys of "femininity" and "togetherness" and attacked women's interest in education and employment. In their 1947 book, *Modern Woman: The Lost Sex,* authors Ferdinand Lundberg and Marynia Farnham posited that women had been created to be biologically and psychologically dependent on men. The desire to be a mother constituted the key to sexual pleasure, they wrote, and the culmination of the sexual act occurred when a mother nursed a child. The authors urged government-sponsored propaganda campaigns to bolster the family through subsidizing psychotherapy for "feminist neurotics," giving cash subsidies to encourage women to have more children, and awarding annual commendations to mothers who had excelled at child raising. Women, they said, could achieve mental sanity only if they reclaimed the home as the central focus of their existence.[19]

Women's magazines joined the chorus with articles like "You Can't Have a Career and Be a Good Wife," "Why I Am against the Equal Rights Amendment," "Are You Too Educated to Be a Mother?" and "Making Marriage Work." The author of the first article, identified only as a "successful career wife," wrote, "Always in double career marriages there is terrific strain. . . . With two strong personalities thrusting forward to success, not all the pull can be smoothly cooperative. . . . A marriage that survives twin careers is the exception; one that can *thrive* on a dual setup is a miracle."[20] In the *Ladies' Home Journal* article "Are You Too Educated to Be a Mother?" the author argues that a woman who has gone to college is likely to have fewer children than a high school graduate and even fewer than a woman who leaves school in the fourth grade. "Thus, our educated women, potentially mothers of children with greater native ability, are guilty of squandering their genetic inheritance. Unthinkingly they are lowering the standards of future generations." Sweden, the author points out, has reversed the unfavorable birth rate among its educated, more financially secure women. "We must learn that we are not too educated to be parents; we must learn that we are too educated *not* to be!"[21] This call for educated women to have more babies doesn't go further to discuss whether or not these women should utilize their college degrees anywhere other than in the bedroom. One can only surmise.

THE HAPPY SUBURBAN HOUSEWIFE UNDER SCRUTINY

By 1960, fifteen years after the end of World War II and the push toward a new kind of domesticity in American life, the media began to dissect the prevailing image of the happy suburban housewife. Newspaper articles, magazines, and television programs reported that the happy housewife was not so happy after all. But in almost all of the coverage, from *Newsweek* to *Good Housekeeping* to CBS television, "everybody who talked about it found some superficial reason to dismiss it."[22] The American housewife was frustrated because of "incompetent appliance repairmen," the distances mothers had to drive to chauffeur their kids around, or because they had had more and more education, which naturally made them unhappy being just housewives. "The road from Freud to Frigidaire, from Sophocles to Spock, has turned out to be a bumpy one," reported the *New York Times* on June 28, 1960. "Many young women—certainly not all—whose education plunged them into a world of ideas feel stifled in their homes. They find routine lives out of joint with their training. Like shut-ins, they feel left out. In the last year, the problem of the educated housewife has provided the meat of dozens of speeches made by troubled presidents of women's colleges who maintain, in the face of complaints, that sixteen years of academic training is realistic preparation for wifehood and motherhood." So, how to solve this problem? Suggestions ranged from barring women from four-year universities (since they wouldn't need a college education to become housewives), hiring them as nurse's aides and baby sitters to substitute love for their angst, and to that age-old issue: sex. Waiting wives, it was theorized, spent all day at home in anticipation of having sex when their husbands returned from the office. But too frequently husbands were tired after a long day at work and weren't interested in sex. Thus, frustrated wives became even more frustrated, with their sexual needs ignored and unmet.

THE FEMININE MYSTIQUE

Betty Friedan, a working suburban mother who wrote for women's magazines, marked the fifteenth reunion of her fellow graduates from Smith College with a survey of their attitudes and accomplishments. Some 200 of her classmates responded. And while the questionnaire raised more questions than it answered, it showed that with all their education, these white, middle-class American women were frustrated in the role of housewife but that they had managed to enlarge it and make it as meaningful as possible. The survey, along with Friedan's interviews of suburban women, eventually became the basis for her groundbreaking book, *The Feminine Mystique,* published in 1963. She later claimed that, as she read over the answers to her questionnaire, she discovered what she would call "The Problem That Has No Name," the deep-seated and confused dissatisfaction her classmates felt but could not fully articulate. She uncovered the baffling fact that women were failing to realize their personal potential at a time when more of them than ever were receiving a higher education. Instead, they had fallen prey to the myth of the "happy housewife"—or what was often referred to as the "feminine mystique"—the myth that defined a woman's major goal as pleasing her husband and raising a family. Friedan explained the feminine mystique this way:

> In the fifteen years after World War II, this mystique of feminine fulfillment became the cherished and self-perpetuating core of contemporary American culture. Millions of women lived their lives in the image of those pretty pictures of the American suburban housewife, kissing their husbands good-bye in front of the picture window, depositing their stationwagonsful of children at school, smiling as they ran the new electric waxer over the spotless kitchen floor . . . Their only dream was to be perfect wives and mothers; their highest ambition to have five children and a beautiful house, their only fight to get and keep their husbands . . . They gloried in their role as women, and wrote proudly on the census blank: "Occupation: housewife."[23]

Friedan's point of view struck a chord. The book sold nearly 3 million copies in its first three years in print. "When this book comes, it comes at exactly the right moment to, in some ways, start a grass fire across suburban America in which women say, 'I recognize myself there. I'm one of those people who's not that happy,'" said historian William Chafe in the Public Broadcasting System's (PBS's) series, "The First Measured Century." Alice Kessler-Harris,

Professor of History at Columbia University, concurred: "Friedan captured a moment in time and a set of feelings," Kessler-Harris said in an earlier segment of the same PBS series. "When Betty Friedan argued that the [home] was not necessarily the only commitment that women should have, she touched a sort of nerve that was already raw among women. . . . So I think the book was the right book at the right time."[24]

By 1963, the majority of World War II wives were in their early forties. Their children were older; some were already out of the house. There was a whole generation of mothers who were aware of new possibilities, new potentials but, at the same time, cut off from them. "If they went to work," said historian and author Sarah Evans, "they went into dead end jobs. Only a few got to be professionals, and those women were regularly told they shouldn't be where they were. The majority may have experienced a good education or a wartime job with real potential, but after the war they did not work outside of the home."[25] Friedan contended that the home had become a "comfortable concentration camp," in which women, with few, if any, positive role models, accepted a "voluntary servitude" in the suburbs. The supposed suburban bliss could be, in reality, a lonely existence, racked by skyrocketing divorce, addiction to drugs and alcohol, and an epidemic of mental illness. "You wake up in the morning, and you feel as if there's no point in going on another day like this," said one woman interviewed by Friedan. "So you take a tranquilizer because it makes you not care so much that it's pointless."[26]

In naming and defining a generation's frustrations, Friedan pointed to a time bomb that was, indeed, about to explode. She gave those women who settled for a life filled with disappointment and lowered expectations a sense of community, a feeling that they were not alone. However, many of the wives of the war generation had their lifestyle and decisions called into question. Understandably, many were defensive. "I had a mixed attitude toward the book," said Barbara Higby. "I thought she presented an extreme picture of women and their roles. On the other hand, I have always felt that women and men are equal and that a woman can't always depend upon a man." Mary Rohlfing also supported equal pay for equal work. But she felt Friedan and many in the feminist movement were "just men haters who had gone too far." Others were conflicted about what they remember as Friedan's take on child care. Though she never "faced the question of which women would take care of the children when white, middle-class suburban housewives turned into ambitious, self-fulfilling professionals,"[27] women who had chosen not to work so they could stay home and raise their children didn't appreciate what they considered an assault. But many of these same women sought new options to enrich their lives. They became active in the parent-teacher association, neighborhood organizations, and other volunteer groups. Some became politically active. And still others, craving more, eventually pursued paid jobs outside the home. By 1960, there were twice as many women at work than in 1940. The median age was 41, and the proportion of wives at work had doubled from 15 percent to 30 percent. Although the number of single working women declined over the same 20-year span, the number of *mothers* at work leaped 400 percent from 1.5 million to 6.6 million. Thirty-nine percent of these working moms had children between the ages of 6 and 17. By 1960, both husband and wife worked in more than 10 million American homes.[28]

FROM "ROSIE THE RIVETER" TO "WOMEN'S LIBBER"

When Bella Gillaspie told her students about her experiences as a "Rosie the Riveter" in World War II, they asked if she was a women's libber. She paused, never having considered her work in a factory with 400 men as anything more than a patriotic act in a time of war. "You know," she told her students after some reflection, "I've never been recognized as a women's libber, but I was probably one who helped start it all."[29] Most historians would agree. The breakdown of traditional sexual roles of a large section of the female population was the most profound sexual consequence of World War II, even though the full impact wasn't felt for another two decades. The publication of Friedan's *Feminine Mystique* galvanized housewives and created the reasons for what would eventually be called the Women's Liberation Movement, or women's lib. Concurrently, the civil rights movement of the 1960s, with its focus on racial inequality, encouraged a readiness to think about the same issues generated by gender inequality. The fight against racism heightened women's awareness of their own oppression and provided organizational and tactical tools they would use in their own struggle. Women in the civil rights movement felt empowered by the slow but steady progress being made in the clamor for racial justice and gained a new sense of confidence in themselves. In 1966, a group of women, including Friedan, met in a New York hotel room and formed the National Organization for Women (NOW), a political action group mandated to "take the actions needed to bring women into the mainstream of American society" with "full equality for women, in fully equal partnership with men."

Although it is not a straight line from World War II to the Women's Liberation Movement of the 1960s and 1970s, the moment of independence and cultural validation experienced by the mothers of the baby boom generation struck a chord that never stopped reverberating in their hearts and minds. As historian Evans suggests, the change in women's economic status during the war may well have shaped the mixed messages they gave to their own daughters, many of whom "proclaimed the rebirth of feminism" 20 years later. "On the one hand," said Evans, "they are teaching their daughters the rhetoric of the feminine mystique . . . you should marry well . . . your life will be defined by whom you marry. But, they are, at the same time, communicating a whole other set of possibilities. And, in some cases, they have perceived the possibilities for themselves and then felt prohibited from choosing them. The very person who is *telling* you that you should get married and put your dreams of satisfying work outside the home on the back burner is *showing* you by her anger and frustration that it is all a trap."[30]

By the end of the 1960s, the stage had been set for a widespread assault on traditional attitudes and values regarding sex roles in America. The issues were inclusive and varied and ran the gamut from domestic violence to a woman's right to choose, from equality under the law to defending a person's sexual orientation. Thousands of different groups and virtually every aspect of American life were affected. For a "Rosie the Riveter" like Mary Louise Mohr who had always been "an advocate of feminism," the goal of equal pay for equal work was paramount. Mohr "would never, ever think a woman should work for less than her male counterpart."[31] Service wife Edith Bennett, who went to college at age 40, earned a degree in history and taught junior and senior high school for 16 years, honored the value of meaningful work for women, no matter how late in life. The issue of reproductive choice was (and is) what got World War II service wife Alice Joniak ready to march.

Wars have always been strong catalysts of social change. Inhibitions are lost, moral and social taboos are broken, and the emphasis on living for the present without thinking about the future inevitably leads to an increase in promiscuity. Once disrupted or broken, traditional values are not easily restored. Millions of married women, many with children, went to work for the first time during World War II. Couples met and married in record numbers without the traditional courtship. There simply wasn't enough time. Young wives left their hometowns to follow their husbands during their stateside military training. Many got pregnant along the way, not knowing if the baby would ever know his or her father. American GIs, far away from family and home, "did things" they might never have done. And young women, emboldened by a paycheck and kinship with other women, experienced a freedom and independence most women had never known. Despite attempts to get back to "normal" after the war and the apparent "togetherness" of the country, World War II set in motion a profound change in relations between the sexes, a change that continues to be rebutted, refined, and reconstructed. Members of the "greatest generation" mobilized to fight a war and, in the process, not only defeated the enemy overseas but unwittingly instigated a seismic transformation in the way American men and women work, love, mate, and ultimately partner with one another.

NOTES

1. Leila J. Rupp and Verta Taylor, *Survival in the Doldrums: The American Women's Rights Movement, 1945 to the 1960s* (New York: Oxford University Press, 1987), p. 15.

2. John Costello, *Love, Sex and War: Changing Values 1939–45* (London: Collins, 1985), pp. 369–70.

3. Greg Knight, "The Suburbanization of America: The Rise of the Patio Culture," http://home.texoma.net/-kgreg/paper.html.

4. Elaine Tyler May, historian, author, professor. Interview by author. July 12, 2002.

5. David M. Kennedy, *Freedom from Fear: The American People in Depression and War, 1929–1945* (New York: Oxford University Press, 1999), p. 857.

6. Nancy A. Walker, ed. *Women's Magazines 1940–1960: Gender Roles and the Popular Press* (Boston: Bedford/St. Martin's 1998), p. 13.

7. Elaine Tyler May, *Pushing the Limits: American Women 1940–1961* (New York: Oxford University Press, 1994), p. 74.

8. "Soap Operas," http://www.bookrags.com/history/popculture/soap-operas-bbbb-02/.

9. "Comedy: Domestic Settings," http://www.museum.tv/archives/etv/C/htmlC/comedydomes/comedydomes.htm.

10. Jessica Rachoza, "The Power of the Gaze: The Stereotypical Image of Women in Advertisements," http://www.msu.edu/-rachozaj/Portfolio/The%20Power%20of%20the%20Gaze.pdf.

11. Walker, pp. v–vi.

12. Jennifer Colton, "Why I Quit Working," *Good Housekeeping,* September 1951, p. 13.

13. Susan M. Hartmann, *American Women in the 1940s: The Home Front and Beyond* (Boston: Twayne, 1982), pp. 110–11.

14. Judith Tarcher, "Most Likely to Succeed," *Good Housekeeping,* June 1948, p. 33.

15. Hartmann, pp. 112–13.

16. William Chafe, *The Paradox of Change: American Women in the Twentieth Century* (New York: Oxford University Press, 1991), pp. 156–68.

17. Isabella Gillaspie, World War II factory worker and postwar teacher. Interview by author. October 29, 2002.

18. Barbara Higby, World War II service wife and postwar certified public accountant. Interview by author. September 18, 2002.

19. Sarah M. Evans, *Born for Liberty: A History of Women in America* (New York: Free Press, 1997), pp. 238–39.

20. Walker, p. 71.

21. Ibid., pp. 115–16.

22. Sara M. Evans, *Born for Liberty: A History of Women in America* (New York: Free Press, 1997), p. 265.

23. Betty Friedan, *The Feminine Mystique* (New York: W.W. Norton, 1997, 1991, 1974, 1963), p. 18.

24. "William Chafe Interview," *PBS, The First Measured Century, World War II,* http://www.pbs.org/fmc/interviews/chafe/htm. http://www.pbs.org/fmc/interviews/kessler-harris/htm.

25. Sara Evans, historian, author, professor. Interview by author. November 20, 2002.

26. Friedan, p. 31.

27. Daniel Horowitz, *Betty Friedan and the Making of the Feminine Mystique: The American Left, The Cold War, and Modern Feminism* (Amherst: University of Massachusetts Press, 1998), p. 208.

28. Chafe, p. 189.

29. Gillaspie.

30. Evans.

31. Mary Louise Mohr, wife of Tuskegee Airman. Interview by author. June 30, 2004.

SELECTED BIBLIOGRAPHY

Abraham, George "Doc." *The Belles of Shangri-La and Other Stories of Sex, Snakes, and Survival from World War II.* New York: Vantage Press, 2000.

Alt, Betty Sowers and Bonnie Domrose Stone. *Campfollowing: A History of the Military Wife.* New York: Praeger, 1991.

———. *Uncle Sam's Brides: The World of Military Wives.* New York: Walker and Company, 1990.

Anderson, Karen. *Wartime Women: Sex Roles, Family Relations, and the Status of Women during World War II.* Westport, CT: Greenwood Press, 1981.

Bailey, Beth and David Farber. *The First Strange Place: Race and Sex in World War II Hawaii.* Baltimore: The Johns Hopkins Press, 1992.

Baker, Vernon J. *Lasting Valor.* New York: Bantam. 1997.

Bérubé, Allan. *Coming Out under Fire: The History of Gay Men and Women in World War II.* New York: Plume 1991.

Brandt, Allan M. *A Social History of Venereal Disease in the United States since 1880.* New York: Oxford University Press, 1985.

Buckley, Gail. *American Patriots: The Story of Blacks in the Military from the Revolution to Desert Storm.* New York: Random House, 2001.

Chafe, William. *The Paradox of Change: American Women in the Twentieth Century.* New York: Oxford University Press, 1991.

Chernin, Ted. "My Experience in the Honolulu Chinatown Red-Light District." *The Hawaiian Journal of History,* 34 (2000): 203–7.

Cooper, B. Lee. "From 'Love Letters' to 'Miss You': Popular Recordings, Epistolry Imagery, and Romance During War-Time, 1941–1945." *Journal of American Culture,* 19 (1996): 15–27.

Costello, Cynthia B., Shari Miles, and Anne J. Stone, eds. *The American Woman 1999–2000.* New York: W.W. Norton & Company, 2000.

Costello, John. *Love, Sex & War: Changing Values 1939–45.* London: Collins, 1985.

Cott, Nancy, ed. *No Small Courage: A History of Women in the United States.* New York: Oxford University Press, 2000.

———. *The Grounding of Modern Feminism.* New Haven, CT: Yale University Press, 1987.

Davis, Flora. *Moving the Mountain: The Women's Movement in America Since 1960.* Champaign: University of Illinois Press, 1999.

Dong, Arthur. *Coming Out under Fire.* Documentary film. Los Angeles: Deep Focus Productions, Inc., 1994, 2003.

Erenberg, Lewis A. and Susan E. Hirsch, eds. *The War in American Culture: Society and Consciousness During World War II.* Chicago: The University of Chicago Press, 1996.

Evans, Sara M. *Born for Liberty: A History of Women in America.* New York: The Free Press, 1989.

———. *Personal Politics: The Roots of Women's Liberation in the Civil Rights Movement and the New Left.* New York: Knopf, 1979.

Farnham, Marynia and Ferdinand Lundberg. *Modern Woman: The Lost Sex.* New York: Harper & Row, 1947.

Field, Connie. *Rosie the Riveter.* Documentary film. Santa Monica, CA: Direct Cinema Limited, 1999.

First Run Features. *Before Stonewall.* Documentary film. New York: First Run Features, 1985.

Forman, Sidney. *"D" Day to Victory.* Tinicum, PA: Xlibris, 2000.

Freedman, Estelle B. *No Turning Back: The History of Feminism and the Future of Women.* New York: Ballantine Books, 2002.

Freedman, Estelle and John D'Emilio. *Intimate Matters: A History of Sexuality in America.* New York: Harper & Row, 1988.

Friedan, Betty. *The Feminine Mystique.* New York: W.W. Norton, 1963.

Gluck, Sherna Berger. *Rosie the Riveter Revisited: Women, the War, and Social Change* Boston: Twayne Publishers, 1987.

Goldstein, Joshua S. *War and Gender.* Cambridge: Cambridge University Press, 2001.

Goodman, Philomena. *Women, Sexuality and War.* London: Palgrave, 2002.

Goodwin, Doris Kearns. *No Ordinary Time: Franklin and Eleanor Roosevelt: The Home Front in World War II.* New York: Simon and Schuster, 1994.

Gordon, Linda. *Woman's Body, Woman's Right: A Social History of Birth Control in America.* New York: Grossman, 1990.

Greer, Richard. "Dousing Honolulu's Red Lights." *The Hawaiian Journal of History,* 34 (2000): 185–202.

Harris, Mark Jonathan, Franklin Mitchell, and Steven Schechter. *The Homefront: America during World War II.* New York: G.P. Putnam's Sons, 1984.

Hartmann, Susan M. *American Women in the 1940s: The Home Front and Beyond.* Boston: Twayne Publishers, 1982.

———. *The Homefront and Women at War with America.* Cambridge, MA: Harvard University Press, 1984.

Hegarty, Marilyn E. "Patriot or Prostitute? Sexual Discourses, Print Media, and American Women during World War II." *Journal of Women's History,* 10, no. 2 (Summer 1998): pp. 112–36.

Honey, Maureen, ed. *Bitter Fruit: African American Women in World War II.* Columbia and London: University of Missouri Press, 1999.

Hoopes, Roy. *Americans Remember the Home Front: An Oral Narrative of the World War II Years in America.* New York: Berkley Books, 2002.

Horowitz, Dan. *Betty Friedan and the Making of "The Feminine Mystique": The American Left, the Cold War, and Modern Feminism.* Amherst, MA: University of Massachusetts Press, 1998.

Kennedy, David M. *Freedom from Fear: The American People in Depression and War, 1929–1945.* New York: Oxford University Press, 1999.

Kessler-Harris, Alice. *Out to Work: A History of Wage-Earning Women in the United States.* New York: Oxford University Press, 1983.

Lingeman, Richard. *Don't You Know There's a War On? The American Home Front 1941–1945.* New York: Thunder's Mouth Press/Nation Books, 2003.

McDermott, George L. *Women Recall the War Years: Memories of World War II.* Chapel Hill, NC: Professional Press, 1998.

May, Elaine Tyler. *Homeward Bound: American Families in the Cold War Era.* New York: Basic Books, 1988.

———. *Pushing the Limits: American Women 1940–1961.* New York: Oxford University Press, 1994.

Mead, Margaret. "The Women in the War." In *While You Were Gone: A Report on Wartime Life in the United States,* ed. Jack Goodman. New York: Simon and Schuster, 1946.

Meyerowitz, Joanne. "Women, Cheesecake, and Borderline Material: Responses to Girlie Pictures in the Mid-Twentieth-Century U.S." *Journal of Women's History,* 8, no. 3 (Fall 1996): pp. 5–28.

Milkman, Ruth. *Gender at Work: The Dynamics of Job Segregation by Sex during WWII.* Urbana: University of Illinois Press, 1987.

Millett, Kate. *Sexual Politics.* New York: Doubleday, 1970.

Mintz, Steven and Susan Kellogg. *Domestic Revolutions: A Social History of American Family Life.* New York: Free Press, 1989.

Morehouse, Maggi M. *Fighting in the Jim Crow Army: Black Men and Women Remember World War II.* Lanham, MD: Rowman & Littlefield Publishers, 2000.

Morris, Gary. "The Bad Girls of M-G-M, 1932." *Bright Lights Film Journal* 17 (September 1996), http://www.brightlightsfilm.com/17/04a_badgirls.html.

Perkins, W. Drew and Bill Reifenberger. *The Tuskegee Airmen: They Fought Two Wars*. Documentary film. Hollywood, CA: Rubicon Productions, 2004.

Rarey, Damon Frantz, ed. *Laughter and Tears: A Combat Pilot's Sketchbooks of World War II Squadron Life*. Santa Rosa, CA: Vision Books International 1996.

Rupp, Leila. *Mobilizing Women for War: German and American Propaganda, 1939–1945*. Princeton, NJ: Princeton University Press, 1978.

Rupp, Leila and Verta Taylor. *Survival in the Doldrums: The American Women's Rights Movement, 1945 to the 1960s*. New York: Oxford University Press, 1987.

Shilts, Randy. *Conduct Unbecoming: Gays and Lesbians in the U.S. Military*. New York: Fawcett Columbine, 1994.

Shukert, Elfrieda Berthiaume and Barbara Smith Scibetta. *War Brides of World War II*. Novato, CA: Presidio, 1988.

Terkel, Studs. *The Good War: An Oral History of World War II*. New York: The New Press, 1984.

Time-Life Books. *This Fabulous Century: 1940/1950*. New York: Time-Life Books, 1969.

Tobias, Sheila. *Faces of Feminism: An Activist's Reflections on the Women's Movement*. Boulder, CO: Westview Press, 1997.

Tuttle, William M. Jr. *Daddy's Gone to War: The Second World War in the Lives of America's Children*. New York: Oxford University Press, 1993.

Virden, Jenel. *Good-bye, Piccadilly: British War Brides in America*. Urbana and Chicago: University of Illinois Press, 1996.

Wald, Carol. *Myth America: Picturing Women 1865–1945*. New York: Pantheon Books, 1975.

Walker, Nancy A., ed. *Women's Magazines 1940–1960: Gender Roles and the Popular Press*. Boston: Bedford/St. Martin's 1998.

Ware, Susan. *Beyond Suffrage: Women in the New Deal*. Cambridge, MA: Harvard University Press, 1981.

———. *Modern American Women: A Documentary History*. New York: McGraw-Hill, 1997.

Wynn, Neil A. *The Afro-American and the Second World War*. New York/London: Holmes & Meier, 1993.

Yellin, Emily. *Our Mothers' War: American Women at Home and at the Front during World War II*. New York: Free Press, 2004.

ADDITIONAL BIBLIOGRAPHY

Anthony, Susan Brownell. *Out of the Kitchen, Into the War: Woman's Winning Role in the Nation's Drama*. New York: S. Daye, 1943.

Appleby, Joyce et al., *Telling the Truth about History*. New York: W.W. Norton, 1994.

Baty, Paige. *American Monroe: The Making of the Body Politic*. Berkeley: University of California Press, 1999.

Bentley, Amy. *Eating for Victory: Food Rationing and the Politics of Domesticity.* Urbana: University of Illinois Press, 1998.

Boris, Eileen. *Home to Work: Motherhood and the Politics of Industrial Homework in the United States.* Cambridge: Cambridge University Press, 1994.

Boris, Eileen and Nupru Chaudhuri, eds. *Voices of Women Historians: the Personal, the Political, the Professional.* Bloomington: Indiana University Press, 1999.

Breines, Wini. *Young, White and Miserable: Growing Up Female in the Fifties.* Boston: Beacon Press, 1992.

Bunch, Charlotte. *Passionate Politics: Feminist Theory in Action.* New York: St. Martin's Press, 1987.

Campbell, D'Ann. *Women at War with America: Private Lives in a Patriotic Era.* Cambridge, MA: Harvard University Press, 1984.

Colman, Penny. *Rosie the Riveter: Women Working on the Home Front in World War II.* New York: Crown, 1995.

Diedrich, Maria and Dorothea Fischer-Hornug. *Woman and War: The Changing Status of American Women from the 1930s to the 1950s.* New York: Berg, 1990.

Ehrenreich, Barbara. *The Hearts of Men.* Garden City, NY: Doubleday & Co., 1983.

Filene, Peter. *Him/Her/Self: Sex Roles in Modern America.* 2d ed. Baltimore, MD.: Johns Hopkins University Press, 1986.

———. *Bitter Fruit: African American Women in World War II.* Columbia, MO: University of Missouri Press, 1999.

Freeman, Jo. *The Politics of Women's Liberation: A Case Study of an Emerging Social Movement and Its Relation to the Policy Process.* New York: David McKay, 1975.

Gallagher, Jean. *The World Wars through the Female Gaze.* Carbondale: Southern Illinois University Press, 1998.

Honey, Maureen. *Creating Rosie the Riveter: Class, Gender, and Propaganda during World War II.* Amherst: University of Massachusetts Press, 1984.

Kerber, Linda et al., eds. *U.S. History as Women's History: New Feminist Essays.* Chapel Hill: University of North Carolina, 1995.

Litoff, Judy Barrett. *Since You Went Away: World War II Letters from American Women on the Home Front.* Princeton, NJ: Princeton University Press, 1978.

Lopata, Helena Z. *Occupation: Housewife.* New York: Oxford University Press, 1971.

Mead, Margaret. *And Keep Your Powder Dry.* New York: Ayer Company, 1942.

Myrdal, Alva and Viola Klein. *Women's Two Roles: Home and Work.* London: Routledge & Kegan Paul, 1956.

Norton, Mary Beth. *Major Problems in American Women's History.* Boston: D.C. Heath & Company, 1996.

Oakley, J. Ronald. *God's Country: America in the Fifties* New York: Dembner Books; distributed by W.W. Norton, 1990.

Rothman, Sheila. *Woman's Proper Place: A History of Changing Ideals and Practices, 1870 to the Present.* New York: Basic Books, 1978.

Ruiz, Vicki and Ellen duBois, eds. *Unequal Sisters: A Multicultural l Reader in U.S. Women's History.* New York: Routledge, 2000.

Scharf, Lois. *To Work and to Wed: Female Employment, Feminism, and the Great Depression.* Westport, CT: Greenwood Press, 1980.

Scott, Joan. *Feminism and History* New York: Oxford University Press, 1996.

Sinnott, Susan. *Doing Our Part: American Women on the Home Front during World War II.* New York: F. Watts, 1995.

Walker, Nancy A. *Shaping Our Mothers' World: American Women's Magazines.* Jackson: University of Mississippi Press, 2000.

INDEX

About the Author

JANE MERSKY LEDER is a freelance writer and journalist. She is the author of the award-winning book, *Dead Serious*, as well as *Brothers & Sisters: How They Shape Our Lives* and *Grace & Glory: A Century of Women in the Olympics*. Her articles have appeared in numerous publications, including *Psychology Today*, the *Chicago Sun-Times*, and *American Heritage*.